ADVANCE UNCORRECTED PROOF

This copy is supplied for review purposes only, and for limited distribution. As the work is still under review by the author and the publisher, there may be corrections, deletions, or other changes before publication. **Not for resale.**

PLUNDER

PLUNDER

*A Memoir of Family Property
and Nazi Treasure*

MENACHEM KAISER

HOUGHTON MIFFLIN HARCOURT

BOSTON • NEW YORK

2021

Copyright © 2020 by Menachem Kaiser

All rights reserved

For information about permission to reproduce selections from this book, write to trade.permissions@hmhco.com or to Permissions, Houghton Mifflin Harcourt Publishing Company, 3 Park Avenue, 19th Floor, New York, New York 10016.

hmhbooks.com

Library of Congress Cataloging-in-Publication Data
Names: Kaiser, Menachem, 1985– author.
Title: Plunder : a memoir of family property and Nazi treasure / Menachem Kaiser.
Other titles: memoir of family property and Nazi treasure
Description: Boston : Houghton Mifflin Harcourt, 2020. | Includes index.
Identifiers: LCCN 2020033851 (print) | LCCN 2020033852 (ebook) | ISBN 9781328508034 (hardcover) | ISBN 9780358449836 | ISBN 9780358449904 | ISBN 9781328506467 (ebook)
Subjects: LCSH: Holocaust, Jewish (1939–1945) — Poland — Sosnowiec (Województwo Śląskie) — Reparations. | Kaiser, Meir Menachem, 1921–1977 — Family. | Inheritance and succession — Poland. | Jewish Property — Poland — Sosnowiec (Województwo Śląskie) — 20th century. | World War, 1939–1945 — Claims. | World War, 1939–1945 — Destruction and Pillage — Poland. | Kaiser family. | Treasure troves — Poland. | Sosnowiec (Województwo Śląskie, Poland) — History — 20th century.
Classification: LCC D819.P7 K35 2020 (print) | LCC D819.P7 (ebook) | DDC 940.53/18144 — dc23
LC record available at https://lccn.loc.gov/2020033851
LC ebook record available at https://lccn.loc.gov/2020033852

Book design by Chloe Foster

Printed in the United States of America
DOC 10 9 8 7 6 5 4 3 2 1

Excerpts from Abraham Kajzer's memoir reprinted and translated by permission of the late author's family members. All rights reserved. English translation by Denise Grollmus. Lines from "A Sixth Finger" from *Or Kalu/Captive Light: Poems* by Mira Meir. Copyright © 1989 by Mira Meir. Used by permission of Hakibbutz Hameuchad, a division of Sifriat Poalim Publishing Group. All rights reserved. Excerpt from *Skarby polskie: Przewodnik dlaposzukiwaczy* by Włodzimierz Antkowiak. Copyright © 1993 by Włodzimierz Antkowiak. Reprinted and translated into English by permission of Bellona Publishing House, a division of Dressler Dublin. All rights reserved.

To Zaidy

CONTENTS

Part I

—

MAŁACHOWSKIEGO 12

1

My father's father, Maier Menachem Kaiser, died in April 1977. This was eight years before I was born—I didn't know him, we had had no grandfather-grandson moments, I'd never given him a hug, he'd never given me gifts my parents weren't thrilled about, he'd never scolded me for running into the street or told me he loved me. To me he was the father my father had once had and that's it. I knew astonishingly little about him, much less than could be attributed to our lives' lack of overlap. What *did* I know? I knew the pit stops in the obituary. I knew he was born in Poland (but not which city); I knew that he survived the war (but not a single detail beyond that); and I knew that after the war he moved to Germany, where in 1946 he married Bertha Ramras and had one child, my uncle; then to New York, where my father and my aunt were born; then to Toronto, where he died, at fifty-six, of heart failure.

Whatever slim conception I had of my grandfather came from what my father told me, usually on the anniversary of my grandfather's death, the yahrtzeit. On that day my father and I had a routine, same every year, fixed, ritualized. Just before sunrise my father wakes me up and we go to shul, where he leads the services and says the Kaddish. Afterwards he brings out a couple of bottles of schnapps, a bag of pastries, a bag of crackers. The dozen or so men gather around, have a shot, have some pastry, and say to my father, *May his neshama have an aliyah.* They say this in the manner one offers holiday greetings—formally, perfunctorily, but not unkindly. My father replies *amein,* thank you.

After shul he and I drive to the cemetery. It is exceptionally well maintained, laid out according to synagogue affiliation, and neighborhood-like, with soft demarcations and ordered avenues: Beth Emeth, Minsker, Stopnitzer, Anshei Minsk. Modest even in the afterlife, the men and the women are buried separately.

We park and walk to my grandfather's grave, where we read Psalms. There are Psalms for every occasion. At a gravesite you say chapters 33, 16, 17, 72, 91, 104, and 130; and then in chapter 119, which is composed of twenty-two paragraphs, one for each of the Hebrew letters, you read the paragraphs corresponding to the spelling of the name of the departed. I read the Psalms very quickly, for me this was yet another spiritual chore, I am practiced at chewing through the Hebrew. But once I am done I have nothing to do, nowhere to go, so I stand in front of my grandfather's grave, bored but not restless, and watch my father. He's a very good-looking man, square jaw, full head of black hair, trim. He's wearing what he's always wearing: Dockers, sensible shoes, white or blue button-down shirt, dark windbreaker, and dark baseball cap (he is entirely indifferent regarding the logo: it could be SWAT or FUBU). He reads the Psalms much slower than I do, slower even than his usual prayer-speed. My father is a man of habit—he extracts a deep comfort, even a kind of strength, from rules and routine—and his intensity reveals itself in the prescribed methods. I don't know what my father feels and thinks about his father. But whatever those thoughts and feelings are, they are displayed, if not quite articulated, when he prays quietly but not silently at his father's grave. He shuts his eyes tight enough that his temple creases. Here and there his voice, caught on a Hebrew word, rises and breaks. My father is crushing the Psalmist's words in his mouth. Most years he does not cry, but sometimes he does—sobless, stoic tears—and I peek out at him, uncomfortable, uncertain as to what, if anything, I am supposed to do. It occurs to me now that these are the only instances when I've ever seen my father cry.

On the tombstone is my grandfather's full Hebrew name, which is my full legal name: Meir Menachem Kaiser. (My parents updated the English spelling of "Maier.") It is strange to see your name engraved on a tombstone. I wouldn't say it's unsettling or disturbing—I'm still young, I don't have many thoughts, profound or otherwise, regarding death—it's just weird. The rest of the tombstone is taken up by a short Hebrew poem, a play on his name—"Meir" is derived from the Hebrew word that means light, "Menachem" from the word that means comfort: *The light* [meir] *of our eyes has been taken from us / We have no comfort* [menachem].

As a poem it's not much, but it is sincere, upfront, unpretentious. I am sure that the poem affected, and continues to affect, those who knew my grandfather.

I never met my grandfather; I am not deeply affected. I am not numb —at a gravesite you feel *something:* you feel the shape of sadness, you feel an empathetic stab that others feel the loss so viscerally—but my grandfather is nearly as abstract to me as is *his* grandfather, whose name not even my father knows. My grandfather's absence is a dry and un-tragic fact. That I bear his name is a circumstance of timing: had either of my two elder sisters been male, he would have been named Meir Menachem, which had been hanging there for eight years, waiting for a boy to fall onto.

When my father finally finishes the Psalms, he and I each take a rock

from the ground and put it on top of the tombstone, a custom whose or-
igins I don't know but which I take to mean: I was here, I remember. As
we drive through and then out of the cemetery, my father—feeling raw,
or plaintive, or perhaps lonely—talks about his father. But he doesn't
say much, and his descriptions almost never go beyond frustratingly
loose generalities; there are almost never any anecdotes, quotes, conflicts,
setbacks, victories, habits, quirks, nothing that could give shape or form
to the dead man we just visited. One year my father told me that my
grandfather was a health fanatic. "He did yoga," my father said, "way before it was trendy. He stood on his head every day." One year he told me
that my grandfather suffered from ulcers and drank Milk of Magnesia.
Another year he told me that my grandfather and I were very similar. I
asked my father to elaborate—how exactly am I like Zaidy? My father
shook his head and said, "I don't know, I just can see it."

There are photographs of my grandfather, but not many, and most of
them are rigidly composed and uncandid. He is handsome, bald, and he
looks good in a suit. He has a wide, clean-shaven face and cheeks that
ball up when he smiles.

We knew that my grandfather was the only one in his family to have
survived the war, that his parents and his siblings had been murdered,
as was nearly all of his large extended family. But as knowledge this was
dark matter. We knew nothing about his prewar or intrawar life. We
didn't know which concentration camps he had been in or what his father had done for a living. We knew nothing about his parents, aunts,
uncles, cousins; my father and his two siblings—let alone my generation—would be hard-pressed to tell you the names of my grandfather's
siblings; they wouldn't even be entirely sure of the number. We knew
they had died, but we had no idea who *they* were. We did not know
where they died, or how they died. And so when my grandfather died,
they died another sort of death.

• • •

I went to Poland for the first time in 2010, for reasons that had nothing to do with family history—I'd just finished a research fellowship in Lithuania and was spending Rosh Hashanah in Kraków—but once I was there I felt I should go to my grandparents' hometowns. It seemed like something I should do. Less an obligation, really, than etiquette. When you're in town you visit your relatives and say hi; when you're in Toronto on your grandfather's yahrtzeit you go to his grave and say Psalms; when you're in Poland for the first time you make the trip to your grandparents' hometowns and take pictures. You go and for the rest of your life you can say you have been.

I called my father and asked him what city his parents were from. He wasn't entirely sure about his mother ("Oświęcim, but maybe Rzesów . . . ?") but his father, he said, was definitely from Sosnowiec, a large city in the Silesian voivodeship, historically notable as the point where the Russian, Prussian, and Austro-Hungarian empires kissed. I checked online and saw that it was only seventy kilometers from Kraków; I could make it there and back in a day, easy. I told my father I was going to go. He said he thought that was a nice idea.

My father had never been to Sosnowiec, and evidently held no burning desire to go; he'd been to Poland a couple of times, on air-conditioned tours of cities, shtetls, camps, and famous rabbis' gravesites, and while I don't think he was actively avoiding his father's hometown—had the guide offered to stop there, my father would have gladly agreed—he had never felt compelled to make arrangements on his own. Overall my father seemed detached: Sosnowiec was where his father was born, where he went through what he went through, it is what it is. Partly this is due to personality: my father isn't a sentimental man, doesn't get attached to objects and places. But it's also clear that my father's ambivalence toward Sosnowiec has been to some degree determined by his father's reticence: our arrangements of meaning, of intrinsic and extrinsic significances, are at least partly inherited. Had my grandfather talked often about his childhood, had he described his home and his school and his block and the ghetto in great and loving and terrifying detail, a sort of nostalgia — untethered, derived, but still real — would have been cemented in his children. They would have dreamt of Sosnowiec. So to ask what Sosnowiec meant to my father is really to ask what Sosnowiec meant to my grandfather. This is a much harder question.

I asked my father if he had any relevant addresses, and he said he thought so, he'd have to dig through some papers. A few hours later he called me back and spelled out *Małachowskiego 12* — where, he said, he was pretty sure his father had grown up. My father also said that my great-grandfather had in fact owned this building; and that after the war my grandfather had tried and failed to reclaim it; and that twenty years ago, at my grandmother's urging, he, my father, had had my grandfather's documents translated, had made some inquiries about reclaiming the building, but had gotten nowhere, everyone said forget it, it wasn't possible or it wasn't worth it. All of which was interesting — I had never heard any of this before — but incidental. What mattered to me was that I had an address, I now had as my destination a particular spot on a particular street, and not an entire big blank city: my map of Sosnowiec now had a kind of memory-topography. When you seek out your origin, specificity of place matters. You want to know which city, you want to know which block, you want to know which apartment, which room. You want to get as particular as possible.

I took a train from Kraków to Katowice, then a second train to Sosnowiec. From the train station I walked toward Małachowskiego. The streets were narrow, potholed, crammed with small angry cars and recalcitrant streetcars and canopied by what seemed like thousands of overhead wires. Sosnowiec, I could see, was no one's favorite vacation getaway spot. Sosnowiec was gloomy and worn down and, in color and spirit, gray. Was I surprised? I don't know. Among American Jews trekking back to the *alte heim,* cameras slung around their necks and myth-memories ringing in their ears, it's become somewhat of a trope to be surprised by the city your immigrant grandparents grew up in. (It's so *urban!* It's so *modern!*) This is a coddled, storybook, sentimental preconception, but it can be hard to resist. While I hadn't pictured chickens and horses and peasantry, hadn't imagined finding at Małachowskiego 12 a modest but sturdy wooden cottage with a smoking chimney and a secret cellar, still, you can't help it, when you imagine your grandfather's Polish hometown you imagine (we have been conditioned to imagine) rural, green, quaint, old worldly, shtetl-ish. Sosnowiec is nothing like that. Sosnowiec isn't a village, isn't a shtetl, and it isn't picturesque. It is a grim postindustrial city. This is true historically, aesthetically, and atmospherically. The dominant industry in the region for centuries was coal mining, and this can be felt — the city feels grimy, heavy, melancholy. The city feels like a cough. The architecture is low, mean, Soviet, concrete: most of the buildings were built or renovated after the war and are utilitarian, curveless, a wrung-out gray or beige.

I found the street without difficulty — Małachowskiego is a major artery that cuts through the city center, made up mostly of boxy apartment buildings and municipal government buildings. Number 12 was one of those boxy apartment buildings. It was, as is standard in this part of the world, attached — it would be more accurate to describe it as the last quarter-section of the no-nonsense structure that runs nearly the length of the block. But the address of the adjacent section was Małachowskiego 14, which was not an address associated with my grandfather, and was thus of no interest to me. Number 12 was five stories high, with two rows of shallow white balconies protruding like ribs. Its color was a bleached beige. It was exceptionally plain-looking, if not quite drab.

I stood on the opposite side of the street and studied the façade, the laundry draped over the balconies and the perched satellite dishes. Feeling soft-hearted, feeling like I was inside a significant moment, I gave permission to my grandfather's history to settle onto, into, this plain-looking building. I confirmed to myself that this must be where my grandfather had grown up. Where else? I didn't have any other addresses so it must be here. I took some photographs. Passersby eyed me and my camera suspiciously. I understood their wariness. I understood that I didn't belong here. I felt it. I was an outsider, I was a sightseer, I was the furthest thing possible from a native. I was dancing my stupid nostalgia dance. The fact that I was from Sosnowiec (in a manner of speaking) and had returned only meant I belonged here even *less*. What I felt most sharply standing there in front of my grandfather's building was not a connection to this place/that time but a sense of *discontinuity* with the past. No matter how literary and metaphorical you wanted to get, this wasn't my home. My grandparents had done everything they could to wipe away this history. And they'd succeeded, no? Despite being the son of two Poles, my father would consider the idea that he is Polish ludicrous. No longing had been passed down. No seeds of nostalgia had been planted.

An old man exited the building and I ran toward him, gesturing for him to hold the door. A gracious and uninquisitive neighbor, he smiled and held the door. Inside was dreary, underlit, but not dirty or un-looked-after. It felt institutional and fireproofed. I walked up and down the stairs. There were four or five apartments on each floor and I looked at each door as if it might reveal itself as my grandfather's. But of course no apartment announced itself as the apartment my grandfather had grown up in eighty years prior. I could have knocked on a door, could have done my best to explain who I am, what I'm doing in this building, what I'm doing at your door. But I felt sheepish. I already felt like I was trespassing. I'd gone inside, I'd gotten as close as I was going to get.

I went to City Hall, where a patient clerk looked up my grandfather's name. It took a while to get it straight—I had assumed that my grandfather's legal name was spelled like mine; I simply handed her my driver's license—but eventually the clerk brought out a large leather-bound book and showed me a handwritten inscription, in gorgeous cursive, covering the bottom half of the page, announcing the birth of my grandfather, Maier-Mendel Kajzer ("Mendel" is the Yiddish diminutive of Menachem), to his parents, Moshe and Sura-Hena.

Then I walked to the station and got on a train. The departure felt final; there was no reason to think I would ever return. Why would I? I'd seen the city my grandfather was from, I'd seen the building he'd grown up in, I'd turned up a handwritten birth announcement, I'd gotten my photos. As a pilgrimage this was strictly a one-time thing. The only reason to return would have been to find answers to any outstanding questions, but I had no questions and felt no need to create any.

Every year hundreds or even thousands of Jews travel to the difficult-to-pronounce towns their parents or grandparents or great-grandparents came from. They fly to Ukraine, Poland, Lithuania, Latvia, Romania, Hungary, Belarus, they schlep onto creaky trains and cramped buses, hire zany guides, knock on ancestral doors, pleadingly ask old people if they recognize this name, have confusing and meaningful interactions with the locals, try to map out the patchy passed-down memories. In general it is a thrilling, fraught, emotional trip (how could it not be?). It is kind of like a memory-safari.

The destination is as much mythological as it is geographical. At the center of these families there is a story. How did he survive? How did she get out? What did he go through? The story might be partially known, or even entirely unknown; but it is known that there *is* a story. It is less historical than anecdotal: it is personal, it is living. These descendants are traveling great distances in order to interrogate, probe, glimpse, touch that story.

The hometown is significant because it is the setting of the story. (Otherwise it's entirely uninteresting, just one of ten thousand shtetls: I wouldn't make a great effort to go to *your* grandfather's Polish hometown.) The regular tourist submits herself to the place ("Can you recommend a place to eat?"). She recognizes, celebrates, and reinforces the local/foreign divide. The memory-tourist, however, is on a mission. She attempts to cajole the place into giving up its buried secrets. The question is not "What is this place?" but "What is the meaning of this place?" She blurs the local/foreign divide. I'm not from here but I'm from here. The purpose of the trip is not to experience place as much as it is to ratify or elucidate or edit the myth of the place. The memory-tourists try to find and speak to ghosts. Sometimes they succeed.

That the descendants will just as likely use the Yiddish name of the town instead of the Polish one makes for a very handy metaphor.

On one level this is similar to the genealogical impulse (*Where do I come from? Who are my people?*) but a thousand times more intense, given that most of the branches of the family tree terminate with horrific abruptness. On another level it's a way of approaching, even if it's only a tiny step closer, an ineffable tragedy. (Here is a great vibrating dissonance: on the one hand, your grandfather lost *every single one of his family members;* on the other hand, his story is unremarkable, almost a cliché.) What are these descendants searching for? Sometimes it's straightforward. Sometimes the questions are answered with a visit to an archive, or a conversation with an elderly local. But I think they are often searching for answers to questions they don't know how to ask, questions that cannot be formed. If you grew up around Holocaust survivors you know what I'm talking about. If not, try to imagine trying to imagine a survivor's inner state.

Over the next few years I spent a lot of time in Poland, sometimes for research, sometimes just because, and every so often my father would mention the building in Sosnowiec, those documents gathering dust in the closet. He'd encourage me to take a look, see if there was anything there, maybe I'd be able to do something. That it took more than four years from when I first learned about those documents until I read them speaks to how unurgent the matter seemed. The file was in Toronto, in my parents' house, and the couple of times a year I visited I'd always forget I was supposed to take a look.

Finally in the summer of 2015 I was in Kraków for a few weeks and my father faxed me a copy of the file. It was a thick sheaf, fifty or sixty pages, in Polish, German, English. And it was a mess: original documents, carbon copies, translations, translations of translations.

After I organized the file a story emerged, though it was a story without arc or resolution. There was only frustration: for twenty years my grandfather had tried to reclaim or at least be compensated for his family's property, and for twenty years he'd gotten nowhere. The bulk of the documents consisted of letters to and from people and institutions who couldn't or wouldn't help him. A lawyer in Sosnowiec demanded a hefty retainer and "the dates and places of death [of your uncle and father] and witnesses who can confirm the information," an absurd, impossible request; my grandfather never even responded. My grandfather asked a Polish friend to check the municipal records to see if there was any possibility of compensation from the Polish or German government; she wrote back that she couldn't get access to the records and that compensation was pretty much impossible anyway. My grandfather wrote to a Rabbi Brandys, the head of the Sosnowiec Jewish community, to request a certificate that he was the owner of the building at Małachowskiego 12; Brandys responded curtly that "the Jewish community is not authorized to issue such a document."

My grandfather's best chance for compensation came in 1957, after the US government established the Foreign Claims Settlement Commission in order to register claims of US nationals against Poland for property that had been expropriated during the war. On my grandfather's application he cites the loss of a building worth 58,000 zloty, about $400 (roughly $3,500 in 2020 US dollars). And in 1960 Poland agreed to pay

$40 million to those with eligible claims; my grandfather undoubtedly heard the news, undoubtedly imagined his form was being processed, his claim being investigated.

But he heard nothing, no confirmation, no rejection even. Nine years after he'd submitted his application he wrote to a lawyer in New York named Alberti and asked him to look into it.

Alberti informed my grandfather that he hadn't submitted his claim properly, in fact hadn't submitted a claim at all: there was *another* form, not available until 1961, that the FCSC required. My grandfather was apparently unaware. I don't understand how he missed the news—the FCSC had publicized this requirement extensively, even setting up an office in New York City to process the claims. By the time he wrote to Alberti it was too late. No claims filed after January 31, 1965, were accepted.

How disappointed my grandfather must have been. For years he had tried to navigate these faraway bureaucracies, had tried in vain to enlist the help of friends, strangers, lawyers. And then the US government had forced open an opportunity, had delivered a chance to be at least partially compensated for what had been taken from his family. But he had misunderstood the instructions. He'd blown it.

In 1967 my grandfather had many of the documents translated into German, and asked two former Sosnowiec residents to write affidavits stating that the Kajzer family owned Małachowskiego 12; it seems he was preparing to file a claim in German court. He also had the building manager, Konrad Moszczeński, with whom he'd been in very sporadic contact, send him a notarized copy of the mortgage register. This was by far the most legally relevant document in the pile. It was a short piece of paper, only four or so inches long, with a large Sosnowiec County Court seal at the bottom, stating that "on the basis of a 22 April 1936 decision of the Mortgage Department of the City of Sosnowiec, the deed of the property at Małachowskiego 12, Land and Mortgage Register number 1304, was transferred to Moshe and Sura-Hena Kajzer, a married couple,

68%, and Shia and Gitla Kajzer, 32%." For some reason my grandfather never filed, or at least we have no evidence that he did; this is the end of the paper trail.

I was unexpectedly moved, reading these documents, tracing this story. To some extent this was due to the fact that I was reading words my grandfather himself had written. Words, even words laced up inside a letter to an attorney or a US government form, are like footprints. But aside from stating his parents' names and revealing the fact that they had owned a textile business, the file revealed little biographical information. This wasn't a journal, there was none of that kind of overt intimacy.

And yet.

I could imagine my grandfather's desperation, his disappointment. I pictured him in his white and pink kitchen ripping open the letters, taking in the words with quickening breath and growing anger. Anger not at the lawyers or Rabbi Brandys or the commission, but at all of them, at everyone who stood in his way, at everyone who couldn't or wouldn't help, at everyone who did this and allowed it to happen, at those who allowed it to go unpunished, at the city of Sosnowiec, the country of Poland, the Germans, the Americans, maybe at God, too. How could he not connect the relatively minor injustice of being unable to secure his inheritance with the unspeakable tragedy that had left him as the only heir? He was very persistent. My grandfather asked and asked and asked: the New York lawyer, the Sosnowiec lawyer, the Sosnowiec rabbi, the Polish government, the American government—everyone was kind and solicitous (aside from the rabbi), but the response was always no.

Throughout the file my grandfather comes across as businesslike, detached. But you cannot help but wonder what's roiling beneath. What did the building mean to him? Was his interminable bureaucratic struggle a stand-in for a deeper, more personal, less articulable struggle? Did my grandfather see this as his only chance at extracting even a little bit of justice? Later my father told me that when his family moved to Toronto in 1963, his father had brought with him savings of $50,000, worth about half a million dollars today. I was surprised. I had assumed, having spent time with the version of my grandfather that had emerged in the file, that he had been severely cash-strapped. "If Zaidy had that much money," I asked my father, "why all the *agmas nefesh* over four hundred dollars?" My father said he didn't know.

Pursuing a seventy-year-old claim on a drab building in Sosnowiec was sentimental and unpragmatic. My father—exceedingly unsentimental and pragmatic, a real cost-benefit kind of guy—had made an effort to look into it on behalf of his mother, but once she passed, that was it; Sosnowiec and everything in it became faraway and forgotten history. It was assumed, to the extent it was considered at all, that some property in some Polish town would be worth very little money—certainly not enough to justify the time and resources necessary to perform who knows what legal maneuvers in a country no one understood or trusted. This had been my stance too.

Although I don't know anything about my grandfather's time in the war, or his history from before the war, it isn't an uneasy ignorance, by which I mean it has never felt to me like a secret, doesn't have a valence of shame or trauma, I've never sensed in this gap the throb of repression, though of course on some level it's there—my grandfather went through what he went through and never told his children—but it has never felt like forbidden knowledge, only lost knowledge, like he died before he could tell anyone, or before anyone asked him. I don't know why my grandfather didn't tell his children about what he'd lost—he was protecting them, or protecting himself, he was creating a new life, I don't know. But whatever it was, his children, my father and his siblings, seem unhaunted—my father has explained to me just how normal it was growing up, how all of his friends' parents were survivors, how no one he knew had grandparents—and it's been passed down, this normalcy: for my siblings and cousins and for me it's become undetailed family history, our grandfather was a survivor, he went through what he went through, it's our legacy, but we, or at least I, have never felt particularly disturbed by this legacy, it's simply always been there.

But then I read the file, saw how my grandfather had tried and failed for more than twenty years to reclaim what his family had lost, and here was an opportunity, I thought, to allow myself to be disturbed. The building, maybe, was a means to access a history, a person, that I'd always thought inaccessible, immutably closed.

2

Yechiel, a Brooklyn-born Hasid who lived in Kraków and had been trying for years to break into the local real estate game, particularly prewar Jewish property, put me in touch with a lawyer known, he said, as "The Killer." "She's good?" I asked. "Of course," Yechiel said. "She's The Killer."

I reached out to The Killer, made an appointment, and a few days later I gathered up the file and took a taxi to a large apartment block in the north part of Kraków. The Killer's ground-floor office was a single rectangular room with two large adjacent desks facing the door, pinching the room into an H-shape. On the wall The Killer's diplomas hung beside unframed posters of kittens and an oversized cat calendar.

It was a mother-daughter-daughter team. The Killer was in her eighties and had a wrinkled, intelligent, severe face, with gray hair cut short. She was sphinxlike—she sat very still and without expression, and she spoke only Polish and in a brisk monotone. She was incomprehensible to me on two levels: we had no common language plus she was totally unreadable. Her daughter Grazyna, polite, patient, middle-aged, was her right-hand woman, her paralegal, and our interpreter. The other daughter, Jadwiga, obviously less critical to operations, sat at an old computer in the corner — the only computer in the office — watching a video of wrestling pandas.

They greeted me warmly, offered me cookies from a package and orange soda. I sat down and we got to it. I showed them the file, told them about the building. The Killer and Grazyna flipped through the pages, commenting to each other in Polish. They asked me clarifying questions — who's this, who's that, who's alive, who's dead. I asked them to explain some of the Polish/German documents. Communication was, if not arduous, then choppy. Grazyna never spoke for herself — any question I had, no matter how minor or procedural, she relayed to The Killer, who responded at length to Grazyna, who translated. Our communication thus felt rather monarchal.

Grazyna kicked her sister off the computer, then went to Google Street View and searched for Małachowskiego 12; I recognized the building immediately. "That's it," I said. "Oh!" Grazyna said. "Super, super." They then sought to determine its value. They asked me how many apartments were on each floor, but I couldn't remember; so, judging from the image on the screen, they estimated: five floors, five apartments per floor. Grazyna brought out a tabletop calculator. Say each apartment was, on average, seventy square meters. That would bring the total square footage of the building to 1,750 square meters; and given that nearby apartments were listed at between 1,100 and 1,600 zloty per square meter, the building was worth between 1.9 million zloty and 2.8 million zloty, about $430,000 to $630,000.

"Super," Grazyna said. "Super."

"Hunh," I said.

Grazyna then went to the municipal website and searched for a deed, but nothing came up. She explained that this was likely because the building hadn't been bought or sold since before the war; the records hadn't been updated. The pre-digital records, she said, would be in City Hall, in a ledger she called the "Forever Book." Right now the status of the building was in limbo, technically speaking it was ownerless: *nieuregulowany stan prawny/nieustalony właściciel.* This meant: *unregulated legal status/undetermined owner.* An accidental testament to absence.

We then focused on my family. Had my grandfather ever received any compensation from the Polish government? No. Was I sure? — because receiving *any* amount of money would mean forfeiture of claim. I said that as far as I knew, he had never gotten any money. My grandmother had received a small pension from the German government. But nothing from the Polish government. Good, they said. They then seemed to imply that if there was in fact documentation to the contrary, it would be best if that documentation were to remain unknown.

The next order of business was to construct the family tree.

Who was your grandfather? Maier was my grandfather. When was he born? In 1921. And who were his parents? Moshe and Sura-Hena, as you can see, here's a photograph of my grandfather's birth announcement. When were they born? I have no idea. Did your grandfather have siblings? Yes. There was a brother, Michoel Aaron, I know this because my father is named after him, and a sister, whose name I don't know but can try and find out. When did Moshe die? In the war. When did Sura-Hena die? In the war. Do you have their death certificates? No. When did Michoel Aaron die? In the war. When did the sister die? In the war. Do you have their death certificates? No. Did Moshe have siblings? Well, there's Shia, he's on the mortgage, he owns 32 percent. Are there others? I don't know. Do you know who were Moshe's parents? No. Did Michoel Aaron or the sister have any children? I don't know. Did Shia have children? I don't know. Can you find out? I can ask, but if Shia, Michoel Aaron, or the sister had children I'm nearly certain none sur-

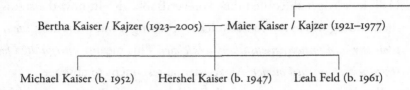

Bertha Kaiser / Kajzer (1923–2005) — Maier Kaiser / Kajzer (1921–1977)

Michael Kaiser (b. 1952)   Hershel Kaiser (b. 1947)   Leah Feld (b. 1961)

vived. I would have heard of them. Do you have their death certificates? No. Do you know Sura-Hena's maiden name? No. Maier was married to whom? Bertha Kaiser. Is she alive? No. Do you have her death certificate? Yes. Do you have her birth certificate? No. And Maier is dead? Yes. Do you have his death certificate? Yes. Do you have his birth certificate? No. And Maier had how many children? Three — my father, Michael; my uncle, Hershel; and my aunt, Leah. Do you have their birth certificates? Yes. Are they still living? Yes. And they will sign power of attorney to you? My father will, and my aunt will. But with my father's brother it might get complicated. It is a very complicated situation. Did Maier leave a will? I think so. I think it was all just left to my grandmother. Did your grandmother leave a will? I think so. Do you have documents that "Kajzer" became "Kaiser"? I think so.

Perhaps as a kind of semiconscious counteraction to the abrupt and to-tal loss of family suffered by their parents, my father and his two sib-lings never strayed far. They settled down and raised their own families around the corner from their childhood home, where my grandmother lived until she died, in 2005, outliving my grandfather by a lot and her second husband, Chiel, by a little. The entire family stayed unscattered, within a three-block radius. Aunts, uncles, cousins, and Bubby were an

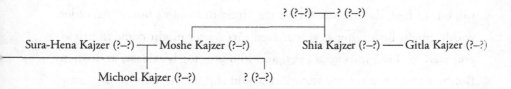

omnipresent part of my childhood. Directly across the street from our house were the other Kaisers, Uncle Hershel's family, whom for some lost reason we called the Kiddies, and one street over were my aunt Leah's family, the Felds.

Even taking into account the proximity, the families were exceptionally close. Our lives were threaded into one another's, and Bubby, if not quite the matriarch (she was too fearful, too unself-possessed, too dependent), nevertheless held the affectionate center of our orbit. We were a large raucous lot. There were six children in my family; in the Felds', five; and in the Kiddies', seven—and a year after Hershel's wife, Sheila, died of breast cancer, he married Naomi, who moved in with her four children, and then, a year later, they had another. Cousins were nearly as essential a feature of my childhood as were siblings. Everyone had at least one cousin who was about the same age and who thus made for a natural companion; we paired up, tripled up, made little interlocking cousin cliques. Up until high school I spent more time with Ari Kaiser, one grade up but only four months my senior, than with any other human being. Sunday mornings Bubby made breakfast, obscenely buttery scrambled eggs, for anyone who showed up anytime between, I don't know, seven and noon. (A great joy of Bubby's was feeding her children and grandchildren—though it was a joy shot through with trauma and fear: if you didn't finish what was on your plate, she would weep.) You'd roll out of bed, daven, walk down the street to Bubby's house. An older cousin might be leaving as you arrived. Ari Kaiser might come in just as you were tucking into your eggs, and join you for breakfast, and when Bubby turned toward the stove Ari would slip on her enormous plastic eyeglasses and blink his now giant eyes and impersonate Bubby's accented sighs and the way she said *bubbele* and make you laugh so hard snot exploded from your nostrils.

That all three families were Orthodox, that everyone led similar lives and obeyed similar religious strictures and schedules, facilitated — supercharged — the closeness. On those long, flat, interminable Shabbos afternoons — when you can't drive, can't ride your bike, can't use electronics, can't do homework — we would drift back and forth between the houses, play Ping-Pong, basement hockey, board games, eat nosh, tease the younger kids, ruin the grown-ups' naps. My cousins' homes were an extension of my own. I knew perfectly those rooms, those kitchens, those basements, those closets of toys and games. I could go over whenever I wanted, I could sleep over whenever I wanted. There was enough cousin-traffic between the houses that you weren't expected to knock; if on the rare occasion the door was locked, then you knew the combination, or where the key was hidden.

On Friday night everyone's Shabbos meals would end when they'd end and everyone would make their way to one of the cousins' for dessert. The adults clustered at the far end of the table and argued, kibitzed, joked, talked Torah, talked travel, compared grocery deals. The kids clustered around the other end and did the same thing in their own key. It'd inevitably get very loud — one argument or bout of hilarity anywhere at the table raised everyone's volume — with lots of chaotic cross-talk. You could dip in and out of conversations like they were TV channels.

My immediate family and the Felds were, on the whole, loud and clever, but next to the Kiddies we were downright meek and slow. The

Kiddies were exasperatingly quick and intelligent, and unyielding in the extreme. This was particularly true of Uncle Hershel. Hershel had a huge, hard belly, thick plastic glasses, thick dark beard. He was very affectionate, though his affections could hurt: he'd greet you by grabbing the skin beneath your chin and say *zeeeeeskeit!*; and in the Kiddies' house you might be subject to tickle torture, wherein Hershel picked you up and put you on the curled end of the bannister and tickled you until you felt you were going to die. Hershel's debate chops were legendary: the only ones who had the tenacity to keep up were, once they were old enough, his sons. Argument for them was a blood sport. The rest of us would watch, stupefied and amused, as they argued endlessly, inexhaustibly, dazzlingly, over politics, history, *halacha,* anything. Hershel was also the single greatest Tetris player I've ever known, which says something, I think, about his focus, obsessiveness, and stubbornness.

Let me go on about Hershel for one more paragraph, because I want to give you some sense of a very complicated man, because the story is about to turn. Hershel had this great oratorical trick he'd perform at family functions. Everyone would deliver their speeches, which were less speeches than *divrei torah:* involved hermeneutical teachings that pulled from the Bible, Talmud, any of the thousands of commentaries. Then Hershel, last up, would improvise his own involved hermeneutical teaching that *combined* all the preceding ones: he'd use all their sources, all their insights and conclusions, and right there in front of us unspool his grand synthesis.

In the mid-1990s the family came apart. For a long time I didn't know why, didn't know what the dispute was about. The falling-out, this fight that cleaved the family, that put my father and aunt on one side and Hershel on the other, was, to us kids, very sudden and very mysterious —we had no idea what had happened, only that it was something exceptionally serious. It had to do with money, we could pick up that much, there were lawyers involved, it had something to do with business, assets, maybe even inheritance, any of the crasser if usually invisible ligaments of Family.

My parents kept us in the dark. They didn't clue us in, didn't intentionally explain and didn't unintentionally let anything slip. But the anger and heartbreak were impossible to miss; it's atmospheric, your parents' emotional state. Whatever was going on became one of those adult conversations that's always under way but just out of earshot. A great invisible monster whose presence we could sense. I remember my father's face when he'd see his brother on the street — which happened often, it was unavoidable, our families lived so close, and on Shabbos when you can't drive, when you have to walk, you and your neighbors will cross paths plenty — how his features hardened, his brow furrowed and his lips a tight line, how he'd stare or conspicuously not-stare.

Hershel's kids were as clueless as we were. Ari Kaiser and I, over the course of weeks and then months, tried to figure out what the heck was going on between our fathers, but we couldn't come up with anything, couldn't piece together why everything had fallen apart.

For a while the fallout stayed confined to that generation. I and my siblings still went to the Kiddies'; Ari and his siblings still came over to us. Hershel would still grab the skin beneath our chins, would still subject us to tickle torture. I suppose it was a kind of intimacy inertia. My father's stated position was that it didn't bother him if we went to his brother's house, even if he himself wouldn't set foot there. But animosity gradually seeps down, parent to child, turns into a more benign but still substantial discomfort. Soon enough we were also staying away from the Kiddies. Gradually our lives diverged. Within a few years there was virtually no interaction between the Kiddies, on one side, and us and the Felds on the other. We adjusted to this Hershel-less reality. Yes I have an uncle but we have nothing to do with him. Hershel became more and more abstract, a character from a past story. The falling-out, the fight, the lawsuit hummed somewhere in the far background of our family life.

When my grandmother died, my father, uncle, and aunt had to sit shiva together. They sat side by side on Bubby's green velvet sofa, minus the plastic cover (if Bubby weren't dead she'd die) and minus the cushions—those in mourning must sit low, close to the ground—looking calm, projecting an air of composure and normalcy, but it was palpably abnormal and awkward: each sibling-faction was pretending the other didn't exist. My father sat in the middle with Hershel to his immediate left, but there might as well have been a hundred-foot wall separating them. The room, the crowd, the array of folding chairs, the conversation divided along this fault line. Visitors offered condolences twice. Once to Hershel, to whom they'd relate a memory or sentiment about Bubby, then say the verse traditionally offered as a valediction to a mourner; and then slide over to my aunt and father, to whom they'd repeat the memory or sentiment, and say the verse again.

One afternoon, when I was in ninth or tenth grade, my father and I were alone in the kitchen and, unprompted—if memory serves this really came out of nowhere—he explained everything. (I don't know what elicited this; my father, for all his pragmatism, can be very impulsive.) He leaned over the countertop, chummy, relaxed; I leaned next to him, mirroring his pose and demeanor. "First things first, you have to understand the context," he said. At the top of a blank sheet of paper he wrote, in his characteristic block letters, APEX. Underneath he drew four lines, radiating outward, family tree–style. "Apex is a real estate company," he said. There had been four original partners, one of whom was my grandfather. My father wrote KAISER at the terminus of the first line. Each partner had a 25 percent stake. "When my father died that twenty-five percent," my father said, drawing three new branches under KAISER, "was split into three. So we have eight and a third, Leah has eight and a third, and Hershel has eight and a third."

During Zaidy's lifetime, my father said, Apex's assets, made up primarily of four residential apartment buildings in Toronto, had never been worth that much. But over the years the value had increased substantially. (I asked how much they'd be worth today. My father shut his eyes and nodded. "A lot.") The Kaiser family had always operated as a single entity.

The fallout, my father explained, had to do with the Apex holdings; I don't see a need to detail or relitigate the alleged wrongdoings here — I'll say only that the general narrative I received that day was that Hershel, true to character, refused to back down, refused to settle, made Talmudic arguments for why he was in the right. That it was more Hershel's stubbornness and tenacity, the doubling down and prolonging, and less the original misdeed that was unforgivable. My father, leaning against the counter, was orderly, detailed, impassive. He presented all this almost like a case study: I could discern no animus in him toward his brother. But I remembered, even if I'd been young and uninformed — I'd seen up close the anger and heartbreak.

Fifteen years after that day in the kitchen I met with The Killer and took those first steps toward reclamation and understood that this story of inheritance could hardly be isolated from that story of inheritance. I looked up the publicly available court documents, followed the Apex lawsuit as it snaked for more than a decade through the Canadian justice system, tracked the judgments and appeals and decisions and further appeals, hundreds and hundreds of (surprisingly lively) pages. I had, then, two piles of documentary evidence pertaining to my family and family property. There was that of my grandfather's building in Sosnowiec, a thin, haphazard, scattershot pile of sources that offered not much more than an outline of an outline of a story, with so many aching gaps and questions. And there was that of Apex, an easily downloadable two-foot-high superabundance of material, the story of a family's dissolution told in glaring detail.

Only in 2011, when the Supreme Court of Canada refused to hear the case, did the lawsuit finally wind down. This didn't mean, of course, that the parties were ready to reconcile. But it was a necessary starting point—the ordeal could now be moved into the past tense. And a few years later my father and Hershel did in fact reconcile, somewhat. With Hershel's wife acting as an intermediary, the brothers reached an agreement: they could be in touch, there could be a relationship, of sorts, they could reenter each other's lives, but neither would mention the past. No accounting, no questions, no confrontations, no clarifications, no apologies demanded and no apologies given. The past was to be put away. To celebrate, my mother, father, Hershel, and Naomi went out to dinner. By all accounts they had a nice, normal time.

Thus their relationship entered a third phase—cordial, friendly, stable, undramatic.

In 2015—right around the time I met with The Killer—Hershel fell ill, and in the span of a few months he lost something like half his body weight. Gone was that huge, hard belly. Even more unnerving was the change in persona. He had always been so quick, so garrulous, all this coiled energy; now he was slow, spacey, quiet, glassy-eyed, helpless. My father checked in on Hershel regularly. He helped with errands, took Hershel to doctor's appointments, pushed him in his wheelchair to shul.

In September 2015 I went to Toronto and sat down with my father and Leah and her husband, Mordy. I explained what I'd learned: Zaidy's father and uncle had jointly owned the building in Sosnowiec; the documentation was actually pretty good; the lawyer I'd retained was confident we could get it back.

"It seems like it'll be a relatively straightforward process," I said.

Overall they were bemused. Sosnowiec was a million miles away, in a left-behind and intentionally forgotten world. They had no sentimental ambition there. Mordy asked me how much the building was worth.

"Four, five hundred thousand dollars, maybe more."

The figure surprised and impressed them, but I wouldn't say it excited them. Any windfall was still very abstract. They were of the opinion —and in this regard they were much more perspicacious than I was —that this process wouldn't be so straightforward. They had no faith in the Polish legal system—to their ears the phrase "Polish court" sounded like a punch line—and believed that the average Pole, judges not excepted, was, if not necessarily an out-and-out anti-Semite, then certainly not rushing to help foreign Jews take back ancestral property, and was probably also an anti-Semite. But here I was, having spent all this time in Poland, saying we had a shot. They were game.

"What I need now," I said, "is your power of attorney. This is your inheritance, not mine." Yes, of course, they said. No problem.

"And you have to decide what you want to do about Hershel."

"What does Hershel have to do with this?"

"He's Zaidy's child too."

It was unlikely, I knew, that they would embrace the idea of getting involved with Hershel, especially not with something as close to the bone as an inheritance proceeding involving real estate. Even if everyone was now on speaking terms, there was plenty of unresolved hurt and betrayal, and there would never again be a sense of comfort and trust. But I had hoped, given that none of them was really going to be involved past these power of attorney forms, that they'd say whatever, okay, go get Hershel's signature, what does it really matter. My father and aunt demurred: there was no way Hershel would simply go along with it, no way he would simply just sign a paper and let others take control. That's just not how Hershel, even a weakened Hershel, works.

I proposed to leave Hershel out of it for now, if there was money at the end we could deal with it then, give him his share, it would be much easier that way for everyone. Everyone agreed. So The Killer prepared two power of attorney forms, one for my father and one for my aunt; as far as the Polish courts were concerned, Maier Kajzer had two children. I didn't give it much thought at the time—it was a decision of expediency, so as not to have the reclamation fail before it started. But in retrospect it was a shameful, and shamefully ironic, decision: in order to proceed with the reclamation—which represented a kind of un-erasing of my family—I had to, or chose to, erase my family, and do so within the official Polish record, no less.

I shipped the power of attorney forms to Kraków and that was that: we'd set the machine in motion and now there was nothing to do but wait, let The Killer do her thing. It felt a little strange, a little uncomfortable—a little unromantic?—how this had so quickly assumed a bureaucratic shape. But that's how it works was what I was told. Your motivations can be personal and sentimental and on fire but the process is bureaucratic and cold and procedural. There was no person or persons to appeal to, no one I could implore, or demand, to sign the deed back to my family. There was no one who *could* sign the deed back to my family. This story doesn't have an antagonist (is "history" an antagonist?). The building was ownerless, lost, and the apparatus to be used to try and force recovery was a legal one.

3

In the months after sending off the power of attorney forms I didn't give the matter much thought. This was an easy story to slip into: I was the grandchild embarking on a mission of memory, I was reclaiming an ancestral building and doing so for the sake of or in the name of or in order to be connected to or something having to do with my grandfather; what else was there to consider, who else was there to consider?

Obviously: the people who actually live in the building, for whom my claim would be an out-of-nowhere hurricane. It took some time for this to sink in but more and more it felt . . . not *wrong* but irresponsible to proceed with the reclamation without at least knowing, knowing of, knowing about the residents. The Killer was against the idea. Don't make trouble, she said. You could cause a panic. You could mess everything up.

I ignored her advice and returned to Sosnowiec. I brought my friend Jason, a photographer who can be, especially when he's photographing (and he's always photographing), relentless and a little shameless—his company makes me bolder—and Larysa, an understated, whip-smart museum curator, as an interpreter. We agreed that if we were to have any hope of having a meaningful conversation with a resident, we'd have to go in soft. "Soft"—I'm making this sound like a practical decision. Which it was, but it was also a cowardly decision. I was going to obscure the truth: we'd say we were interested in researching and writing a history of the building, which, while not inaccurate, we *were* interested, nonetheless suffered from a grave omission. At the time it seemed honest enough—I *wasn't* scoping the place out, I was genuinely just trying to meet the residents. But in retrospect this is a weak justification.

We got inside without incident. Jason and Larysa took in the dull green walls, the sterile stairwell. "This doesn't look like it's from before the war," Larysa said. "This looks like a building from Communist times." I shrugged. Who knows what the story was. Maybe it'd been renovated. Anyway, I said, here's a plan? Let's be methodical? We can start at the top, knock on doors, work our way down?

It was mid-morning on a weekday, and very quiet. The only sign of life was a middle-aged man entering his second-floor apartment, which, as we could see even from the hall, was under renovation.

Top floor. We chose a door at random and Larysa knocked. Jason and I stood a few feet back, far enough that we seemed (we hoped) unscary but close enough to indicate that we were of the same party. No answer. Larysa knocked on the next door; again no answer. We tried a third door. This time the door opened, but only a couple of inches, only as far as the chain would allow. Peering out at us through the gap was an old, thin, unsmiling woman. Larysa said the bit we'd prepared in the car. But the woman was having none of it. I didn't have to understand the conversation to see that it wasn't going well. *Nie, nie, nie.* She was unpersuaded, unconvinced, untrusting. The pretext we'd crafted—that we were American researchers interested in learning about the history of the building etc.—was useless. Our presence was threatening, Jason's camera was threatening, our interest (in her life, in her home) was threatening.

We tried the other doors on the floor; no one answered, which was disappointing, but also, given how tense it had gotten with the old woman, somewhat of a relief.

We held a whispered meeting and decided to abandon the plan of trying each door and instead to walk down two flights to the apartment being renovated, because, one, we knew someone was home, and because, two, that someone, as we'd seen on our way up, was young, in his late thirties or early forties and therefore, we figured, much less likely to be spooked.

The man was standing in his doorway as we came down. We (that is, Larysa) introduced ourselves and offered our undercooked spiel. He agreed to be interviewed without hesitation. His name was Bartek. He was friendly, amenable, forthright. He had a wide noble forehead, made wider and nobler by his receding hairline. Dark hair with matching thin goatee and sharp-angled eyebrows. He looked like a pudgier, kinder Lenin. His t-shirt and sweatpants were covered in home improvement splatter, caulk and paint and white dust.

Bartek apologized for the state of his apartment and suggested it might be easier if we talked in the hallway. He brought out a chair for me and a chair for Larysa and a toolbox for himself, which he stood on its side and used as a stool. Jason stayed standing and took photos. It was tight; the four of us took up all the space in the stairwell.

Bartek asked us how he could help, what it was we wanted to know. He was so welcoming and unsuspicious—it made it that much harder to deceive myself that what we were doing wasn't deception. On some level I *wanted* Bartek to be wary, or at least to be a little warier—wary enough so that my lies felt not so heavy but not too wary that he didn't want to speak to us. Perhaps it was a generational thing, perhaps it was a temperamental thing, but Bartek wasn't wary at all, he was only receptive, only wanted to be helpful to these strangers, an American writer and an American photographer and their Polish handler who showed up without warning at his home claiming to be researchers.

Bartek said that although he could understand and even speak a little English, he felt more comfortable speaking in Polish. Of course, I said, Larysa will translate. Jason was photographing continuously—the visuals here were irresistible: cold hard stairwell as foreground; gorgeous mess of an apartment as background; and Bartek, in his filthy sweats, perched on his toolbox, as subject.

I opened the interview—and I say "interview" because at the outset it felt formal, stiff—by reiterating our cover story: "We're doing a project to understand the building, the history of the building, and to that end we want to know your story, your memories."

Bartek matter-of-factly sketched his bio. He was born in a nearby town called Czeladź but when he was two years old he moved to Sosnowiec, to this apartment, to live with his grandparents. In the thirty-six-square-meter apartment, he said, lived seven people: his grandparents, his great-grandparents, him, and the sixth and seventh I didn't catch—perhaps an aunt and uncle.

"How long ago was that?" I asked. I acknowledged it to myself in the moment and I should acknowledge it here: though I was interested in Bartek's narrative I was also pushing, fishing, for details relevant to my family's narrative.

"I'm forty-two years old now," Bartek said, "and I moved here when I was two. So forty years ago."

"So you've been in this apartment essentially your entire life?"

"*Tak,*" Bartek said, then, in English, "This is my family's house." My heart skipped; these were startling words to hear. Bartek didn't mean anything by it, it wasn't said defensively or threateningly, he only meant to show off his English; he had no reason to feel threatened or to act defensively—well, he did have a reason but he was unaware he had a reason. I'd been telling myself this was *my* family's building, and so it was startling to hear him say, "This is my family's house"—here was his story intruding on mine, or my story intruding on his—and in that moment I regretted coming here, asking for interviews, meeting and getting to know and becoming attached to people who would be, no matter how generous my outlook, no matter how right-minded my intentions, adversaries. Bartek had no idea and I hated that he had no idea.

If you want to understand this building, Bartek said, you have to know that it is connected intimately with the theater. Most of the apartments had been designated by the Communist government for the cast and crew of Teatr Zagłębia, a renowned provincial playhouse. "The theater lived here," Bartek said, in English. All the residents were theater people. There were actors, actresses, directors, costumers, secretaries, administrators. Bartek's grandfather? He was a leading man. Even today, Bartek said, many of the residents are involved with the theater. That woman upstairs who had been so suspicious? Her name was Teresa, and her late husband was an actor. One floor below her lived one of the leading actresses, across the hall from a woman who worked in the theater office. "Many actors used to live in this building," Bartek said. "On Fridays and on Saturdays, after the premiere, they'd come home and throw huge parties. The whole building was a party. We are strangers but somehow, because of the theater, we are kind of family, even today."

While we were talking a few residents squeezed by to go up or down the stairs. They were polite but aloof. If they were curious about what was going on, why these three strangers, one with an open notebook and another with a camera, were interviewing their neighbor, they did a good job hiding it.

I asked Bartek (disingenuously? It was getting more and more difficult to tease out my interest in Bartek and his story from my interest in my own) if he'd share any early memories of the building, of those parties, of his neighbors, of his family. He reminisced softly for a bit, nothing very specific, more image than narrative, then, of his own accord, circled back to the story of how he'd come to live with his grandparents. He corrected and expanded what he'd told us before. He didn't in fact move here when he was two. Rather, it was at that age that he began spending more time with his grandparents than he did with his parents; Bartek didn't say why, and I didn't ask. At age six, he said, he decided to move to Sosnowiec for good.

Jason interrupted with instructions for a pose: "Bartek, can you put your hands on your knees?" Bartek put his hands on his knees. "That's perfect," Jason said, camera up against his face.

Bartek, as he held the pose, told us that he didn't see his mother, not once, for the next thirty-five years, even though she lived only four kilometers away. And then one day he got a message on Nasza-klasa, a kind of Polish Facebook, from a brother he had never known existed, inviting him to his wedding, where he met not only the groom but also four other brothers, *and* saw his mother for the first time in thirty-five years. "We had," he said, "an impromptu family reunion."

I asked (what else could I ask?) what that was like.

Bartek said, in his overpronounced English, "It was amazing," then switched back to Polish. Initially, he said, he was very moved, very touched, maybe even more moved than his brother, who was the one getting married. He had hoped that after the wedding his mother would stay in touch, would restart their relationship, but she never reached out; she died six months later. Bartek saw her only once more, in the hospital, for fifteen minutes.

The conversation—in that natural and unnatural way we move on from difficult subjects—turned to Jason asking Bartek if he could take a portrait shot inside the apartment; Bartek was happy to oblige. Then Larysa and Bartek had a conversation, in Polish, I don't know what about, and while they were talking Jason pulled me aside. He said he thought I had to come clean with Bartek, tell him the real reason we were here. Given how raw and honest Bartek had been with me, it would be, Jason said, unpardonable to let this deception deepen. I said to Jason, You're right.

The interview resumed. I said, "I want to say thank you."

"It was no problem," Bartek said. "It was very nice to meet."

"The truth is," I said, nervously, awkwardly, "my family was from Sosnowiec. My family was actually from this building. Before the war my grandfather lived in one of these apartments."

I said it like a confession—a partial confession, I know, I know: *still* I was omitting the hardest part—but it didn't have any noticeable effect on Bartek, who simply asked me for the name. I said "Kajzer" and he said he didn't recognize it; he called his aunt, who didn't recognize it either.

We went inside the apartment to take the portrait of Bartek. Bartek's wife, also in sweats, watched us, tickled by our interest in her husband and their apartment. A huge shaggy dog followed Bartek around. I didn't even try and imagine this as anything but Bartek's apartment, as the apartment he'd inherited from his grandparents. That this may once have been where my family lived didn't register, didn't matter.

Of the dozen or so photographs Jason took inside the apartment that day, my favorite shows Bartek standing behind a small folding table in his living room, red t-shirt tucked into his gray pants, drawstrings a-dangling. The dog is kneeling beside him. On a small folding table is lunch. A couple of covered pots; a bottle of fruit drink, colored an unnatural red; and a loaf of sliced bread in a clear plastic bag.

Bartek offered to introduce us to other residents. Thinking aloud, he ran through who in the building would be good to speak to, who'd be available, who'd be amenable. Touchingly, not only did Bartek know all the other residents in the building, he *knew* them, was close to them. This woman would be good but had the flu. This man was out of town. That neighbor was also renovating so it might be too hectic. Ah, Bartek held up a finger—the best person to talk to would be, no question, Hanna.

Bartek escorted us down the stairs to the first floor and knocked on apartment number 2. He introduced us to Hanna, who was in her sixties, short gray hair, friendly, trusting, very shy, but happy to speak with us.

Hanna's apartment had all the markers of a space lived in a very long time; it was extremely tidy but you could see, feel the accumulation. The apartment was full of put-away boxes and books—shelf after shelf dedicated to philosophy, criticism, architecture. The four of us sat at a small square folding table in the living room. On the wall and on the side tables were many framed photographs, nearly all of which were of the same cute blond boy, Hanna's grandson.

We opened the conversation—it felt much less formal than it had with Bartek, maybe because we'd eased into it by now, maybe because Hanna was so approachable—with a recitation (sounding stupider and stupider) of why we were here, how she could help, etc. Hanna lit up. She wasn't the type to get overly excited but even so you could tell that our interest in the building delighted her. Where should I start, she asked. (She didn't speak any English; all of our conversation went through Larysa.)

Why not start with when you moved here?

"I moved into the building right after it was built," Hanna said, "in 1955. I was ten years old. I've lived here ever since, through my marriage, through my divorce."

I thought: That can't be right.

Jason, catching my eye, confirmed: "Nineteen fifty-five?"

Hanna nodded. *Tak, tak.* She was sure of the date because she was sure she was ten years old when her family moved in. Her family hadn't lived far away, just a few blocks over, and she remembered the construction, remembered anticipating the move.

I thought: If the building was built in 1955 then the building did not exist before 1955; and if the building did not exist before 1955 then what had my great-grandfather owned before the war? Where had he lived if not here? What had my grandfather tried to reclaim for twenty years? What was I trying to reclaim now?

I asked Hanna if she knew what had been on this plot before this building was built. Maybe, I thought, there'd been a building here before the war but at some point between 1940 and 1955 it was knocked down and in 1955 this building, the building Hanna said she'd moved into when she was ten, was built.

Nothing, Hanna said. There was nothing here before.

Nothing? An empty lot?

"Just a small wooden house, where an old lady lived. There was an apple tree in the yard. The kids in the neighborhood used to steal apples from her."

It was clear that one of the histories here—either Hanna's or, much more likely, mine—was wrong. But I didn't know how to raise this point with Hanna; I did my best to keep the conversation on track. I asked Hanna why her family had moved to this building in particular, if her family had anything to do with the theater.

Hanna said that her father was, like her, an architect, and though he did some work for the theater, the reason they had moved here was that the conditions were better. Hanna pointed out a couple of framed photographs of her father, who looked like you'd expect a prewar Polish architect to look: dignified, hat, glasses, mustache. (We'd find out later that he was more than just an architect—he was the city planner.)

I asked Hanna, as I had asked Bartek, if she could share childhood memories of the building. With a kind of sheepish glee, she told us about the theater parties. Everyone would get very drunk; she laughed. Very rambunctious. The police had to come often. Once the police came to break up a party but were subsequently called away, to a more urgent emergency, but they left their attack dog at the door of one of the apartments, to make sure the party didn't restart, but then they, the officers, didn't come back, so the dog stayed there all night, and in the morning an actor, trapped inside his own apartment, had to scream out of his window for help: he was late, he had to get to the theater. And once on Christmas Eve Bartek's grandmother came over and asked Hanna's parents if they'd had Christmas dinner; they said yes; she said, Good, because there are some actors here who haven't had Christmas dinner and we'll do it here, your apartment is bigger, and she threw open the doors to reveal a dozen hungry actors waiting in the hall. And back in the fifties and sixties, Hanna said, her parents had the only television in the building, and every once in a while all the residents would cram inside and watch a broadcast of the National Theater. Those were great parties, she said. She looked down at the table, looked up, offered a slight, wistful smile.

Then she said she wanted to show us something, and got up and retrieved from a shelf a bunch of rolled-up papers, which she proceeded to spread out over the table. They were maps. But not everyday tourist maps. These were large, historical, precise, like official city surveys, which was what in fact some of them appeared to be. At least half a dozen maps, covering the whole table, hanging off the edge like stacked tablecloths.

Hanna thumbed through the pile of maps and extracted one from the middle and put it on top. It was a city map, drawn, she said, in 1936. She pointed out the landmarks—train station, City Hall—and explained the legend: if a lot is striped it means there is a building; no stripes means the lot is empty, or contains an "unofficial" structure (such as a small wooden house with an apple tree). Where on the map were we? With her finger Hanna followed Małachowskiego until it intersected with Targowa and stopped on a stripeless lot. There was no building here in 1936.

Hanna gestured for us to be patient and got up to fetch something from the next room. As soon as she turned the corner the three of us, with sitcom timing, began to whisper-argue. Larysa said, "I told you this building looked new."

"It doesn't make sense!" I hissed.

"What doesn't make sense?" Larysa said. "The building was built in nineteen fifty-five."

"But how?"

"Do you think she's lying?" Jason said. "She seems to really know what she's talking about."

"I don't think she's lying," I said, "I'm just saying it doesn't make sense. I've got records of a mortgage on this building from nineteen thirty-two!"

Hanna returned to the room with another large, official-looking map, this one from 1966. But before we began examining it I, flustered, confused, came clean, told her that my family had lived at Małachowskiego 12 before the war.

Okay, Hanna said. She was unperturbed. She wasn't challenging my narrative, nor did she see me as challenging hers, even as our respective narratives could not, it seemed, both be true.

I asked: "This building definitely did not exist before the war?"

"This building did not exist before the war," she said.

"Did the numbers change? Is that possible?"

Hanna said she didn't know. When she moved in in 1955 this was definitely number 12 and it definitely stayed number 12 ever since. I'm very confused, I said. I explained to Hanna that I had a document from 1967 that referenced a 1932 mortgage on this address, so whatever building was Małachowskiego 12 in 1932 was still Małachowskiego 12 in 1967.

Hanna shrugged apologetically, then stood up and brought out yet *more* maps. At this point stacked on the square table were at least a dozen extremely detailed, professional-grade maps. In this small, full, tidy apartment was more and better cartographic information regarding Sosnowiec than, I'd be willing to bet, anywhere else—maybe even including City Hall. (Later we asked Hanna how she'd gotten these maps; she said that years ago she had helped her brother with his master's thesis, which examined the history of Sosnowiec's cityscape, and they had borrowed copies of these maps from City Hall and no one had ever asked for them back.) How bizarre, unexpected, moving, to encounter such prodigious expertise on Sosnowiec real estate—from the daughter of the city planner!—in the very building I was trying to reclaim (or maybe it wasn't the building I was trying to reclaim, by then I had no idea).

We were all standing, leaning over, elbows on tables, plotting the city out. We looked at the map from 1966, compared, analyzed; we looked at a German wartime map; we looked at a pre–World War I imperial map. In a book celebrating the city's 110th anniversary was a photograph of City Hall from before the war, with open space on either side, no apartment blocks in sight. It wasn't photographic evidence that the building didn't then exist—this plot was outside the frame—but the photograph made it even easier to imagine this building not being here.

We tried but couldn't make sense of how this building could exist and also not exist. I showed Hanna all my documents, including the mortgage, told her that my great-grandfather had not only lived in but also owned Małachowskiego 12—which may or may not have been this building—and that I was trying to reclaim it. Which meant that—if this was in fact the correct building—I was trying to reclaim her home. But Hanna seemed unfazed, seemed to see this only as an interesting research question. I asked her if she recognized the name "Kajzer." She did not.

We stayed another couple of hours. We talked about the city, its history, its architecture. Hanna's love for Sosnowiec was abundant and heartwarming, in the way that a learned, earned love of a place always is. Hanna asked if my family was Jewish. I said yes (relieved that it was not assumed), and Hanna pointed out on the maps the synagogue, factories from before the war. I tried a few times to ask Hanna about her life, about her own history, but she'd demur, steer the topic back to Sosnowiec, to the theater, to the building, her home.

Part II

—

RIESE

Silesia

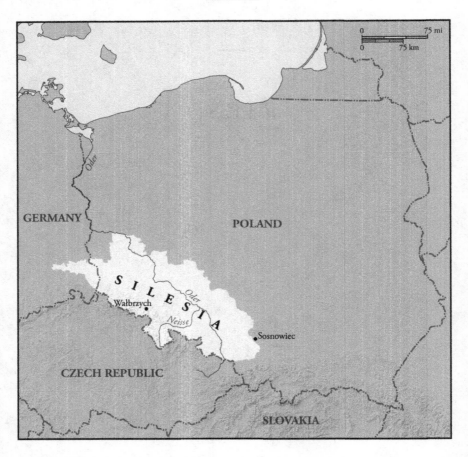

4

The historical region of Silesia lies in the basin of the Oder River, which begins in the Czech Republic and flows north-northwest through Poland and marks, along with the Neisse River, the Polish-German border. Most of Silesia lies within Poland, with bits in Germany and the Czech Republic: it is a borderland if there ever was one. Silesia is both Poland and not-Poland, and the seams show—it has a different feel, a different look, a different mood from the rest of the country. There is no continuous national narrative here. To skate over a lot of turbulent history, Silesia has belonged to Moravia, Bohemia, the hyperfragmented Piast dynasty, the Bohemian Crown Lands, the Austrian Empire, the Prussian Empire, the German Empire, the Weimar Republic, Germany, and, finally, contemporary Poland. Pre–AD 500 populations include Corded Warers, Jordanovians, Lusatians, Bylanians, Celts, Venedians, Przeworskers, Scythians, Sarmatians, Marcomanni, Vandals, Goths, Huns, Gepids, and Heruli. So whose land is this, historically? Depends who you ask. There's a Polish narrative that lines up contemporary Poland with the Piast dynasty and the Lusatians (1300 BC—500 BC), who are positioned as a kind of proto-Slav population. There's a Czech narrative that spotlights the Moravian/Bohemian empires. The German narrative runs from the Goths and Vandals (100 BC—AD 500) through the Prussian Empire and the unification and the Weimar Republic and ends abruptly with the Potsdam Conference, in 1945, at which point the border was pushed westward to the Oder-Neisse line.

Silesian identity, then, can be a slippery thing. It's a layer cake of nationalities, loyalties, allegiances, languages. Today it's pretty indisputably Polish, at least in the everyday sense (though with lots of visible if subdued Germanic elements: architecture, cityscapes, cemeteries; there's even a Polish word for this—*ponimiecki,* or "post-German"), but this is a recent and largely engineered development. In the years after the war, millions of ethnic Germans in Silesia—which had very suddenly become Poland—were expelled. And more than a million Poles from the Kresy—the eastern part of the interwar Polish state that had been annexed by the Soviet Union—emigrated, or were forced to emigrate, to Silesia, which was part of what the Polish Communist government officially called the "Recovered Territories." And the considerable Jewish population of Silesia had been wiped out.

It is a land of displacement. A population removed; a population deleted; a population installed. There is a sense of rootlessness, strangeness, unfamiliarity that, once you know what to look for—once you learn how to read the ruins—is everywhere. There is an entire genre of Silesian stories about people finding valuable and unexpected things in their literal backyards: imperial crowns, Austrian silverware, Jewish corpses, Wehrmacht helmets. There is an identity of the land that is independent of the identity of its people.

The displacement, the turnover, the roiling demographics—it's fertile ground for myth. There are so many lost, terminated, extinguished, transplanted cultures and peoples. I don't believe in ghosts but I feel totally comfortable asserting that Silesia is haunted. (Out of all the things that can haunt, ghosts are probably the *least* interesting.) The residue, the shards of history, will find their form in narrative, in stories often implausible and unverifiable — but plausibility and verification aren't really the point. It's myth, mystery. It's a narrative form of the question *What happened here?*

At the center of this Silesian culture of mystery is something called Project Riese, a series of seven underground complexes dug by the Nazis, or, rather, by Jewish slave laborers, in the Owl Mountains, about seventy kilometers southwest of Wrocław. The complexes are in various states of completion and range massively in size — the largest contain kilometers of tunnel, with multiple stories and cavernous ten-meter-high rooms. Exactly why the Germans built Riese, at enormous expenditure and up until the last days of the war, has never been conclusively determined; there are essentially no primary documents. Riese is a genuine enigma; it is Silesian mystery on a grand, indisputable scale.

I first heard about Riese in 2015, when Piotr Koper and Andreas Richter, referred to in the media as "explorers" and "treasure hunters," announced to the world that, using radar technology, they had discovered the location of the so-called Golden Train, a legendary train full of looted gold that the Nazis had hidden inside a mountain near the city of Wałbrzych. Koper and Richter's claim was taken *extremely* seriously. Treasure hunters from across Poland and beyond flocked to the site. Government representatives from Israel, Germany, and Poland held meetings to determine to whom the gold rightfully belonged. The military got involved. Press from around the world, including the *New York Times, The New Yorker,* the BBC, and *National Geographic,* descended on Wałbrzych. But as the Golden Train offered little in the way of visuals — What was there to see? The ground the Golden Train *might* be under? — the stories tended to focus on the treasure hunters and the enigma that *did* exist: Riese. The photographs — brooding underground complexes in the lush Silesian countryside, with secret entrances and underwater rivers and beefy red-faced Polish treasure hunters — were spectacular.

Despite having been to Poland a dozen or more times, and despite the fact that I'd been engaged in World War II–related research for years, I had never come across anything about Riese, secret Nazi tunnels, treasure, the Golden Train . . . It was as if I'd stumbled onto an alternate Poland, where the history was of a different mode, a different mood. In the Poland I knew, the Poland I'd spent so much time in, the history of World War II was bleak, morose, grayscale, was about oppression, suffering, death, concentration camps, ghettos, German brutality, Polish complicity, Jewish genocide. But in this alternate Poland, World War II history was shiny and adventurous, all about mystery and treasure. Obviously this is a false dichotomy. It's of course inseparable, it's of course all part of the same country- or even continent-sized historical mess. Nazi treasure and Nazi brutality are hardly unrelated. What it comes down to is where the emphasis is placed. And here, in this alternate Poland, located apparently in Silesia, the emphasis was on mythical trains and mysterious tunnels, sexy and exciting stuff. The Jews — the ones who'd dug the tunnels, who'd died digging the tunnels, the ones from whom much of that gold (wherever it was or wasn't) had been stolen — were abstract and incidental.

I was entranced. I wanted, felt compelled, to see Riese, to visit this alternate Poland. Part of the draw was, simply, how strange it all was. But it went beyond that, it was more than curiosity. This was right around the time I'd met with The Killer, had begun my own search, my own hunt, and on some level I felt a bizarre kinship with these treasure hunters. I can't really explain it. Our ambitions were obviously very different but on some level I think I felt they rhymed.

I reached out to a woman named Joanna Lamparska, the cited authority in seemingly every Golden Train and Riese article, to ask if she'd be my Silesian guide. She agreed, and a couple of weeks later I, along with Jason and another friend, Maia, met Joanna in a supermarket parking lot in Wrocław. Joanna was in her late forties or early fifties, with dark hair cut short—one immediately got the sense that this was less about style than utility—and big eyes that blinked rapidly, giving a (false) impression of guilelessness. She introduced herself to us, we introduced ourselves to her, we climbed into her safari-ready Land Rover, and we were off; there was no tour-guidey opening spiel. We made our way out of the city. The one-lane highway, flat fields on either side and brooding mountains on the horizon, was punctuated by roundabouts and one- or two-intersection villages. Parts of Silesia are fairy-tale gorgeous—forests, mountains, castles—and parts are hellishly derelict: many of the towns are former mining towns, gray, depressed, half-abandoned; most of those castles are ruins.

It was an hour-and-a-half drive to the day's first stop. Joanna was excitable, funny, personable, keeping up a patter about the history and mystery of Silesia: the geography, geology, language, mines, crypts, churches, castles, Upper Silesia versus Lower Silesia, Teutonic Knights, prehistoric cults, something called the Amber Chamber, the Golden Train, Project Riese . . . we had some trouble following, though knowing what I know now I'll offer in our defense that this is the sort of information that isn't really received, it's very gradually absorbed; it's frankly too weird to comprehend via lesson; you go along for the ride until maybe it starts making some sense or, rather, until you learn to accept how little sense it makes. Also, Joanna wasn't really a guide in the traditional sense. She knew everything about Silesian mystery, knew all the players, this was her world, her life, but it quickly became clear that this trip wasn't just about the sites we were visiting or the people we'd be meeting. This was a culture, with its own mores, orthodoxies, heresies, histories, sensibilities; it wasn't as if there was some route or spiel that could handily explain this. Joanna talked and talked and we asked and asked, pausing only when

Joanna's phone rang. Who was calling? Treasure hunters. They called with tips, updates, news, gossip, complaints, plans; this was a large and active community, with lots of factions. Joanna was a kind of hub: she was trusted, knowledgeable, on good terms with everyone. After each call Joanna would tell us who had called and why. "This is the explorer from Chernobyl. Very interesting and dangerous explorations." "They are searching the forest near Łódź for mass graves." "His wife is a psychic and they use her powers to look for treasure." The way she talked about these treasure hunters/explorers (she used the terms, as far I was able to tell, interchangeably) was strikingly maternal: loving, critical, proud, somewhat embarrassed, somewhat exasperated.

The first Riese site on the itinerary was Sobon, the smallest and least accessible of the complexes. Joanna had arranged for a couple of explorers, Andrzej and Janek, to be our guides; we rendezvoused at a local restaurant. As we pulled up I could tell the two were already there, because in the parking lot was a Land Rover, identical to Joanna's—same model, same color, also with a roof rack, also with raised air intake.

Andrzej had a wide, handsome, ruddy face, with soft gray hair that fell onto his forehead and a thick colorless mustache. He wore army green cargo pants, a plain black tee, black no-nonsense boots, and the kind of wide wraparound sunglasses that men who are extremely serious about their outdoor activities wear. He looked like an off-the-clock Polish drill sergeant, with a fancier haircut. Janek had a large round belly and a tight goofy grin and thinning curly hair cut short. He wore pants similar to Andrzej's and a camo jacket that had on its arm a German flag insignia that he'd Polonized by whiting out the black and yellow bands, leaving it white/red. Janek was quiet and deferential, clearly the sidekick to bluff, voluble Andrzej, who did all the talking, all the deciding, all the explaining. Andrzej was polite but extremely serious, if not quite grave —as if he sought to project to us how unfrivolous a venture this was.

In the car Joanna had described Andrzej and Janek as "very serious explorers." They were respected, had a history of discoveries big (entrances, shafts, etc.) and small (World War II–era firearms, typewriters, currency, etc.), and had the necessary equipment, know-how, determination, physical ability, chutzpah, time, and obsessiveness for what was, I was quickly learning, something considerably bigger than a weekend hobby.

Andrzej announced that it was time to see Sobon.

Maia and Jason went with Joanna in her Land Rover and I, at Joanna's urging, went with Andrzej and Janek in Andrzej's Land Rover. They didn't speak English and I don't speak Polish, but Andrzej knew a smattering of German and I'd taken four semesters of Yiddish in college, which meant we could pretend we were communicating. Andrzej said many things about the landscape that I'm sure were very interesting. The interior of the car was as expeditionary as the exterior, full of high-end, well-used gear—helmets, ropes, harnesses, belay devices, tents, lanterns, clothing, electric generator, a couple of axes, a couple of metal detectors. I was taking in the treasure hunter aesthetic—military, unpretentious, utilitarian, tough. Explorers yes but not of the foppy gentlemanly variety. Indiana Jones but more commando. More perplexing were the various very authentic-seeming Nazi tchotchkes scattered about, such as the *Reichsadler* badge—the imperial eagle gripping a swastika in its talons—pinned right beneath the A/C controls. I was less offended than curious; I imagined (I hoped) it meant something very different to Andrzej than it did to me. I didn't ask about it because, one, Andrzej and I didn't have a common language, and, two, I would have no idea how to articulate a question like that to a person like this.

We turned off the highway onto a steep unpaved road, which we followed for about half a mile before turning onto another road—ignoring multiple no entry signs—that was less a road than a narrow muddy path. The Land Rovers were making more and more of a case for themselves. It was all hilly woods; the path was strewn with rocks and logs and riven by deep ditches. We came to a small clearing and parked. I got out of the car and searched for any hint—a hole, say, or unnaturally flat ground—of the underground complex. But as far as I could see we were in a spot of uninterrupted forest. It was beautiful, serene, forest-quiet and -cool: totally unsuspicious (and thus, I suppose, totally suspicious); no Nazi tunnels anywhere.

Joanna pulled up beside us. Maia and Jason got out of the car and, just like I did, tried to espy the tunnel.

Three bumbling American Jews vainly scanning the forest in search of a secret Nazi tunnel: Andrzej and Joanna, enjoying our cluelessness, let us stay bewildered for a few minutes. Then they led us maybe fifteen meters in and with unmistakable pride—they were Silesians; this was *their* mystery—pointed out the tunnel entrance. Of course we'd missed it: we'd been looking for a subway entrance; this was hardly more than an air duct, and it was angled, the top reaching barely to my calf, which made it seem even smaller. From a standing position, it looked like a shadow, maybe an alcove. I could have passed this a thousand times without suspecting anything.

We returned to the Land Rovers and geared up. From the back of hers Joanna fetched two pairs of rubber overalls, one for myself and one for Jason, and a couple of military-grade flashlights. (Maia, chary of confined spaces, would stay aboveground with Joanna.) Andrzej and Janek, from the back of their Land Rover, got rubber boots, headlamps, and pullovers. Then Andrzej clipped to his belt a pink stained-glass lantern, which seemed bizarrely out of place, but everything that day was bizarre and out of place; I didn't give it a second thought.

We huddled together and Andrzej delivered a short safety speech: stay together, Andrzej stays in front, Janek stays in back, don't wander off. Capeesh? Capeesh. Andrzej then showed us a map of the complex.

Our route was straightforward: we'd enter the tunnel at entrance 2,

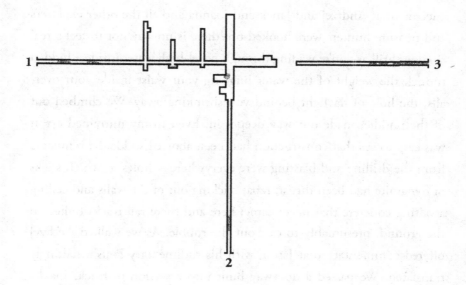

go straight down the corridor until we could go no farther—about 170 meters—then turn around and come back out.

The entrance was low enough and narrow enough that to enter you had to lie flat on your back, feet poking in, and drag yourself forward and downward—immediately there's an incline—until your feet touch flat ground. Andrzej went first; he wormed his way in briskly and with dust-raising gusto. Jason, not a small man, rested his Leica on his chest and maneuvered his way in. Then me, then Janek.

And we were inside Complex Sobon. How can I describe it? In the most immediate, material sense it was as you might imagine. What I mean to say is that it was extremely tunnel-like: dank, cold, dark, just wide enough to walk in pairs and low enough that I could reach up and touch the ceiling, which was, along with the walls, unsmooth rock; the tunnel was unreinforced, unfinished. A deep mountain cavity. We walked up a small slope and then down a small slope and then through a puddle that went up to my navel. Here I had my first shiver of experi-

ence of what Andrzej and Janek and Joanna and all the other explorers
and treasure hunters were hooked on: there is no way not to feel a real
ringing thrill as you're wading through navel-high water inside a hidden
tunnel, the weight of the water hugging your waist inside your overalls, the hole of daylight behind you shrinking away. We climbed out
of the puddle, made our way deeper in. Even to my untrained eye it
was easy to see that construction had been aborted suddenly: remnants
from the drilling and blasting were everywhere—holes in which sticks
of dynamite had been thrust; rebar sticking out of the walls and ceiling
awaiting concrete that never came; here and there rail tracks bolted to
the ground, presumably to cart out the rubble. As we walked Andrzej
offered commentary that Jason, with his rudimentary Polish, haltingly
translated. We passed a doorway built into a section of brick. Inside,
Andrzej said, was a *magazyn:* a storage space, probably for dynamite,
maybe for weapons. We passed beneath a couple of wooden A-frames,
darkened by age but still sturdy-seeming; they looked vaguely religious,
these strikingly man-made structures set against the cold rock. We followed Andrzej deeper yet; it got colder, darker, danker; not to belabor
the point, but the tunnel was really very tunnel-like. Thus far into this
paragraph, I've stuck pretty much to a material description: I want you to
be able to picture it. But know that a material description here is wildly
insufficient. There're the visuals and then there's the sensation. Because
this place, Sobon, this aborted underground complex, made no sense.
It didn't add up. You crawl inside a precisely planned and engineered, if
unfinished, Nazi tunnel hidden in the side of a mountain and your mind
reels, tries to process but can't quite, grasps for rationale, motivation,
narrative. You are besieged by the mystery of it. Okay a tunnel, all very
tunnel-like and everything, but *why?* Why is there a tunnel in the middle
of the forest? To what end? The mystery of these tunnels, which on the
Internet had struck me as something unaggressively curious and weird,
was now—once I'd donned rubber overalls and inch-dragged my way

inside, and touched the walls of rock, and walked beneath the wooden A-frames, and waded through navel-high puddles, and ducked under the rebar, and examined the dynamite cavities—so *forceful*. What is going on here? What was it they were trying to accomplish? And on top of that the mystery is itself a mystery: Why don't we know? How is it possible that a project like this is off the historical grid?

I was beginning to understand whence the obsession.

Even with Jason stopping every few feet to take photographs, it didn't take long for us to reach the end of the tunnel. An abrupt wall of un-dynamited bedrock—you could literally see how sudden the cessation of work had been. Andrzej unclipped the stained-glass lantern from his belt, set it on the ledge, and from his pocket fished out a lighter and a tealight. He lit the tealight and placed it inside the lantern. The effect— given that we were 170 meters inside the earth—was dramatic. Pink-yellow light danced upon us and upon the stone. Andrzej said something about honoring the memory of those who had died here. Jason and I were quiet and confused. Andrzej was quiet and making a show of piety. That might not be fair. Like I said, we were confused. Did he do this mini-ceremony every time he came down here? We'd met Andrzej only a couple of hours ago but this didn't seem like him. The gesture struck us as performative, more than a little absurd. But what did we know?

Then Andrzej told a story about once finding, in the very spot where we were standing, a Jewish ring. (I don't know what a "Jewish ring" is, I don't know if the ring had some sort of recognizable Jewish marking, or if it was an otherwise unremarkable ring that Andrzej assumed had be-longed to a Jewish slave laborer.) He said he'd found the ring but hadn't taken it—he'd left it down here out of respect. (I wondered: respect for what exactly? For the ring? For the nameless Jew it ostensibly belonged to? I also wondered: Is leaving the ring in the cold, dark, dank Nazi tun-nel a gesture of respect? Genuine question.) The next time Andrzej came down the ring was gone, presumably taken by another (less respectful?)

explorer. Andrzej shook his head and told us he regretted he hadn't taken the ring when he had the chance. Jason and I listened and hmm-ed. The anecdote was difficult to parse. Was Andrzej's regret born of a sense that while *he* would have shown the proper respect (whatever that meant) toward this ring, the explorer who'd taken it was in all likelihood treating it disrespectfully, i.e., as unsentimental bounty, a mere Nazi curio? Or was Andrzej's regret rooted in greed? Or, less harshly, did Andrzej simply wish he possessed that which he'd found—that the ring was rightfully *his* Nazi curio? Or maybe these distinctions aren't so useful here. Maybe when it comes to Andrzej and the rest of the treasure hunters, it isn't so easy to demarcate motivations, to disentangle something like respect from something like greed.

After Sobon all of us, Andrzej and Janek included, drove back to the restaurant where we'd initially met to schmooze, drink, unwind. The details of the conversation I don't really recall; it was informal, strange, fun; Jason, Maia, and I were giddy, giggly, overwhelmed and pleasantly stupefied by everything we'd seen that day. We had a thousand questions for Andrzej and Janek—about their work (they were electricians by trade), treasure hunting, Riese, etc. Really only Andrzej spoke; Janek stayed silent or, if asked a direct question, offered a quick shy answer.

But at some point Maia asked a much heavier question. It went something like: How do you take into account all the people who died digging those tunnels? Is *that* part of the story you tell yourselves? Like, what do you *do* with that information? Are you affected by it? Does it matter to you? Does it change how you relate to the tunnels? Sure, Riese might be a grand exciting mystery, but it's also, if not quite a mass grave, then a stark physical testament to mass murder.

The question wasn't put aggressively, but it was unapologetic and to the point. And it clearly touched a nerve. I wouldn't say Andrzej got defensive but he certainly got animated. He leaned forward, hands on table, and started off on a passionate and emphatic answer that quickly outpaced Joanna's translation and soon turned into a dialogue between the two of them, Andrzej and Joanna, in Polish, with Joanna less translating than offering periodic bullet points. Memory. Jews. Slaves. Honor.

Jason, Maia, and I sat back and waited until we could ask Joanna what it was that she and Andrzej were getting so worked up over; we were patient, we were accustomed to delays in comprehension. Andrzej and Joanna's conversation in Polish would have washed right over me but I kept catching something inside Andrzej's otherwise impenetrable speech — I kept hearing my last name (which Andrzej, as far as I knew, did not know). Polish Polish Polish Kaiser Polish Polish. The first time I assumed I misheard. The second time I asked Maia and Jason if they'd heard what I heard — they said they thought so but weren't sure. The third time they confirmed they had.

I interrupted to ask Joanna: Is Andrzej saying "Kaiser"? Because I keep hearing "Kaiser."

Yes, Joanna said, Andrzej is saying "Kaiser" — he is referring to Abraham Kajzer, a concentration camp prisoner, extremely famous among the treasure hunters. Kajzer, she explained, had managed somehow to keep a diary while working on many of the Riese sites, and this diary was published in Poland in the early sixties and, owing to the Riese-relevant details recorded therein — campsites, worksites, construction material, digging methods, layout, etc. — had become required reading for the treasure hunters. They'd all read it. Apparently they'd all *studied* it. Kajzer's diary was, I was made to understand, pretty much the only primary source on Riese. You want to learn about Riese you start with Kajzer. Silesian Treasure Hunting 101. Okay, interesting, I said. But why'd he come up just now? What was Andrzej saying about him? Joanna explained that Kajzer had come up because Andrzej was talking about the slave laborers — the Riese victims — the Jews — and Kajzer was the go-to example, even a kind of stand-in. A conversation about Riese's Jewish slave laborers is a conversation about Abraham Kajzer.

Leaving Maia's question unanswered, we pivoted to the subject of Abraham Kajzer. This was much safer territory for Andrzej. He could be effusive instead of defensive. He and Janek heaped praise on Kajzer's book, on Kajzer's person, on his bravery, on his attention to detail, on his literary talent, on his historical contributions. They waxed rhapsodic about how significant Kajzer was to the explorers, the honor he's accorded, the esteem in which he's held. "A great, great man," they said. "One of the most important men who went through the war, Jew or Pole."

This was very strange, encountering this sort of mythos, on the part of Andrzej and Janek and apparently *all* of the treasure hunters, regarding a Jewish Holocaust survivor. Aside from a handful of heroes and writers, like Mordechai Anielewicz or Jerzy Kosinski, exceedingly few individual Holocaust survivors or victims have made a mark on Polish collective memory. The Shoah is almost always told and taught and remembered as a large-scale tragedy — not names but numbers, not persons but populations. Yet these two middle-aged Polish electricians, both of whom had lived their whole lives in small rural Polish towns, who evinced no special affinity for Jewish memory, who were very interested in history but only insofar as it pertained to treasure hunting, were obsessed with this Abraham Kajzer and his book.

You know, I said, my last name is Kaiser.

Ha ha! Wouldn't that be something, Andrzej said, sipping his beer, if it turned out that the two of you were related.

That *would* be something. What city was he from?

Janek said Kajzer was from Łódź, a city disappointingly far from Sosnowiec, which meant that Abraham was probably not related, or at best distantly related, and that this Kaiser-Kajzer thing seemed destined to remain little more than a cute coincidence.

The second Riese complex we visited was Osówka. Osówka has an entirely different flavor from Sobon, and the difference is clear from the get-go. This is a family-friendly tourist attraction. There are signs directing you from the highway, paved roads all the way through, plenty of parking. There's still mystery here—it's still a subterranean Nazi complex—but with institutional, if tasteful, packaging. The guides had neat haircuts and wore branded polo shirts. A couple of dozen tourists, mostly families, with excited kids (and equally excited dads), ambled about, eating ice cream cones, getting ready for their excursion inside the tunnel or, if they'd just exited, blinking under the bright sun.

Inside the large and extremely unhidden entrance it was, like Sobon, cold, dark, dank. But, unlike Sobon, it was *enormous*—the complex is more than 6,700 square meters. About 7 percent of the complex is concrete-reinforced—and in these harshly angled concrete corridors and dead-gray rooms it feels positively nefarious, sinister, downright villainous—but most of the complex is unfinished rock; it looks and feels extremely industrial, like a state-sponsored infrastructure project (which is in fact what it is). There are rooms and passageways more than eight meters high. There are open spaces more than fifty meters long.

The place was dumbfounding, though in a different sense from Sobon. At Sobon what assaults the imagination is the mystery, the strangeness; at Osówka it's the *ambition*. Sobon had you wondering; Osówka had you marveling. The intended purpose might not be clear but the scope and scale certainly are. It's an entire cave neighborhood. It's so preposterously outsized, so ludicrous, so cartoonish. It's a full-on underground Nazi lair/headquarters/factory/whatever.

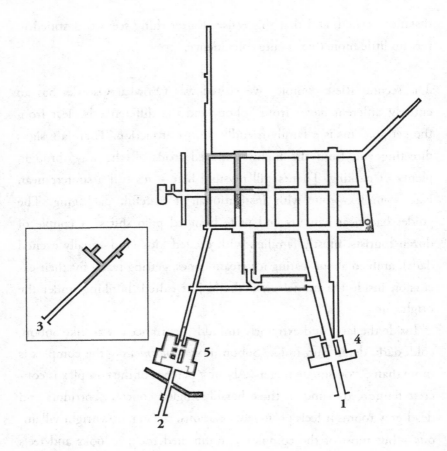

And to get a sense of the ambition of Project Riese in its entirety, multiply Osówka by seven. As best we can tell, Riese was meant to cover more than thirty-five square kilometers; the Nazis were going to hollow out a mountain. Albert Speer, Hitler's chief architect, mentions in an endnote in his memoirs that 150 million marks—equivalent to more than $1 billion today—were spent on Riese (which doesn't factor in the unpaid labor), and that in 1944 the project consumed more concrete than the entire German population had at its disposal for air-raid shelters. Add to that all the necessary infrastructure work: roads, pipes, bridges, railways, massive earthworks, etc.

All of which really adds fuel to the conspiracy fire. Riese's bizarreness and grandiosity tweak your imagination. Erode your reality checks. Suddenly the myth of the Golden Train seemed just a tiny bit less mythical. There was plenty of room down here for a locomotive. If Hitler & Co. were capable of Riese—I mean technically, I mean in terms of sheer chutzpah—who's to say they weren't also capable of parking a train full of looted gold inside a mountain?

Osówka, like the other Riese complexes open to the public, is best understood, I think, not as a museum or memorial (the underlying narrative is too murky; we don't quite know what we're looking at/preserving/ memorializing) but as a ruin. It is something of a man-made wonder. It's an unusually raw and unmediated glimpse of Nazi ambition and also the partial successes and ultimate failures of those ambitions. It's Riese but it's bigger than Riese. It's world domination. It's precisely engineered mass murder. It's genocide. Look what the Nazis set out to do, my god. Look how far they got. Look how fast they got there. Riese inspires a kind of heavy-hearted awe. In that sense it's demonic.

My sense is that the tourists come to Riese to be astonished. The treasure hunters come for their own complicated reasons but the tourists are not here to explore or mourn or celebrate; the victims are invisible and the enemy is long gone. No, the tourists are here to be astonished. What's on display is the engineering.

Osówka had a gift shop, naturally, with Riese-themed key chains and shot glasses and books, including a couple of Joanna's, and, featured prominently, Abraham Kajzer's. So this is what Andrzej and Janek and Joanna had been talking about. Titled *Za Drutami Śmierci*, which Joanna translated as *Behind the Wire of Death*, it was a thin paperback, about 140 pages long, with a decidedly Holocaust-y cover, a blurry monochrome photo of a barbed wire fence. I bought it. Of course I bought it. Not to read, but as a souvenir. Show my family this other Kajzer, Abraham, so famous among Silesian treasure hunters.

• • •

That night, back in the apartment we'd rented in Wrocław, Jason and Maia crashed and I, bored but not yet sleepy, flipped through *Za Drut-ami Śmierci*. I couldn't understand a word but still I tried to commune with it a little. On the first page there was a grainy black-and-white photograph of Abraham, dated 1962. Abraham is sitting outside, on a lawn chair, maybe a rocking chair, arms on the armrests, a relaxed and candid pose. He's facing someone or something a few degrees to the left of the photographer. He's half in the sun and half in the shadow. Abraham is lean, his face a little gaunt, weathered, with deep, distinguished laugh lines. He's got a big leading-man nose, thick dark eyebrows that nearly meet, and a shock of white-black hair sticking straight up. He's handsome, roguish even. He is wearing a wide-collared light-colored short-sleeve shirt, dark pants, no accessories save a wristwatch, and if you look long enough you'll notice that he's got only four fingers on his left hand.

This edition was published in 2013 by the Gross-Rosen Museum. (Gross-Rosen refers to both a sprawling network of concentration sub-camps—among which were the ones the Riese laborers were interned in—as well as the main camp, which is where the museum is.) It included a preface, which even through the Polish I could see was heavy on biography, on names, dates, places. The first line was *Abraham Kajzer urodil sie 15.02.1914 roku w Będzinie,* which even I could understand: *Abraham Kajzer was born on February 15, 1914, in Będzin.* So Janek had been incorrect. Abraham Kajzer was born not in Łódź but in Będzin, which is the city adjacent to Sosnowiec. This changed the nature of the coincidence considerably.

With my phone I scanned the first couple of pages of the preface and ran the text through an online translator. The result was choppy, but comprehensible.

The preface, weirdly comprehensive, listed not only the names of Abraham's parents—Fyvush and Udla—and the names of their seven children—Shprintza Gitel, Necha, Chaskiel, Abraham, Michael Rubin, Maier, and Fyvush Wolf—but everyone's birthdates as well. Maier, Abraham's younger brother, was born on March 6, 1921. My grandfather, also named Maier, was born on February 18, 1921. Which meant that, given Ashkenazi practices of legacy-naming, it was probable that both Maiers were named after the same person, a Maier who had died not long before. Less conclusive but still interesting evidence came a couple of paragraphs down: in 1932 Abraham Kajzer (then eighteen years old) and his wife, Chana, had a son, whom they named Moshe, not after my great-grandfather—who was still alive at the time; we name only after the dead—but perhaps after whoever my great-grandfather had been named after.

At this point it seemed very likely that Abraham Kajzer and I were in fact related—but how, exactly? Here I got lucky. I had data. I had spreadsheets.

The first thing The Killer had set out to do for the reclamation was establish who was who in my great-grandfather Moshe Kajzer's family and who was who in his brother Shia Kajzer's family. We needed to know who else, dead or alive, might have a claim on the property. This entailed a sweeping search of wartime, interwar, and pre–World War I records, stretching back to the 1880s, when Moshe and Shia were born. This was a daunting task. Polish municipal archives are no picnic. You have to pull from different eras, empires, jurisdictions, languages. There are Russian marriage records, Polish birth announcements, German ghetto censuses, etc. To that end, The Killer had consulted a man from Montreal who had compiled one of the most extensive and best-organized historical records of Polish Jewry. In a few weeks' time he provided The Killer with six color-coded spreadsheets, more than thirty pages in total, listing any Sosnowiec or Będzin records in which a "Kajzer" or "Rechnic" (maiden name of Sura-Hena, Moshe's wife) appears. These entries included birth records, marriage records, death records, and census data.

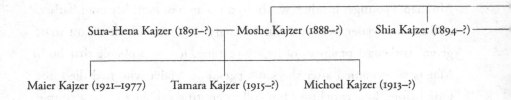

Sura-Hena Kajzer (1891–?) ── Moshe Kajzer (1888–?)   Shia Kajzer (1894–?) ──

Maier Kajzer (1921–1977)   Tamara Kajzer (1915–?)   Michoel Kajzer (1913–?)

Up until now I hadn't looked too closely at these spreadsheets; there hadn't really been a reason to. We'd pulled the significant information (birth dates; the name of my grandfather's sister, which was Tamara) and noted the information that was absent (any dates of death; any record that my grandfather had had more than two siblings). But otherwise the spreadsheets hadn't seemed that relevant.

But that night in Wrocław, Jason's snores floating into the living room, I opened them.

I found a 1912 marriage notice for Moshe and Sura-Hena, my great-grandparents, that included the names of Moshe's parents: Dovid and Ester Kajzer. My great-great-grandparents. Hello, I said to their ghosts.

Then I searched for other marriage notices where Dovid and Ester Kajzer were the listed parents. I found four. Necha, who married Marek; Shia, who married Gitla (the minority owners of the building); Maier, who married Blima; and Fyvush, who married Udla, and who were the parents of Abraham. My great-great-uncles and -aunts. Hello, I said to their ghosts.

So how were Abraham and I related? Abraham's father, Fyvush, born 1886, was the older brother of Moshe, born 1888, my great-grandfather. Which meant that Abraham and my grandfather were first cousins. Or

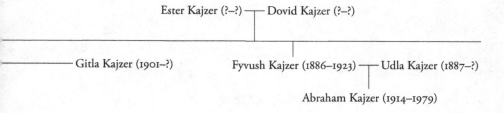

Ester Kajzer (?–?) ──┬── Dovid Kajzer (?–?)

── Gitla Kajzer (1901–?)   Fyvush Kajzer (1886–1923) ──┬── Udla Kajzer (1887–?)

Abraham Kajzer (1914–1979)

put another way: Abraham was my grandfather's closest relative to have survived the war; it seems Abraham and my grandfather were the only two, in fact, from all the children and grandchildren of Dovid and Ester to have come out of the camps alive. The preface mentioned also that two of Abraham's siblings had gotten out of Poland before the war — his brother Chaskiel had moved to Argentina (as a stowaway, I'd later learn) in 1927, and his sister Necha had gotten married and moved to Palestine in 1939. I read all this and thought: here was an entire new branch of the family. Just like that the family went from extinct to not-extinct.

Abraham and his two siblings were also heirs to the building: they have just as much a claim on their uncle Shia's 33 percent stake as my grandfather does. But this wasn't simply about new relatives, more heirs. This was also a new legacy, a wartime story I was able to enter. My grandfather was a blank, past-less, but Abraham was a celebrity.

5

It would come up in conversation that I was reclaiming my great-grand-father's property in Poland. Most people were into it. They thought it was an interesting and meaningful thing I was doing. Particularly enthusiastic were those with parents or grandparents or great-grandparents who'd fled eastern Europe, or really anywhere, or those who were themselves refugees—in other words, those who had in their family a narrative of flight. These people tended to see the reclamation as a kind of crusade, they believed I was righting a wrong, taking up the cause of my survivor grandfather, exacting a tiny but nonetheless significant act of Holocaust justice.

But not everyone was into it. I encountered plenty of ambivalence, skepticism, criticism. This was especially the case in Poland, where the cost and consequences of the war are so much more immediate, the narratives so much messier. Friends and friends of friends, Jews and non-

Jews, locals and expats raised their eyebrows and wondered, more or less accusingly, more or less confrontationally, if what I was doing in Sosnowiec was in fact, beneath the sentimental surface, beneath this lovely little story of taking up my dead survivor grandfather's cause, an act of appropriation, or something like appropriation, or even if it wasn't really appropriation it nonetheless smelled like appropriation, it had the same ugly goal and result. People live in this building? they asked. I said, Yes, it's an apartment building, people live there. Okay, they said, so correct me if I'm wrong but at the end of the day you're taking away their homes?

These rebukes, these gentle or not-so-gentle pokes at the ethical underpinnings of the reclamation, really rankled. Even if I didn't subscribe to the crusade narrative—I didn't claim that what I was doing was in any way heroic, or about justice, or amounted to any sort of moral declaration—I refused to accept that what I was doing was *wrong*. To posit otherwise demonstrated, I felt, an outrageous myopia. As if this were a case of an evil landowner abusing the legal system in order to displace helpless tenants. As if this were happening in a vacuum, all history melted away. As if World War II never happened. As if the world reset in 1945 and nothing before counted.

As you can probably tell, I would get very defensive.

I'd say: How is this in any way appropriation? We aren't *taking* anything. The building was my great-grandfather's. He was murdered so it passed to his son, and then his son died so it passed to his children. Where exactly is the moral snag here?

You have nothing to do with this building. You never even knew about this building until a few years ago. And now you're coming out of nowhere to claim it.

Maybe the root of our misunderstanding is semantic. Let's use a different terminology—let's drop "reclaiming." "Reclaiming" implies a transfer of ownership, a seizure, and I can understand how that might make some people uneasy. So let's drop "reclaiming" and instead use "asserting." So not "reclaiming the building" but "asserting ownership of the building."

Call it what you want, but the fact of the matter is that you don't live here, your family doesn't live here, no one in your family has lived in Sosnow-iec for decades, and you don't plan on living here, ever. You come to Poland for a couple of months a year, you're really not much more than a glorified tourist, and you saw an opportunity to take — I'm sorry — to "assert owner-ship" of this building.

It's true, I don't live here, my family doesn't live here, and hasn't lived here for a long time; it has been a seventy-year absence. However, there are very good reasons for that absence. The delay to the process has no bearing on the ethics of it.

It certainly does have a bearing. This country did not stand still the past seventy years, waiting for you.

Let us pretend, for a second, that my great-grandfather lived out his life in Sosnowiec, as did his son, as did *his* son, and that I was born and raised not in Toronto but here, in Poland, and you and I, in this parallel universe, where World War II never happened, or happened on a sig-nificantly smaller scale, where history continued unbroken, were having this same conversation about my family's property. You wouldn't dream of saying to me, That building your family owns in Sosnowiec, it's just not right, it's immoral, how could you do such a thing. The reason my family is no longer in Sosnowiec is that they were all murdered. It is baf-fling and frustrating to me why you seem to believe that this fact should undermine our claim.

Do you have any idea how many people lost their property during the war, during Communist times?

Many people, I know. But the claim we have on the building isn't competing against any other claim; the building is, currently, technically ownerless. This isn't a zero-sum game. The fact that many people suffered an injustice shouldn't mean that justice is denied to all. Why shouldn't our claim be honored?

You have to consider the massive upheaval the country went through. The trauma. The displacement and death.

You're speaking to me as if I'm out to destroy something. I don't represent a movement, and I don't represent a philosophy. I represent only my family. All we want is the return of something that is rightfully ours.

I can't help but wonder if it's all as innocent as you're making it out to be. That you had to hire a lawyer speaks volumes about the nature of your little quest.

This isn't being done via any illegal or semi-legal mechanisms, nor are we taking advantage of any loopholes or arcane Polish laws. There is no abuse of power here. We're forced to do this via the court because, thanks to historical circumstances and the wholesale erasure of my family, the extremely prosaic laws of inheritance haven't been applied. We're not using the courts to gain an edge or to manipulate the system; we're using the courts to return the state of things to their normal course, viz., property that belongs to you is passed on, after you die, to your kin. It is such a boring, everyday occurrence. Someone dies and their children inherit. Nothing remarkable here. So unless you're arguing against the very concept of private ownership, I don't see why my family should be denied its rights.

The fact of the matter is that the concept of private ownership was suspended, or at least severely eroded, in this country for nearly fifty years.

Is the argument here that the property should belong to no one? That post-Communist Poland is entirely detached from pre-Communist Poland? But that's simply not the case. Communism ended, the country reverted to a democracy, property laws were upheld. Prewar claims are valid. There is, even if fractured and glued together, a continuity in this country, historically, legally. And I am pursuing the rights granted to me according to the law of the land.

It's not a legal issue. It's an ethical issue. People live in those apartments. What about those people?

What *about* them? No one is taking away their property—they do not own the apartments they live in. Not legally, not technically, not in spirit. They do not own those apartments because they never bought those apartments. They never bought those apartments because they never had a chance to buy those apartments because the only people who could sell those apartments were murdered.

So this is about the money.

You can question my motivations, which may be more pecuniary than I'm willing to admit, especially in light of how much the building is apparently worth; it isn't easy to demarcate motivations, to disentangle something like respect from something like greed. But in any case my motivations are one thing; my legal and moral rights are another.

You are remarkably callous. I keep asking you about people and you keep answering me about property. The people who live in those apartments have rights.

No one is planning to deny the residents of Małachowskiego 12 their rights.

Those apartments are people's homes.

I am not planning to raze a residential Sosnowiec block in order to build a mall. I am not planning on evicting anyone.

You know as well as I do that if you do get that building back, and sell it, or manage it, or whatever, then rents are almost certainly going to rise.

That is a separate issue. You want to argue that I have an ethical obligation to not *sell* the building because it'll have an adverse effect on the tenants? Maybe. That strikes me as an important conversation. But right now we are not talking about selling, and we are not talking about evicting, we are not talking about rents. We are talking about the simple fact of ownership.

You still don't get it. You're not thinking, at all, about the residents. Put aside the question of their rights, your rights. Forget for a minute about the legality, the morality, forget all that. Just think about them as people, who live in those apartments, their homes, who have in all likelihood lived in those homes their entire lives.

A hundred times I had this conversation, a version of this conversation, with others, with myself, until it finally sank in, this embarrassingly banal truth: that the residents of Małachowskiego 12 were more than the abstract, incidental inhabitants of the building my great-grandfather owned and lived in before the war. Did I have any compunctions regarding the legality or morality of the reclamation? No. See above. But the least I could do was acknowledge that I was messing with people's sense of security. They would be fearful, of course they would be fearful.

I was a Jew coming back for his family property—this is a veritable trope in Poland. Consider for a second how much property had, before the war, belonged to Jews: hundreds or even thousands of towns and villages were mostly or wholly Jewish; many of the largest cities had been 40, 50, 60 percent Jewish. Three million Jews, dead. A few hundred thousand more who'd fled. In the wake of the war there were a *lot* of vacant homes and properties.

Since the 1990s, since Poland became a democracy and allowed, at least in principle, claims concerning private property to be put forward, reclamation has been a sticky political and cultural issue. (There are no restitution laws: if a property was nationalized, there are no mechanisms to get it back or receive compensation; my claim was, in contrast, an inheritance claim.) I don't speak or read Polish, I'm not really qualified to properly parse public opinion—those pockets of support, scorn, compassion, fear—but I have hung around long enough to understand how threatening reclamation, real or imagined, can seem. In Sosnowiec, pretty much the entire downtown core was Jewish. Kraków, Warsaw, Łódź, Wrocław—huge swaths of these cities, and very central swaths, were Jewish. Reclamation is an issue with monumental demographic, political, and social stakes; it has been a central issue in more than one national election. Sometimes the conversation can take on a regrettable tone: occasionally the greedy foreign Jew will show up in cartoons or political sloganeering, hungry to take advantage of his historical "windfall." But there are legitimate questions of costs, responsibility (Is this Poland's problem? Why shouldn't Germany be responsible? What about Jewish property that had been nationalized by the Soviets?) and of logistics (How best to enable lawful reclamation? Avoid abuse and fraud? What about statutes of limitations?).

Again—I can't really parse this. To try and plumb the psyche of a nation that isn't mine and whose language I don't know—how useful or meaningful would my contribution be? My scope here is narrower. Let's imagine just one building, one home, and let's imagine you and your family have lived for fifty, sixty, seventy years in this building, with a pre-war history that is, let's say, murky, and, as far as you're concerned, better left unexamined, you don't think about it, best not to, this is your home, you've lived here your entire life, and yet you never feel entirely secure, entirely at home, because you worry that one day there'll be a knock on your door and the former owner, or the former owner's grandson, will thrust papers in your face and say: This building? This building is mine.

That Jew is mostly myth—the fear of the phenomenon is massively disproportionate to the phenomenon itself—but, yeah, occasionally it does actually happen.

It can be difficult, in the face of this much tragedy, instability, displacement, to keep everyone in the frame. From a distance reclamation can seem straightforward: what was ours remains ours, intervening years be damned. Up close it's so much more complex. How to approach it humanely and compassionately? Develop an ethics? How to listen, receive, integrate (or reject?) narratives that clash?

There are cases that are cut and dried. The Poles who were complicit in the deportation or murder of their Jewish neighbors and/or who knowingly took advantage of Jews' extreme vulnerability—their claims are easy to dismiss. But what about their children? Grandchildren? Great-grandchildren? Does the fact that they have no idea of the deeds of their progenitors matter? And of all the cases where Jewish property became Polish property during and after the war, I imagine the ones featuring evil, murderous, plotting Poles to be a small fraction (which isn't to say it's not sizable; rather, it's a small fraction of a massive number). What about the situations where the property was taken unknowingly? Or half-knowingly? When suddenly there was a vacancy and a family didn't ask questions and moved in? Or were compelled to move in? Does their belief that they own the property matter? I don't mean legally. I am uninterested in a debate about squatters' rights. I am interested in the moral calculus, that is, how we receive the descendants' narrative. Does the calculus change in ten generations? Fifty?

The story of any given property is made up of multiple stories that split, stop, restart, that are layered, fragmented, winding.

All this moral waffling, I'll be honest, runs counter to how I was raised, to the tenet I received if not explicitly (but often explicitly) then by osmosis: the Poles were (are) our enemies. The Poles who saved Jews were the exception but your average Pole was—at best—perfectly content to see Jewish neighbors carted off to the ovens. If you want to split hairs you might say the Poles were not the killers (but still sometimes the killers) but the abettors of the killers. My father tells me that my grandparents hated the Poles more than the Germans. That they routinely referred to the country as a country of filth and murder, to its citizens as brutes and scum. Does this sound extreme? Unfair? Unnuanced? Guilty of painting with too wide a brush? I don't know what to tell you. This was a received truth among my relatives. My own sympathies, my openness, are suspect to them. That I routinely travel to Poland, drink Polish beer in Polish bars, socialize with Poles, visit Poles' homes, swim in Polish quarries, and go to Polish concerts and give readings in Polish bookshops — if my grandparents were alive I imagine they'd be furious; I imagine they would be heartbroken. But I can't address their pain. It's too big, and too removed, and was never articulated to me; I won't pretend to be able to speak to it.

Regardless of rights, my rights, the residents' rights, our stories were now entangled, and it would amount to a kind of emotional fraud to pretend otherwise. I *wanted* the story to fragment, those cracks to emerge. And oh did the story fragment — the story broke clean in two: it was no longer even clear when or where the building *existed*. Though it was maddening, not knowing if the building was the building, this is what I had sought: I'd declined the easy comfortable linear myth in favor of narrative incompatibility.

I reread my grandfather's documents (which, now that I had Abraham's memoir — which I was having translated — felt like a relatively puny source text for a legacy). Maybe I'd missed something, maybe there was something in there that could help explain how my great-grandfather had owned a building that wasn't. But I couldn't find anything that clarified. Number 12 was still number 12 and so therefore could not be number 12.

I did find something, though: Małachowskiego 12, though certainly owned by my great-grandfather, had *not* been his childhood home. It had been an investment property. Home, as written plainly on one of my grandfather's letters, was on Targowa Street, just around the corner.

The mistake can be traced to the first time I'd visited Sosnowiec, before I'd ever seen those documents, before I'd ever entertained the idea of trying to reclaim the building. I had had a single address regarding my grandfather, Małachowskiego 12, which was where, my father said, his father had grown up. This is what I wrote in chapter 1, that my father said that, and I think that's true, I think he did say that, but I'm not certain, I wasn't taking notes. So maybe my father said that this was my grandfather's home or maybe he said it was maybe his home or maybe it made so much narrative sense that I jumped to that conclusion on my own. I went to my grandfather's hometown to see an address associated with my grandfather, so of course this was his home.

Four years later, when I finally read the documents, I missed that detail, that this was an investment property. I don't know how I missed it. I suppose on some level I refused to see it. The story I was telling was that I was reclaiming the building my grandfather had grown up in: the narrative had gotten stuck in a kind of sentimental default. Visiting an ancestral home is more meaningful than visiting an ancestral investment property, no? Reclaiming an ancestral home is a better story, or at least feels like a better story, than reclaiming an ancestral investment property. I'd gotten caught in a myth of my own making.

Did it matter that I'd gotten it wrong?

On the one hand, though it was a jarring correction, it was also somewhat beside the point. This had never really been about my grandfather's home (investment property). It was about my grandfather's decades-long futile attempt to *recover* his home (investment property). The verb, not the noun. The building itself—even while I'd been under the impression that it had been my grandfather's childhood home—didn't promise any sort of access to my grandfather or the memory of my grandfather or the meaning of the memory of my grandfather; as a physical structure it was spiritually sterile. But with respect to the reclamation—here I did feel I was or at least could be in some kind of conversation with my grandfather or the memory of my grandfather or the meaning of the memory of my grandfather. The reclamation was something I could restart, build upon, improve upon, fulfill, or even fail at as he did.

On the other hand, yes, of course it mattered. You get something so basic so wrong and the whole mission starts to feel shaky. Where the building was, when the building was, if the building was, what my grandfather's relationship to the building had been: the mounting uncertainties—not to mention the lies I'd been peddling—have an effect. You begin to question what it is you're doing and why you're doing it; the sentimental underpinning begins to erode.

6

Joanna spread the word among the treasure hunters that I was Abraham Kajzer's kin and very quickly the story became that I was his grandson, because that story makes more sense, because that story is the better story. It was as if he'd become a kind of alternate grandfather, one whose legacy was celebrated and mythologized, unlike my own grandfather, who was mythless, whose legacy was obscure, hazy, hidden at the center of a bureaucratic and legal maze.

The explorers wanted to meet me, wanted to show me the mines, crypts, tunnels, abandoned castles, ancient pagan sites, medieval battlefields, bunkers; show off their maps, secret documents, aerial photographs, georadar scans, exploration equipment; tell me their theories, hunches, accomplishments, grievances. They wanted to know if maybe I had some heretofore unknown Kajzer-related information. They wanted to be interviewed. They wanted to be written about. I said yes to everything.

I learned quickly that the treasure hunters are not easily lumped together, are not easily categorized. You've got organized and sometimes even sponsored exploration groups employing lidar, georadar, magnetometers, advanced mapping software, satellite imagery; and you've got guys walking around with third-hand metal detectors and divining rods. The "treasure" being hunted might be wartime artifacts, undergrounds, adits, artwork, mines, secret Nazi technology, mass graves, but usually it's nothing that grand, usually the explorers are just, well, exploring —the catchall term for what they're after is "mystery." There are those whose mission is plainly preposterous, like the self-identified count who claims to know the location of a Nazi/alien underground city, and there are those engaged in meaningful historical research. Jerzy Cera, a doyen of the explorers, and one of the first to explore Riese in the early 1970s, publishes high-quality maps and brochures of the Riese complexes, used by museums and researchers all over Poland and beyond. An explorer named Krzysztof brought me to a regular-seeming field outside Świdnica, where, he said, there had been a concentration camp, now gone and forgotten, wiped off the map. Krzysztof had spent years researching the camp, tracking down documents, interviewing locals, surveying the land, figuring out where exactly the camp had been. He led me through a sea of tall grass, it was dusk, it was stupidly picturesque, and in the middle of the field Krzysztof showed me a line of cemented-in bricks, mostly buried and nearly invisible, the remnant of the foundation of what had, Krzysztof said, likely been a prisoners' barracks. Sometimes the explorers find something truly remarkable or bizarre (if there is something to be found, they will, eventually, find it). A crane operator named Janek took me to the site of the Sienawka concentration camp — converted after the war into a mental hospital, later abandoned—and showed me, in the basement, in a small square white brick room, a sort of Nazi laboratory, with two parallel cement basins, too large and too deep to be an operating table or an autopsy table but still pretty clearly medical-related: they had that semi-ritualistic, ceremonial, altar-ish feel about them; these were tables upon which bodies or parts of bodies were set, displayed, stored, drained, something. None of us, not Janek, not Joanna, had any idea what the answer to this mystery was, only that it wasn't a happy one. (Months later, in a photograph taken at the Natzweiler-Struthof concentration camp, in France, I saw a similar basin—and it was filled with severed arms. The mystery wasn't entirely solved—we could not find documentation as to what the arms had been used for, or why they'd been severed—but the function of the basin was now clear.)

There is a monthly trade magazine of sorts, *Odkrywca* (Explorer). Circulation is more than fourteen thousand, and the website hosts an active online forum (though in recent years the explorers have moved en masse to Facebook, the perfect platform on which to boast, organize, complain, shit-talk, float conspiracy theories, get nastily factional). I visited *Odkrywca*'s office, which looked like the office of any small magazine— four flights up, dusty wooden floors, harried editors, everywhere stacks of loose papers—if with more military-themed tchotchkes lying about, including a couple of antique guns the editors assured me were decommissioned. On the wall was a huge display of recent *Odkrywca* covers, a panoplied dreamscape of explorer images: castles, mines, tanks, bombs, various swastika-ed stuff, soldiers, tunnels, trains. The most recent issue included a feature about the German engineer who'd sabotaged Hitler's secret nuclear program; an essay about a fortress museum; an account of a recent discovery of a mine; and reviews of various exploring equipment, in particular metal detectors. The editor in chief and I had an interesting discussion about newsworthiness. Discovery is always news, he said. Like a new tunnel entrance, for example, or a new adit, but in his opinion there hasn't been a truly significant discovery in decades. This work is very gradual. Explorers are like historians, he said, except more active and more curious and more brave and also much crazier.

Exploring in Poland is a regulated activity. You may not explore—

can't even scan the ground with a metal detector—without a government-issued permit. This law is widely flouted, however. Marek Kowalski, the bureaucrat in charge of issuing exploring permits in the greater Wałbrzych area, probably the most explorer-concentrated region in the country (there are more than 1,600 applications a year), estimated that only about 5 percent of those exploring are doing so legally; though when it comes to more intensive explorations, those that include excavations or rely on high-end equipment, then, Marek said, about 90 percent are legal. Violators face up to five years in jail (though that very rarely happens) and/or fines of thousands of zloty.

There are regulations regarding the treasure itself, too—you can't just keep whatever you find. Anything classified as a heritage item belongs by law to the state and must be relinquished; an object is considered "heritage" (1) if it was discovered underground and (2) if it makes historical sense that it's there. Anything found in an attic, for example, would not be a heritage item. A Chinese coin in the ground would also not be a heritage item. A gold filling found in the ground, however, would be a heritage item. Upon relinquishment, the explorer receives a reward of 10 percent of the value of the discovery. I asked Marek how often that happens, that someone turns in a treasure and gets the 10 percent. All the time, he said. Usually it's old coins, he said, which occasionally can be very valuable. So those guys who said they found the Golden Train, I asked, if it turned out they were right, that there was in fact a train full of gold, they'd get 10 percent? It is complicated, Marek said, because they had not gotten the proper permits to explore in the first place. But I can tell you that there were discussions very high up in the ministry whether they should get a reward.

There are a handful of profiteers (and plenty more hapless wannabe profiteers), largely in the business of digging up and smuggling and selling antiquities and World War I/World War II artifacts, as well as opportunists. One of the largest Riese sites, Włodarz, is operated by an explorer named Krzysztof who, having somehow finagled a long-term lease with startlingly few restrictions, has turned the site into a kind of bizarro military theme park: artillery and tanks are strewn about like lawn ornaments; the employees, in army pants, boots, and fleece pullovers, look like an out-of-shape paramilitary unit. When I visited, Krzysztof was in the final stages of installing his latest attraction inside one of the tunnels: a replica Golden Train. It was about the size of the locomotive that snakes through theme parks and zoos, and was of a heavy solid metal painted a deep black with gold accents and lots of gold Nazi insignia: gold swastikas, gold *Reichsadlers*. In large gold capital letters złoty poçiag (golden train) was emblazoned on the side. Krzysztof explained that the route will be 160 meters and feature ten points of interest; along the way riders will see mannequins wearing stripes who are "digging," and mannequins in German uniforms who are "overseeing" the mannequins in stripes.

But the vast majority of these guys are hobbyists with less nefarious, more complex motivations—an unstable mix of pride, delusion, greed, curiosity, camaraderie, destiny, responsibility, adventure, and, of course, the plain fact that it's a lot of fun. It's something like a brash combination of amateur historian, extremely amateur archaeologist, spelunker, and conspiracy theorist.

It makes sense why the explorers are so drawn to World War II—the history is bottomless, there is so much that is unanswered, inexplicable, strange. Poland is veritably pockmarked with World War II mystery. This is particularly true in Silesia, which was German land, the Nazi frontier. (Relevant also is Silesia's centuries-long legacy of mining—primarily coal, but also gold, silver, cobalt, uranium, and other minerals; here is a legacy of *actual* treasure; and where there is a legacy of actual treasure there is, always, a legacy of mythical treasure; in many ways contemporary treasure hunting is but the most recent iteration of a very old narrative.) All that destruction and dispossession and displacement created countless voids, of which the undergrounds are the most literal and most explorable example. And Riese is the central mystery, is in a sense the center of all the mystery. Its size; that it's subterranean; that it's Nazi infrastructure; that there's so little documentation; that so much of the complexes is still inaccessible and unexplored. You can see why its grip on the explorers' imagination is so strong, why its myth-capacity is so enormous, why it's accorded a kind of sacredness. And why, in turn, Abraham Kajzer and his book are so revered.

I came to think of exploring as a *response*. To what? I can't say exactly. To a kind of disturbance. To the traumas that are stored, literally and otherwise, in the ground. It's something like an unease, an apprehension, a discontent with this particular land and this particular history, with these sites and their stories and secrets and tragedies. You hang out with these guys long enough and you start understanding just how metaphorically powerful the concept of "underground" is. The metal detectors, scanning the ground for what's not supposed to be there. The conflation of buried treasure and buried bodies and buried answers.

Andrzej invited me, via Joanna, to come to his sanctuary. "It is a very big honor," she said. "What do you mean, sanctuary?" I asked. "Like his house?" "Yes it is his house," Joanna said, "but not his main house. It is his home for treasure." I didn't understand but I rarely did.

The sanctuary was a handsome two-story house at the end of a long steep driveway surrounded by a lovely landscaped multilevel terrace. No one was home when Joanna and I arrived; we waited outside in a couple of deck chairs. This could have been a rich man's cottage. "I still don't understand what this place is," I said to Joanna. "Does Andrzej live here?" "No." "He lives close to here?" "Oh yes," she said. "A few minutes away." "I don't understand anything," I said. "Oh you will see," she said.

Presently Andrzej arrived and greeted me very warmly, huge smile, huge hug—and with him were his wife, daughter, and son-in-law. They were casually clothed, no camo, no indication they cared much at all about the underground mysteries of World War II. I'd only ever seen Andrzej in blustery explorer mode, so intense and overbearing it was hard to picture him otherwise. But here was his family, friendly and endearing and extremely civilian. Andrzej introduced me as the grandson of Abraham Kajzer. I corrected him, said that Abraham wasn't my grandfather but my grandfather's cousin, but it didn't register: as Andrzej told his family the story of Abraham and his diary, he referred repeatedly to Abraham as my grandfather. I tried again to correct him, but again it had no effect, Andrzej was deep into the story, extolling Abraham's legend, explaining the significance of his book, and wouldn't or couldn't change course: as far as he was concerned, Abraham was my grandfather. I let it slide. Andrzej's family listened to Andrzej and smiled bashfully and shook my hand. I was an honored guest; Andrzej was showing me off. Were they humoring him? It didn't seem like it, though how would I be able to tell, really. My interest in treasure hunting and in Andrzej in particular conferred a sort of legitimacy that Andrzej on some level clearly relished and that his family seemed genuinely impressed by.

We went inside and sat down at a large oak table in a wood-paneled room. The sanctuary had a clubhouse kind of feel. On the wall were framed maps, a large metal ornamental *Reichsadler,* a spoked steering wheel of a ship. An antique typewriter was on display in the corner. Lots of very fine woodwork. The table's centerpiece was a three-foot model of the Eiffel Tower. Next to it was a heap of explorer-related documents —maps, permits, applications, sketches of Nazi UFOs.

After some tea and cake and small talk Andrzej ushered his family back into the car and sent them off. Whatever it was that we were going to discuss, the gesture said, it wasn't family appropriate. As they were leaving, Janek, the sidekick, pulled up. He grinned and waved, but didn't get out of the car. Instead Andrzej got in, and they drove off, leaving Joanna and me alone in the sanctuary. They'll be back soon, Joanna said. They want to bring you something. A surprise.

Fifteen minutes later they returned with an eighty-six-year-old man named Edward Spiranski. Spiranski was in bad shape: he had recently suffered a stroke, and was weak and barely ambulatory. Andrzej and Janek helped him out of the car and stood on either side of him, gripping his arms. But Spiranski still had trouble walking, so on the count of three they lifted him from under his armpits and from under his knees and carried him down the stairs and inside the house and installed him at the head of the table. A still-grinning Janek said good-bye and left.

Spiranski wore a blazer with what looked like a small war medal pinned to the chest. He was a little hazy, a little hard of hearing, but overall very present, if docile, displaying the sort of bottomless patience you see in the elderly who have nowhere else to be. Spiranski has very interesting things to say, Joanna said, and he promptly introduced himself (Joanna translated throughout) and swore emphatically that everything he had to say was one hundred percent true. Using his one good arm he brought out some documents from his bag: a letter he'd recently written to the veterans' office, asking for help with medical costs; a photograph, dated 1951, of himself and two friends in undershirts and military caps sitting by a river playing guitar.

Why had Andrzej brought Edward Spiranski here? To talk to me about his time in the war, of course — Spiranski was nine years old when the war broke out, had spent its duration on a German farm where his parents and siblings were forced laborers. (The setup of our meeting — that is, the way Spiranski talked and the way I listened — in fact felt very familiar, reminded me of any number of interviews I've conducted with elderly Holocaust survivors. They speak; it's often scattershot, non-linear; it's the recall of a nightmare, though not without nostalgia; it's sometimes banal, you've heard stories like this before, you remind yourself what it means that stories like this are banal; you listen and you listen; you receive.) But it was also true that on some level Andrzej was exhibiting Edward Spiranski. He was a prop, a talking relic that Andrzej (whose life was largely devoted to collecting relics) had literally picked up and carried inside in order to display his explorer's bona fides. (If that sounds cynical it's only because you don't yet know what's in the next room.) But it was also true that Andrzej was devoted to Spiranski —who was alone, impoverished, in poor health—in a way that no one else in the world was. Andrzej cared. Maybe Andrzej cared for reasons not purely altruistic—because Spiranski had potentially useful information; because via Spiranski, Andrzej could get a little bit closer to a time and events that he clearly fetishized—but still, he cared. The explorers would teach me this lesson a hundred times over: a motivated love can still be love.

Spiranski said that he liked Jews a lot. His father had rented their home from a Jew named Mortke, and had worked in a beverage company for a Jew named Rensky. Mortke was a very good person, Spiranski said, then began to weep. All the Jewish people and all the Polish people remember Mortke. I don't know what happened to him. As far as I know, all the Jews were gathered by the Germans, and probably killed.

Joanna comforted Spiranski, and, once he regained his composure, he turned back to me and said he had two stories about encountering Jews in the war, both of which took place in Furstenstein, a Gross-Rosen subcamp (where Abraham Kajzer had been interned for a couple of months). During the war young Edward would walk past Furstenstein all the time—the camp was located between the farm his family lived on and the village his mother sent him to with ration cards to buy bread. The bread was black, Spiranski said. White bread was only for wounded soldiers, and there were a lot of wounded soldiers. (As Spiranski talked and Joanna translated, Andrzej, like an impatient child showing off his toys, kept bringing Nazi paraphernalia to the table, ostensibly for Spiranski to inspect and authenticate but in reality to show me. He took down the ornamental *Reichsadler*, as long as my arm and just as heavy, and put it on the table. For the rest of the conversation it lay there like a taunt.) One day, Spiranski said, he saw Jewish prisoners building a road, and another group of Jewish prisoners — "people wearing stripes and as many people as elves" — building a small railway station. Edward was eleven years old and some of the prisoners, he said, were no older. (Andrzej laid out his colorful collection of Hitler Jugend badges.) He was walking in his wooden shoes, nibbling on a piece of black bread, when he came face-to-face with a very young Jew; he stopped in his tracks; he and the young Jew stared at each other. The guard was looking in the opposite direction. Edward extended his piece of black bread to this young Jew but just then the guard turned his head and spotted them; he cocked his rifle and took aim. (Andrzej opened a binder full of plastic sheaths containing Nazi currency; he flipped through and extracted some choice examples and passed them around.) The Jewish boy began to cry and Edward turned and ran home in his wooden shoes. Another time, Edward saw two trucks full of Jews surrounded by some smaller vehicles filled with SS officers. The Jews were singing; Edward could hear them singing. One of his friends corrected him — the Jews weren't singing, they were praying. One of the Jews jumped from the truck, as if to escape, but broke his leg. (Andrzej put a Nazi-era five-mark silver coin on the table and asked Spiranski, What could you get with this during the war? Spiranski replied that the wooden shoes had cost nine marks.) One of the German officers said, Kill him; another officer shot and killed him.

Spiranski had some questions for me — this was the first time he'd met a Jew since the war, he said. The last Jews he had known were Mortke and Rensky. There were many things he was curious about.

What kind of factories do you have in Israel?

In Israel? There are all kinds of factories. Electronics, furniture . . .

Are women working in the factories?

Sure.

Are those factories private?

Sure.

Do you need coal to heat the house?

I don't understand . . . ?

If you want to heat the house, do you need to have your own coal?

Oh, I see. No — most houses in Israel are modern construction, just like here.

Are there chimneys in Israel?

Yes.

Do you have potatoes?

There are potatoes in Israel.

Do they grow their own potatoes?

That's a good question. I don't know.

What do they grow in Israel?

Oranges? Citrus? Pomegranates?

The orange trees are in private gardens or big farms?

I think both.

Do you have windows in Israel? We have windows in Poland, do you have windows in Israel?

Sure.

Do you have villages in Israel, or big cities?

Both.

So Jewish people are working?

In Israel?

Yes.

Sure, they are working.

So they are working, and not only trading?

Ah. Yeah, of course.

What happened in Lebanon? What do those Arabs want from you?

The truth is I am not Israeli, I don't really know that much about Israel.

Okay. Hitler was a clown, from the circus. I don't know what he wanted from Jews. What did he want from the Jews?

This is a good question.

Can you tell me what he wanted from the Jews?

No. I don't know.

So it went for a while—Spiranski asked me many questions about New York City, the subway, black people, Arabs, Jews—until Janek arrived, and it was time for Spiranski to go home. We said good-bye and Janek and Andrzej picked Spiranski up and loaded him into the car.

Fifteen minutes later Andrzej returned. Now time for the tour, Joanna said. Andrzej, visibly excited, rising to his toes, opened a door and gestured proudly at the—I don't know how else to describe?—war museum he'd set up in the bedroom. Hundreds of artifacts were displayed in closed glass cabinets. On the far wall, above the narrow bed freshly made with yellow rose-patterned linen, was a pair of World War II–era rifles, an antique pistol, a collection of sabers. (And below the bed was a pair of blue slippers, a brain-breaking detail of hominess. He slept in here?) Everything in here, I asked, you found? Of course, Andrzej said. The room was a startling testament to the man's obsession and, I suppose, skill as a treasure hunter. (When I asked whether this was the largest treasure collection among the explorers, Joanna and Andrzej scoffed. Not even close, they said.) My reaction to the room was complicated. I was surprised, impressed, mortified, and very curious. Whatever look I had on my face didn't bother Andrzej in the slightest. He beamed. He was exceptionally proud.

He gave me a tour of his collection, section by section, artifact by artifact. On his face throughout was a look of mischievous pride; he kept glancing at me for affirmation, which I readily supplied.

We began with the fancy metal detector in the corner, then moved on to a set of swastika-engraved cutlery. Then a gorgeous compass; a collection of Nazi identification cards; glass/plastic artificial eyes that Andrzej claimed had belonged to Nazi officers. Many, many bullet cartridges; a couple of massive mortar rounds; dozens of Nazi/Iron Cross badges, buttons, and pins. Heaps of Nazi coins, bills, ration cards. Various pieces of jewelry. (Is this where the "Jewish ring" would have ended up?) Canisters; grenades; clips; a miscellany of rusty metal things I recognized as parts of weapons but have no idea what they're called. What looked like a stick of dynamite but according to Andrzej was a kind of dynamite-stick holder. Two clocks (or devices that looked like clocks); old military phones; a Russian radio, which Andrzej fiddled with, saying all it needed was new batteries. An enormous gun with a very long chain of bullets (which he must have attached himself; he certainly didn't find it like that): capable, he said, of firing 1,100 bullets a minute. Many more *Reichsadler* badges. A humongous Continental typewriter. A long row of military helmets, many with Nazi insignias, but also of Soviet, American, and British origin. Andrzej put on a helmet and said it was the same helmet the famous Polish spy Hans Klause used to wear. A massive, beautifully illustrated 1906 atlas. A Napoleonic saber so rusty it was serrated, which Andrzej, still wearing the helmet, brandished like a soldier ready to strike, or like a child pretending to be a soldier ready to strike. Andrzej took one of the guns down from over the bed, cocked it. I asked if it still worked. No, it's just for reenactment, he said, you cannot shoot with it, but he said this with a very mischievous smile. On the floor was a large wooden trunk with a *Reichsadler* stamp. Inside were Nazi knives, which Andrzej, of course, unsheathed and brandished.

What to make of all these cherished swastikas?

I remembered how startled and confused I had been by the Nazi paraphernalia in Andrzej's Land Rover. Even if a *Reichsadler* dangling from your rearview mirror doesn't necessarily mean you identify as a Nazi, surely you must be aware that some people might in fact make that assumption, right? The fact that Andrzej apparently did not care, that he had no problem flaunting his swastikas, was worrisome. Where I come from you do your absolute best to put to bed even the slightest suspicion that you are into the Third Reich.

But seeing Andrzej's museum-room, witnessing his pride over his collection of hundreds of artifacts marked by imagery that I'd always understood as obscene and prohibited, helped put Andrzej's Nazi-philia into context. All these swastikas, *Reichsadlers,* Iron Crosses, etc. — these weren't marks of affiliation, they were trophies. Or scalps. Plunder from a fallen enemy. (When I later learned the extent of Andrzej's hatred toward Germans, including those living today, I found it far more disconcerting than whatever inanimate objects he kept in his sanctuary.) This was how he ordered, measured, displayed, and celebrated his treasure. Yes, he prized these objects; he stored, cleaned, fetishized them in a way that I find difficult to relate to; but at the end of the day it was less about what they represented than the fact that he had found them. Andrzej was not a skinhead, even if the skinhead and Andrzej might have similar ideas regarding interior design. In the United States a swastika is hard to see as anything but a deliberate provocation and a sign of affiliation with Nazi ideology. But here? These were literally buried artifacts. They stood for what was dead and gone.

7

It took more than a year but finally, toward the end of 2016, our papers were in order, and The Killer filed with the court in Sosnowiec. The first order of business was to validate the deaths of my dead relatives. We had to make it official, in other words. At present they were in limbo. My great-grandfather and his brother and their wives, the owners of the building, and my great-uncle and great-aunt, the other two heirs, had died during the war, but no details were known, they'd died in the great unrecorded void, and so legally speaking these citizens weren't yet dead. "Death," as far as government is concerned, isn't something automatically conferred just because you happen to no longer be alive: it is a status that must be applied for, approved, granted.

It was a bizarre if metaphorically rich undertaking. Bureaucratic reality forked from regular reality. Because these people *were* dead: it was an incontestable truth that these people were dead. I knew this because my grandfather knew this and my grandfather knew this because the war happened and he never saw them again. Which doesn't constitute incontrovertible proof, I know, but it's much more than supposition. Of the eighty thousand or so Jews who lived in the region before the war, maybe a thousand survived. That one or more members of my grandfather's immediate family survived is unlikely; that he/she/they survived yet somehow remained unknown to my grandfather for thirty-plus years is just about impossible. But even then, even if they had survived the war *and* somehow remained unknown to my grandfather, they'd *still* be dead —otherwise my great-grandparents would be closing in on 140. (My great-uncle and -aunt, granted, would be only 108 and 106, respectively.) So they were definitely dead, if not definitively dead.

Most people I mentioned this to were of the opinion that what the court was asking was unjust, perverse, insensitive, borderline anti-Semitic. They saw it as an affront, however judicially wrapped, to my family's Holocaust narrative. It's an understandable reaction. This is a fraught arena. We guard our histories very zealously. But the truth was that I didn't see the process as particularly unfair. Absurd, sure, and very annoying, but absurdity and inconvenience are features of bureaucracies everywhere. In our case the absurdity and inconvenience were more pronounced than usual, but still—death requires paperwork. The process was clunky and frustrating, but nothing about it—at least at the outset —struck me as pernicious.

The argument The Killer prepared for the court was one of common sense: that what was plainly real should be acknowledged as bureaucratically real. The only relevant document we had was a 1967 affidavit from Rabbi A. J. England, friend of my grandfather's, stating that he had known the Kaisers in Sosnowiec and that only my grandfather had survived. Which was something, but, in terms of evidence, not much, because England doesn't say how he knows they died; he could be and in all likelihood was repeating hearsay (or whatever you'd call the unde-

tailed knowledge of the deaths of Holocaust victims). We had no concentration camp lists, no testimony that they were in this camp or that
they died there. Extensive searches of databases of Holocaust victims and
survivors turned up nothing.

Step one in having someone declared officially dead is a public pro-
nouncement. The Killer took out an ad in the *Gazeta Prawna* newspaper asking for anyone with information regarding the deaths of Moshe,
Sura-Hena, Shia, Gitla, Michoel Aaron, and/or Tamara Kajzer — or, for
that matter, anyone who may have seen them recently — to come forward within sixty days. No one came forward.

We were then informed by the court that, on the basis of the last
known addresses of the persons whose deaths we were asserting, our case
had been split into two cases and would be administered in two jurisdictions. The death status of my great-grandfather, great-grandmother,
and their two children (my grandfather's immediate family) would be
decided in Sosnowiec; and the death status of my great-grandfather's
brother and his wife would be decided in Będzin, as they showed up on
a 1939 Będzin census.

The judge in Będzin, understanding that this was a matter of ac-
knowledging the obvious, was quick, professional, courteous; I never
even had to make an appearance. He made it official: Shia and Gitla
Kajzer were dead. Mazel tov, I said to my father.

The judge in Sosnowiec, however, requested I testify, or, rather, requested Michael Kaiser and Leah Feld testify; I'd go as their proxy. Our
trial was set for July 26, 2017. The Killer wasn't worried. I wasn't worried.
My dead relatives' deaths were extremely apparent. The confirmation
thereof would be, The Killer and I assured each other, a formality.

One week before the trial — as if the gods were warning me not to take
anything for granted, not even the basic independence, integrity, and

functionality of the Polish judiciary—the government passed a series of laws that threatened to undermine the basic independence, integrity, and functionality of the Polish judiciary.

This hadn't come out of nowhere; this was but the latest escalation of a political crisis cooking for two years, since 2015, when PiS (Law and Justice) had won both the presidential and parliamentary elections, marking the first time since the fall of Communism that a single party held unified control of the government. PiS's platform was nationalist, Euroskeptic, anti-immigrant, Catholic, right-wing, populist. Its leaders were openly contemptuous of democratic limitations, particularly those imposed by the courts, the only branch of the government not under their control. Their opening act was a brazen takeover of the Constitutional Tribunal, Poland's highest court, tasked with deciding matters of constitutionality and settling disputes between government branches.

The country's turn inward, its closing-off, was readily apparent. In 2016 PiS attempted to make some of the most restrictive abortion laws in Europe more restrictive. Not long after, the government made it a crime, punishable by up to three years in prison, to accuse Poland of complicity in the Holocaust—you were no longer allowed to say or write the phrase "Polish death camps." (Following an international outcry, the Polish government backtracked, a little, making it only a civil offense, not a criminal one, and permitted it outright if it was published or said in an "artistic or scientific" context.) But I felt these things at a remove, admittedly. I wasn't a citizen, I wasn't a resident, I couldn't vote, I couldn't speak the language. As far as I could tell, the political situation wasn't affecting my reclamation efforts.

Then in July 2017, one week before my trial, the Sejm, the lower house of parliament, passed three legislative acts that targeted, respectively, the Supreme Court; the National Council for the Judiciary (KRS), the body responsible for the appointment, assessment, promotion, and discipline of judges; and the lower courts. This was a careful, comprehensive assault on the judicial system.

The laws targeting the Supreme Court received the most attention, especially the proposal to lower the retirement age for judges, effective immediately, which would result in a huge number of Supreme Court vacancies—which the PiS-controlled Sejm could then fill. The other two acts were arguably just as pernicious, if less flagrant and more insidious.

Following massive protests in cities across the country, the president vetoed two of the three acts—the proposed reform of the Supreme Court and the proposed reform of the KRS. (As was widely suspected, however, the vetoes were a diversion tactic, a way to buy time and deflect attention; the laws were soon reintroduced with cosmetic alterations and the president duly signed them.) The reforms of the lower courts he signed into law. Immediately the minister of justice, empowered by the new laws to dismiss court presidents and vice presidents without cause or explanation, did just that: dozens of court presidents and vice presidents across the country were removed and loyalists were installed. PiS had tightened its grip on the judiciary.

On the morning of the trial I met The Killer and Grazyna in the fumy basement of the central bus station in Kraków. My lawyer did not look particularly lawyerly. She wore a pink velour tracksuit with the jacket unzipped, revealing a t-shirt with an enormous lion's head, and a pearl necklace that did not at all go with but also absolutely completed the outfit. She carried a large shopping bag emblazoned with kittens. Mother and daughter were in a very good mood. They teased me about my weak handshake, about my being a writer, about my being their third-smartest client. I told them that the next time we went to court I was going to wear a matching tracksuit.

The bus to Sosnowiec took about an hour. From the city center we took a taxi to the courthouse, an extremely municipalish building—nondescript, angular, concrete, brown and gray.

We'd given ourselves a lot of time to get to the courthouse; we were very early. We planted ourselves on a couple of benches at the end of a hallway. The Killer went to the bathroom and returned wearing a barrister's gown—black, with complicated ruffles and an elaborate white bow/cravat thing—and now looked extremely lawyerly, pearl necklace and all. (It did give me a certain pleasure and confidence knowing that underneath the gown was that lion's head t-shirt.) I prodded The Killer to prep me—What was the judge going to ask? Was there anything I should make sure to say? Make sure not to say?—but in so many words she told me not to worry. Her only direction was that if the judge asked what my father's profession was I should say he was a businessman. Also my grandfather. I should say he was also a businessman. The judge, The Killer said, will be very happy with this answer.

I asked what the plan was regarding my uncle Hershel—he's not on the claim, I said, and if it comes up I'd really rather not lie in court. No no, The Killer said, today we are here to decide the deaths of Moshe and Sura-Hena and Michoel and Tamara. The Killer and Grazyna rarely answered my questions directly; they tended just to reassert something tangentially related to the question. If I wanted answers I had to press: And what if it does come up? What do I say? We are here to discuss the deaths of Moshe and Sura-Hena and Michoel and Tamara, The Killer said, again. The case in Będzin went very well for us. I said, again, that I'd really rather not commit perjury. They said, again, that the case in Będzin had gone very well. At that moment our translator, Małgorzata, arrived—she was nerdy, polite, professional, spoke reassuringly good English—and the matter was dropped.

Eventually we were beckoned inside. It was a decidedly ungrand room —windowless, low ceiling, fluorescent lighting, in every direction that coughed-on institutional white—but still it was recognizable as a court-room. The judge's bench was a large cluttered desk set on a foot-high platform. At the far end of the bench, a court reporter sat behind a computer, and a second monitor had been set up for the judge so she could read and amend in real time. Behind the judge's bench was a large and well-polished Polish coat of arms. In front, on either side of a simple podium, were a couple of wooden benches, one for the plaintiff and one for defendant.

I said hello to the judge, an exhausted-looking middle-aged woman with thick blond hair pulled into a tight ponytail. Her manner was brusque and severely professional. My greeting was not returned.

The judge, riffling through heaps of papers, began what I assumed was a necessary preamble to the hearing. On this day in this place concerning this matter etc. I caught a few familiar words—"Kaiser," "Małachowskiego." The court reporter scrambled to keep up; the judge had to repeat herself often. She had a loud sharp voice, which could be heard clearly over the construction noises coming in from outside. The Killer, Grazyna, Małgorzata, and I stood before the bench awkwardly. Małgorzata tried to keep me abreast, whispering in my ear what the judge was saying, about me, my father, my aunt, my grandfather, but it was very disorienting. I was lost in a Polish bureaucratic fog.

There was some back-and-forth between the judge and The Killer —who was, I have to say, totally in her element: the robe, the stoic fierceness; she cut an intimidating figure—and then we were directed to sit. The four of us squeezed onto a single bench, which felt and must have looked ridiculous.

The judge went on declaiming a few more minutes, and then I was called to testify. I stood up and took my place behind the podium, Małgorzata beside me.

My back-and-forth with the judge was very slow—the question had to be translated, and then my answer had to be translated, and then my answer, or the relevant parts thereof, had to be repeated/clarified by the judge so they could be put on the court record. The following is a more or less unedited transcript — my voice recorder was on and hidden in my pocket — of my testimony, or at least the parts that were comprehensible to me.

THE COURT: Have you ever been charged with perjury?

THE CLAIMANT: No.

THE COURT: You would be criminally liable for perjury. In such a case you would be sentenced to eight years in prison.

THE CLAIMANT: I understand.

THE COURT: Do you know the reason why you were called as a witness to the court?

THE CLAIMANT: To give testimony regarding the deaths of Moshe Kajzer, Sura-Hena Kajzer, Tamara, Michoel Aaron.

THE COURT: We'll be starting with Moshe. What do you know about him?

THE CLAIMANT: My grandfather was his son. I didn't know him personally. He died way before I was born. But I know that he died.

THE COURT: What were the circumstances of his death?

THE CLAIMANT: I don't know. I just know that it was between 1941 and 1944.

THE COURT: How do you know that?

THE CLAIMANT: That's what my grandfather told my father, and my father told me. It is known in our family.

THE COURT: So you don't know what happened to Moshe?

THE CLAIMANT: I don't know exactly but he was never seen again.

THE COURT: Is it likely that he was in the ghetto?

THE CLAIMANT: He was definitely in the ghetto and it's possible he was shot, or taken to one of the camps. Where he would have died.

THE COURT: Do you know of any survivors of the ghetto?

THE CLAIMANT: I know of a few. Plus my grandfather.

THE COURT: Why are you certain that Moshe didn't survive if other people did survive the ghetto?

THE CLAIMANT: Because they would have found each other after the war.

THE COURT: How old would he be today?

THE CLAIMANT: Almost 140.

THE COURT: Have you been searching in organizations?

THE CLAIMANT: Many.

THE COURT: What were the results?

THE CLAIMANT: Nothing.

THE COURT: Okay, What was the name of his spouse?

THE CLAIMANT: Sura-Hena.

THE COURT:. What do you know about her?

THE CLAIMANT: Very little.

THE COURT: Was it possible that she survived?

THE CLAIMANT: No.

THE COURT: How old would she be if she were alive today?

THE CLAIMANT: She was born in the 1880s, so between 130 and 140 years old.

THE COURT: How many children did they have?

THE CLAIMANT: Three.

THE COURT: What were their names?

THE CLAIMANT: Michoel, Tamara, and Maier.

THE COURT: Do you know if they were taken to the concentration camp?

THE CLAIMANT: I don't know. I know my grandfather was.

THE COURT: He survived?

THE CLAIMANT: My grandfather? Yes.

THE COURT: What happened to Michoel and Tamara?

THE CLAIMANT: They died.

THE COURT: Where?

THE CLAIMANT: I don't know.

THE COURT: Is their death connected in any way with the war?

THE CLAIMANT: Yes. What? Yes.

THE COURT: How old would they be?

THE CLAIMANT: Michoel was born in 1913, so he'd be 104, and Tamara
would be about 102.

THE COURT: So only Maier survived of all the children?

THE CLAIMANT: Yes.

THE COURT: When did he die?

THE CLAIMANT: 1977.

THE COURT: What estate did Moshe and Sura-Hena leave here in
Poland?

THE CLAIMANT: They left property.

THE COURT: Where is it?

THE CLAIMANT: It's at Małachowskiego 12. I think. It's complicated.
It might be somewhere else. But it was number 12 before the
war.

(The Killer and Grazyna unhappily grumble to each other.)

THE COURT: What are the grounds on which you base your conviction that these people are dead?

THE CLAIMANT: That they're dead, today, in the year 2017?

THE COURT: Yes.

THE CLAIMANT: No one found each other after the war, that's number
one. Even with very extensive searching by my grandfather, after
the war, for thirty years. If they were alive then, my grandfather
would have found them. And then my own searching with organizations in Israel, the US, Canada, and Poland. If they were

alive now I would have found them. And number two, they're dead, because it's 2017. Even if they had survived the war they would be dead by now.

(The Killer stands and conducts an examination of the Claimant.)

THE KILLER: Was your grandfather ever charged with perjury?

THE CLAIMANT: No.

THE KILLER: Was he incapacitated?

THE CLAIMANT: Not until right before he died

THE KILLER: What was his profession?

THE CLAIMANT: Businessman.

THE KILLER: And you were born in?

THE CLAIMANT: 1985.

THE KILLER: So you got the information from your father?

THE CLAIMANT: Yes.

THE KILLER: Was your father incapacitated?

THE CLAIMANT: No.

THE KILLER: Was he charged with perjury?

THE CLAIMANT: No.

THE KILLER: What was the profession of your father?

THE CLAIMANT: Businessman.

(The Claimant sits.)

THE KILLER: I am requesting the Court to declare Moshe Kajzer, Sura-Hena Kazjer, Michoel Kajzer, and Tamara Kajzer legally deceased, and the Court to give an approximate date of their death.

THE COURT: The Court obliges the claimant to place an advertisement in a periodical to announce the disappearance of the persons in question and to request that anyone with information come forward within a period of sixty days.

THE KILLER: This already has been done. The advertisement ran in *Gazeta Prawna* on January 22, 2017.

THE COURT: What was the result?

THE KILLER: No one came forward.

THE COURT: The Court obliges the Claimant to search the records of the concentration camps.

(The Killer objects; the Claimant is called back to the stand.)

THE COURT: What would you like to add?

THE CLAIMANT: All the major databases of concentration camps have been checked already.

THE COURT: Which ones specifically?

THE CLAIMANT: Yad Vashem, United States Holocaust Memorial Museum, there is one run by the German government. The Jewish Historical Institute in Warsaw, the museum in Auschwitz, Museum of Gross-Rosen, and something called JewishGen, which is a collection of many databases. To name a few.

THE COURT: Anything else?

THE CLAIMANT: Individual ghettos, whatever is available.

THE COURT: Anything else?

THE CLAIMANT: This was an exhaustive search in English, Polish, German, Hebrew, and Yiddish. Every available database has been searched.

THE COURT: Anything else?

THE CLAIMANT: My point is that they were not found on any list.

THE KILLER: Are there any sources that you neglected to check?

THE CLAIMANT: No. I'm very familiar with the available resources.

THE KILLER: And the results of the searches?

THE CLAIMANT: No details of any deaths were found.

THE COURT: Anything else?

THE CLAIMANT: We also checked US and German refugee aid organizations that helped after the war, and there were no results. Again, this was an extensive search.

THE COURT: So you should enclose all those documents.

THE CLAIMANT: What documents?

THE COURT: Of all the registries you have checked.

THE CLAIMANT: But how—

THE COURT: Here there is only one list. What is this list?

(The Claimant approaches the bench to inspect a list that had been submitted as evidence.)

THE CLAIMANT: That is the census of the Będzin ghetto. Where some of the Kajzers were, as you can see.

THE COURT: But this is the only list you submitted. What about the other lists?

THE CLAIMANT: What other lists?

THE COURT: All the other lists. The databases you searched.

THE CLAIMAINT: But they don't show up on the other lists.

THE COURT: But you said you searched the other lists.

THE CLAIMANT: I did.

THE COURT: But you didn't submit the lists to the Court.

THE CLAIMANT: Because there was nothing to submit. They weren't on the lists.

THE COURT: You should submit all the lists you searched.

THE CLAIMANT: You're saying I should submit the lists and databases they *don't* show up on?

THE COURT: Yes.

THE CLAIMANT: But how do I show a non-entry?

THE COURT: You said you checked the lists?

THE CLAIMANT: I did.

THE COURT: So you should submit those lists.

THE CLAIMAINT: I should submit those lists? In their entirety?

THE COURT: Yes.

THE CLAIMANT: But there would be hundreds of thousands of entries, maybe millions.

THE COURT: Understood. Anything else?

We debriefed in the hallway. The Killer and Grazyna were annoyed that the judge had asked about the property: our claim concerned only the deaths of my relatives; matters of property/inheritance should not have been relevant. The Killer was already talking about an appeal. I asked Małgorzata how she thought it had gone. She said that the judge had seemed a little stern, and that some of the questioning had been a little ridiculous, but all in all nothing about the proceeding had struck her as overly unusual. This was reassuring to me. So we'll wait and see, I said to The Killer and Grazyna. Maybe the judge will rule in our favor. We will appeal to the court in Katowice, Grazyna said. But maybe we won't have to, I said. Yes, she said, we can appeal to the court in Katowice.

The court reporter exited the courtroom, carrying a tall stack of folders that she secured with her chin, followed by the judge, who had changed out of her robe into a floral print dress. They avoided making eye contact with us, or at least it seemed that way. The Killer changed out of her robe and back into her pink velour jumpsuit and we got ready to head back to Kraków. On the way out, Małgorzata asked me whether I believed in the Bible. It's the Bible, I said. Are you happy? she asked. That's a big question, I said. She nodded sympathetically, and slipped me some pamphlets urging me to embrace Jesus.

8

Not far from the Riese sites there is a so-called technical military museum that has as its main attraction an enormous and enormously strange cement structure—picture a cement ring 150 feet in diameter held aloft by a dozen fifty-foot-high cement columns, like a gargantuan abstract sculpture of a coliseum. This, the museum claims, was a testing rig for Haunebu III, a flying saucer built by the Nazis, and which was not only built, but operational: the aircraft recorded nineteen flights, according to the display, and its propulsion system was based on antigravity technology that gave it a top speed of Mach 10, about 12,000 km/hr. "The drive of this ship probably consisted of electro-gravity generators: powerful electromagnets of Van de Graaff generator and type of Marconi spherical dynamos containing a sphere of rotating mercury."

Among the exploring community there is a pronounced, shall we say, lack of skepticism regarding Riese. It would come up all the time. I'd ask, Why did the Germans build Riese? and I'd be told: nuclear weapons, underground cities, antigravity, time travel, telekinesis. There is a very pronounced para-history here.

Riese was meant to have been a bunker system and/or a factory. Despite the weird dearth of conclusive evidence in any direction, the argument that it was a bunker/factory is nonetheless a persuasive one —because this is what the Nazis did with their undergrounds, they used them as bunkers and factories. In other words this is an extremely strong default explanation, and any assertion to the contrary demands extremely compelling evidence, especially if what's being asserted is generally known not to exist. (Though there is one alternative theory that I really like, it makes a kind of delicious sense, though as far as I know there is no evidence to support it: that Riese served *no* purpose other than to divert massive amounts of Nazi cash—German officials who understood that the war was all but lost funneled money out of Berlin via this quixotic mountain-hollowing infrastructure project.)

For a while my instinct was not necessarily to ignore but certainly not to engage, to not hurt my head trying to understand Van de Graaff generators and Marconi spherical dynamos. A treasure hunter would tell me that the Nazis had built a time machine and I'd nod and take notes and leave it at that. I saw no reason to take these discussions seriously because *there was no reason to take them seriously.* Even to justify why I wasn't taking them seriously is in effect to take them seriously; I did believe and still do believe that it is a valid position not to engage the crazy. What would be the purpose? To methodically demonstrate the dubiousness of Nazi time travel? The conclusions we would eventually reach are the conclusions we have immediately reached. On top of that —and not to pierce the illusion of the author as a tirelessly inquisitive information-gatherer but—my interactions with explorers could be terrifically exhausting, and when things went off the rails, when the subject turned to antigravity or ancient occult civilizations, it'd be that much worse: you feel besieged, bludgeoned, by the absurdity. Half-consciously

I grouped the conspiracy theory stuff in with the rest of the weird: the actual history was strange; the people were strange; the quote-unquote alternative history was also strange. I don't know. People believe crazy things. You will break your brain trying to understand why they believe what they believe. I thought of the conspiracy theories as harmless, unromantic, hard-edged myths. Or — myths gone rampant, sprawling myths that have shed the metaphor or symbolism that kept them tethered and allowed them to be undogmatically appreciated.

But as I got deeper in, as I met more treasure hunters, the conspiracy theory stuff piled up until I had no choice but to confront it, to at least try to make sense of it. It was too prominent a feature of the community to ignore; it was also too prominent a part of Riese mythology to ignore.

I dove in. I tried to dive in. Much of the material was impenetrable, an impossibly dense tangle of pseudohistory and -science. I did what I could. I read many long posts on the Internet. I watched many videos on the Internet. I read the books available in English and asked others to read the books that were only in Polish. I looked up the sources and then I looked up the sources' sources. I spoke to and eventually met a man named Igor Witkowski, the author of more than seventy books, including *Hitler's Werewolves, Japanese Wunderwaffe,* and *Christ & UFOs,* and who more than anyone else is responsible for the strangely tenacious myth of *Die Glocke,* the Nazis' bell-shaped device that could manipulate time and gravity. I wish I had more to report about our meeting — Witkowski, cagey and reticent, tried to pass himself off as a run-of-the-mill military historian, if with fewer hang-ups about things like gravity — but it did help me understand just how seriously the believers believe. They aren't trolling.

Anyway, I immersed myself or tried to immerse myself and I'm here to report back that it gets much, much stranger. Antigravity and *Die Glocke* are just the tip of the conspiracy theory iceberg. Project Riese is the epicenter, the catalyst, the cauldron for all sorts of fantastic, absurd, lunatic beliefs about the Nazis. Pull on any thread and very quickly you get to ancient civilizations; aliens; ancient alien civilizations; UFOs; Roswell; the JFK assassination; Operation Paperclip; Hollow Earth Doctrine; World Ice Theory; Twin Space Program; Nazi occultism; and many postwar Nazi plots, including ODESSA (Organisation der ehemaligen SS-Angehörigen, or Organization of Former SS Members), infiltration into NASA, operational Nazi bases in Antarctica, South America, on other planets.

It is important to understand that conspiracy theories, given the space to fully unfurl, are not beliefs; they are systems of beliefs. These are not standalone delusions. The theory actually has to make sense on its own terms. Which means that one out-there supposition necessitates an entire bouquet of other out-there convictions. I will give you an example. Suppose we grant the premise that the Nazis did in fact successfully deploy antigravity technology: we've connected the dots, we've called BS on those obdurate historians and myopic scientists, and we are reasonably sure or at least are open to the possibility that antigravity is a thing and the Nazis had it. Okay, great. But that's only step one. Now we have to flesh it out. Any objections raised have to be addressed. Here is an objection: If antigravity not only is possible but was in fact deployed in the 1940s, how is it that no one since has figured it out? How is it that the technology no longer exists? Answer: the technology *does* exist and the reason you don't know about it is that it has been suppressed by governments, corporations, cabals. Okay, but objection: What about all the nongovernment research going on? All those universities, all those start-ups, all those tinkerers? Surely not all are part of the conspiracy! Answer: no, they are not part of the conspiracy, but they *are* being actively misled; for decades those governments, corporations, cabals have suppressed the true physics and promoted an alternative field of physics (what you and I know as "physics") in order to "disprove" antigravity. You can see how this goes—one delusion, followed through, implies a radically different understanding of the world. Eventually it's one giant conspiracy. Everything fits together. Once you've established that there is a near-omnipotent invisible power behind the scenes pulling the strings, everything suspicious—and for those so inclined, *everything* is suspicious—suddenly *makes sense,* the cover-ups are transparent, the dots connect, the pattern emerges.

Some conspiracy theorists take it very far, some take it less far, but there tends to be a consistent underlying framework, a set of attitudes or philosophies that allow these beliefs to take root, a special blend of skepticism and unskepticism, of irrationality and hyperrationality. So while most of the explorers who believe in Nazi antigravity, time travel, etc. aren't full-blown conspiracy theorists—only a handful of explorers ever said anything to me about a Nazi-extraterrestrial alliance (though I suppose a handful is still a lot)—they are, I submit, nonetheless subscribing to or at least aligning themselves with this underlying framework.

So in our effort to make sense of the conspiracy theories, let's not get lost in the theories themselves—it isn't worth the immense amount of time and effort it would take to understand, say, how the US-Soviet space race was in fact an orchestrated charade. What would be the point, beyond us having a good time gawking? The much more pressing question is, what do we do with all this? What intellectual, historical, even moral stance do we assume toward it? Can we understand the appeal? The purpose, so to speak? Let's get sociological?

Let's get sociological. Richard Hofstadter, in his essay "The Paranoid Style in American Politics," diagnoses conspiracy theories as a form of collective psychosis, a group's implicit or not so implicit rejection and reorganization of reality. And World War II, Hofstadter says, was a psychic rupture; it reset the baseline of plausibility, it loosened the imagination's constraints. (The only adjective not defeated by World War II and the Holocaust is, I submit, "unimaginable.") The conspiracy theories are, then, a kind of traumatic response. "Certain social structures and national inheritances, certain historical catastrophes or frustrations may be conducive to the release of such psychic energies," Hofstadter writes, and the war has given a "vast theatre for [the paranoid's] imagination, full of rich and proliferating detail, replete with realistic cues and undeniable proofs of the validity of his suspicions." It's a confronting of the incomprehensible via invocation of the impossible. If you wanted to give this a psychoanalytic tweak you could say that the conspiracy theories are a means of aversion, an avoidance of the horror, that the overemphasis on technology and mystery is in fact a looking-away from the death and inhumanity. It's a swapping out of one kind of "unimaginable" for another, more palpable one. World War II is psychically a lot easier when it's about antigravity and time travel than when it's about gas chambers and stacks of corpses.

It's the war in general and the Nazis in particular. It is as if the Nazis were so dementedly evil that some threshold was exceeded, a barrier was broken, and now anything goes, any act, no matter how nefarious or absurd, can be attributed to them: their perceived ambitions and capabilities seem to have limitless stretch. Even within more mainstream circles the Nazis are talked about as if they were supernaturally evil, not quite of this world, something irrational and incomprehensible, something that should have been impossible had the laws of nature held. And though most of us have not fully surrendered our skepticism — most of us are not ready to believe that the Nazis had a time machine — we have still surrendered quite a bit. It's important to recognize that our historical conceptions are to some extent informed by myth, especially when it comes to something as imagination-taxing as the Nazis. Which helps explains why those explorers who claimed they'd found the Golden Train were taken as seriously as they were. Or the bottomless obsession over various Nazi mysteries. Or the enduring trope of Nazis in science fiction (not to mention science fiction masquerading as history). The Nazis already *feel* surreal. This is fertile ground for conspiracy theories.

Riese is interesting because it actually *is* extremely mysterious. Which doesn't make the theory of antigravity any more credible, of course, but it does introduce an epistemological gap, a wedge, a vacuum—conspiracy theory, which is at heart a solution or set of solutions, feeds off mystery. Riese has mystery in spades. From Riese you don't have to do nearly as much conceptual heavy lifting to get to antigravity as you would if you were starting from scratch. Your imagination is stretched to the point where it can just about fit a Nazi UFO.

And the explorers' general attitude toward history and knowledge is already very conspiracy theory-ish; you might say the cognitive prerequisites are already in place:

(1) The adamant, quasi-dogmatic belief that there is a great deal about the war, about Riese, about Nazi secrets, whatever, that is still unknown, or known to extremely few people.

(2) The reason why what is unknown has remained unknown is that it was intentionally and often ingeniously hidden, covered up, obscured. The corollary is that uncovering the unknown requires great effort, courage, perseverance, and insight.

(3) The fact that something is widely believed or even universally believed means bubkes. The attitude toward mainstream sources and so-called experts is somewhere between bemused and disdainful; much of what is "known" is wrong or incomplete. Hand in hand with this goes exceptional self-confidence.

(4) Given (1), (2), and (3), the truth is never obvious, never apparent, is revealed only extremely incrementally. Any shard of truth—such as addled testimony or ambiguous documentation—thus assumes an oversized significance, is understood as a peek behind the curtain.

(5) Given (1), (2), (3), and (4), there is tremendous suspicion toward everything and everyone.

You might say that the treasure hunters are primed for conspiracy theories, or even that they already possess the underlying misconceptions, the conceptual scaffolding.

If you wanted you could be a lot more generous. Since Hofstadter's essay, which was first published in 1964, there has been a marked trend, within the admittedly small world of conspiracy theory research (though it mirrors the trend in any number of disciplines), of depathologization. Don't judge, these researchers exhort: these beliefs, no matter how preposterous and irrational, should not be diagnosed, condemned, mocked, or even thought of as "preposterous" or "irrational"; whether or not the beliefs map onto the quote-unquote actual world is not the point. Rather the conspiracy theories should be thought of as a set of beliefs whose meanings and causes are obscure, and the only way to responsibly de-obscure is by considering the beliefs on their own terms, from the inside, generously, nonjudgmentally, ethnosociologically. Conspiracy theories are thus framed as something like religious convictions: not assertions about reality but beliefs that have meaning and purpose. You could be even more generous. You could argue, as some researchers have argued, that once context is taken into account—once you consider what the adherents know, what they don't know, the social context, cultural context, historical context—conspiracy theories should in fact be considered *rational* reactions. You could argue, as some researchers have argued, that conspiracy theories are a coded critique, a form of resistance against the dominant narrative, a means of casting aspersions on the entrenched power structure.

I am not so generous, however. Personally I am comfortable pathologizing beliefs in Nazi time machines.

So actually let's not get sociological; it's the wrong approach, it's irresponsible, in fact: these explanations, justifications, interpretations, however insightful and interesting, obfuscate a dark and pernicious underside. Because beneath the outlandish assertions lurks an insidious claim — that your understanding of the war is wrong. That you missed the point. Yes yes, fine, the Germans did some murdering and the Jews did some dying but let me tell you the real story. The conspiracy theory insists on reshaping the narrative, redetermining what does matter and what does not matter. The conspiracy theory radically overemphasizes the Nazi agenda and radically deemphasizes the dead. The genocide is made incidental. One cannot help but notice, when reading these extremely long and involved treatises by men who consider themselves to be world-class World War II historians, how little mention there is of any Nazi wrongdoing. Perhaps the most repulsive bit of Joseph P. Farrell's extremely repulsive *The SS Brotherhood of The Bell* — one of the most "authoritative" and best-"researched" books on the *Wunderwaffe* — is his claim that The Bell, the Nazi antigravity and time machine, was "perhaps the most important story to come out of World War Two." I'll note only that I would disagree with Mr. Farrell *even if The Bell were real* — that is to say, even if it turned out that the Nazis actually had an actual time machine it still would not be the most important story to come out of World War II.

This trivialization is a particularly noxious form of revisionism. It's slippery, it comes at you sideway: it isn't blatant denial, there is nothing to counter directly. The number of murdered Jews isn't usually disputed, for instance. Rather the murders are recontextualized, are inserted into a "grander" narrative, usually one with a technological or occult arc. You don't have to tread that far into the muck to come across claims that Auschwitz was a uranium enrichment plant. Or that the crematoria were part of an elaborate occult ritual. The deaths are redefined and the Nazis are, in effect, let off the hook. They did what they did but they had a reason. The suspension of moral agency is a pervasive subtext throughout the conspiracy theories. Hitler was possessed, the Nazi agenda was a kind of manifest destiny, it was all done at the behest of aliens, it was all determined by ancient occult forces.

The moral narrative of the war is thus subverted, inverted, perverted. The Nazis' misdeeds are minimized, whitewashed; they become the protagonists, even the heroes. The real bad guys are the forces pulling the strings, the conspirators, the ones hoodwinking the world into believing that antigravity is impossible. And where you have behind-the-scenes powers you have, inevitably, Jews. They're at the levers, they're controlling the banks, the corporations, the governments. The conspiracy theories are positively soaked through with anti-Semitism. Mostly it's the usual tropes but some of it is truly bizarre. Farrell casually but insistently refers to the research field of physics, the physics the bad guys seek to fool all of us into believing is real, as "Jewish relativistic physics." The Jewish involvement was, Farrell says, part of the reason the Nazis rejected it. It's surprising at first, it feels so out of place, unnecessary, gratuitous — Wasn't this about Nazi time travel? Whence all the Jew-bashing? — until you understand that there is a kind of moral seesaw here, with Nazis on one side and Jews on the other. Given the goal, stated or otherwise, of rebalancing the war's moral weight, it isn't surprising to see how popular conspiracy theories are among Holocaust deniers and revisionists. The objectives converge. Ernst Zündel began his Holocaust-denying career by publishing books like *UFOs: Nazi Secret Weapon?* and *Secret Nazi Polar Expeditions.*

The point is, it's ugly stuff, and should be treated accordingly. Just because it's preposterous doesn't mean it's innocent. (Zündel suggested several times over the course of his career that he didn't actually believe the conspiracy theories he had promoted, he just used them to garner publicity and attention.) While it's all but impossible to chart the effects of ideas, to epidemiologically trace beliefs and attitudes, it is only too clear that ideas *do* have effects, and can infect, and can have very serious consequences. Two days after I'd begun writing this chapter, a man named Robert Bowers walked into a synagogue in Pittsburgh and gunned down eleven Jews. Bowers's social media activity revealed that he had bought in to a whole host of anti-Semitic conspiracy theories, particularly in regard to the caravan of refugees supposedly approaching the border. However it is that Bowers came to believe what he believed, the preposterousness of the theories was, clearly, no deterrent. Your rationality isn't all that helpful a guide to what is and what is not dangerous.

This extends beyond conspiracy theories. Our cultural obsession with the Nazis—which can function, regardless of our intentions, as a kind of valorization—should be examined in this light: What are we emphasizing? Deemphasizing?

To indulge the theories, even via mockery, is to grant them a power. Consider this an argument against a kind of historical prurience. I know how cranky this sounds, I know how much more fun it would be to discuss Nazi flying saucers. But there is a cost to laughing at what should be condemned.

Part III

—

MAŁACHOWSKIEGO 34

9

Two years after beginning the reclamation process—in which I felt I'd made little progress, had gotten no closer to getting the building back, no closer to my grandfather, he was still frustratingly abstract—my mother remembered that she had in the basement a shoebox full of 8mm film cartridges, forty- and fifty-year-old family videos that hadn't been watched in decades, if ever. (In our family, to store is to cherish.) This isn't because no one would be interested—on the contrary: the older the videos got the stranger and more compelling they'd be—but because, absent a concerted effort, a shoebox full of Super 8s in the basement will remain a shoebox full of Super 8s in the basement.

The next chance I had I fetched the shoebox and had the tapes digitized and burned onto a DVD, and on a cold weeknight in March I set my laptop on my coffee table and slid the disc in.

There were about two and a half hours of footage—grainy, flickery, spotty, shaky, over- or underlit, sped up one notch past real-life-speed. I watched beginning to end, without break. In one sense it was perfectly predictable; I don't think there'd be much that would surprise or interest a viewer unrelated to the Kaisers. This was quintessential family video, stolen or staged moments from the lives in the sixties and seventies of a middle-class Jewish American-Canadian family with three children. (That they were relatively recent immigrants and Holocaust survivors doesn't come through, or at least I couldn't recognize the giveaways.) Overall it was unrelentingly banal. Backyard birthday parties; teasing siblings; trips abroad; summer vacations; bar mitzvahs; engagement parties; graduations; new outfits; new car; new house; first day of school; strolls in the park; close-ups of the newborn. Proud happy auspicious moments.

So yes in a wide sense the videos were predictable but — of course — in a more personal sense they were anything but. I sat and watched and I was heart-walloped. It was engrossing, eerie, sad, sentimental. It was a time capsule. It was time travel. I suppose seeing unfamiliar versions of familiar people will have this effect. When I say "unfamiliar" I don't just mean "younger." Here was Bubby but a lovely, vibrant, carefree version of Bubby, a version of Bubby that seemed impossible, a version that seemed so much further away from the war than the Bubby I'd known, even though in a literal, chronological sense the opposite was true. Here were my father, aunt, uncle, trusting and goofy and silly and teasing. My father was a pudgy kid and a striking young man. My uncle Hershel was beautiful and slim till well into adulthood. My mother, gorgeous and shy.

And, of course, my grandfather. Here he was. There he is. He cuts a striking figure. Slim, dapper, almost always in suit, tie, fedora, freshly shaved. He looks like he smells good. How he moves, how he walks, hugs, smiles, stands, holds his children. He has an easy grace (something none of his children or grandchildren have inherited) and a charisma my father and others have referenced but which I never really understood until I saw it. What did I see? I saw his liveliness, his joy, his spirit, his seriousness. This wasn't a new version of my grandfather — I had never known another. The image on these tapes wasn't working against a stored image; this man was entirely unfamiliar to me, and as I watched I realized how *unimagined,* how empty his person — his person as imagined by me — had been. Family sans familiarity is still family but is at the same time something very different. I'd seen photographs of my grandfather, I recognized him, of course. Nonetheless. A photograph captures essence, maybe, sometimes, if you're lucky. But in movement, even or especially in silent movement, there is something so signature, personal, palpable. "Charisma" and "grace" and "spirit" and the rest of the words I'm using to describe my grandfather are, I submit, inherently dynamic attributes: they can be expressed only when there's resistance, when there's movement through (against?) the world.

One clip was particularly arresting, revealing, strange. My grandfather comes home, sits on the sofa, opens the Yiddish newspaper. My grandmother bounces a smiling baby Leah on her lap. My father is practicing the piano. But the three of them (not the oblivious baby) are, it's clear, acting, and they're terrible at it; you can see the strain of performance in their movements, on their faces. They're stiff, unnatural, uncomfortable, even though they're playing themselves. They do multiple takes, assume their positions, open the newspaper, bounce the baby, play the piano. (Who is holding the camera, directing, pushing for another take, demanding the actors be more "natural," be more "themselves"?) What was it about this clip that got me? I don't quite know. The artifice, maybe. That family is in fact a kind of theater. That responsibilities can be understood as roles, however natural or imposed. That maybe the essence of family is pretending to be family.

A few weeks later my family gathered for Passover and I showed them the videos. I rented a projector, draped a couple of white sheets over the living room cabinet for a makeshift screen. My parents, siblings, and nephews and nieces piled into the room, squeezed onto the sofa and armchairs.

We watched, it was a party atmosphere, we shouted and laughed, we squealed every time a familiar face appeared, every time we saw someone we knew in a bathing suit, every time Zaidy kissed — on the cheek, on the mouth! — a woman he wasn't related to. Look how young, how beautiful, how skinny, how handsome, how not-dead these people were! We debated who looked like whom, who got whose nose, eyes, build. We made fun of and admired the outfits. My father's pudginess was obviously cute and hysterical. Hershel's svelteness was obviously cute and hysterical. We had so many questions, which we directed to my father: Who's that? Who's that? Who's that? What is that place? What is going on? When was that?

It was a lot more fun watching with my family than it had been watching alone but that cut both ways — we were an impatient audience, we were eager to be entertained, we were having too good a time to reflect. What had been strange and compelling was now slow, dull, repetitive. Plot, so to speak, became a lot more important. We didn't watch straight through — is four minutes of a family in a park more interesting than one minute? (the answer is yes, it is, but only if you're trying to get closer to the subjects; if you're just watching to see what happens, then no) — but we did watch most of it, a good couple of hours, delighted.

My father, in the leather recliner, feet up, looking much more grandfatherly and patriarchal than usual, was greatly enjoying himself. His childhood knowledge was suddenly useful and interesting. He rarely lets himself indulge in nostalgia; I think he thinks it's impractical, pointless, unproductive (something, perhaps, inherited from his parents, this disciplined focus on the present and future). That night, though, surrounded by his wife of more than forty years and his six children and whichever of his thirteen grandchildren had been allowed to stay up, watching his childhood literally projected onto the wall—even the most unsentimental man would go soft. He was endearingly embarrassed, wistful. He groaned and shook his head at what he and everyone else used to look like, at the attention his parents lavished on his younger sister, at his engagement party, more than forty years ago, at his bar mitzvah, almost fifty years ago. My siblings and I watched the videos and simultaneously watched my father watching the videos.

My father exclaimed: That's Blue Paradise, we used to go there in the summers. That was the day before Hershel's wedding in Israel. That must have been a going-away party before we moved to Toronto. On the screen the men danced in a circle and one by one my father identified them. That's Mr. Mermelstein, that's Mr. Zolty, that's Mr. Levy. That's Harry Ostry, my father said, my father saved him in the camps. What? I said, I've never heard that—what happened? I don't know, my father said, I don't know any details. Did you ever know the details? I don't think so, my father said, I just always kind of knew it, it was a story we always knew. That's Shloimie, that's Max! Oh my god, it's Alan.

We watched my grandfather make havdalah, the ritual that closes out Shabbos with a flame and wine and something pungent to smell. He added a custom we'd never seen before. After extinguishing the flame and drinking the wine, he dipped his fingers into the saucer, picking up drops of wine, and dabbed the corner of his eyes, three times; and then re-dipped his fingers into the saucer and put drops in his front pockets, also three times. We were mystified. Not by the act itself—we were well accustomed to varieties of ritual—but by its absence in our family, that the tradition had apparently been dropped. My father couldn't explain it. "I remember my father did it," he said. "I don't know why I don't." He said he'd start doing it again, there was no reason not to, if it's what his father did it meant it's what *his* father had done, and so on.

The next morning I was with my father in the car, waiting for my mother. My father was wearing white shorts, a baseball cap, and clip-on sunglasses, looking again like his handsome, successful, focused-on-the-present, sixty-three-year-old self. Usually when forced to wait he gets impatient. Usually in this scenario he'd ask, Where is she, I don't understand, we said we'd leave at nine so why isn't she ready at nine? But today he was quiet and reflective. "I have to tell you," he said, "watching those videos, seeing all that, it was very depressing. I woke up feeling very depressed."

"I'm surprised," I said. "You seemed to be really enjoying."

"It didn't hit me until later. When I was trying to fall asleep. When I woke up." Overnight the experience had turned sour.

"Is it because of your parents? Because you miss your parents?"

No, my father shook his head. It was more than that. "Everyone's dead," he said. "All those people in the video—they're all dead."

A week after Passover it was my grandfather's yahrtzeit, and I went to Toronto to be with my father for the weekend, he'd asked me to come. My mother was out of town, none of my siblings live in Toronto, it'd be just us two.

Friday night, my father and I had Shabbos dinner at my aunt's. A couple of my cousins and their spouses were there too. There was, inevitably, an argument—or rather the entire conversation was knitted from mini-arguments, and one argument happened to stick and fester. I don't remember what it was about—political correctness, abortion, Trump, it could've been anything. It wasn't even particularly heated, but I felt outnumbered, ganged up on, and in the argument's wake I grew quiet, sullen, sulky.

After dinner my father and I walked the couple of blocks home quickly and in silence, a silence that got more pronounced once we got inside; it's a large house and it was empty. In the dining room my father and I took off our suit jackets, draped them over a couple of chairs. My father then took off his white button-down shirt, draped it over another chair—a habit he has when my mother's not home—and stood before me in his undershirt and tzitzis. Can I ask you something, he said. He was upset. His voice was hard and low.

"Yeah?" My voice was also hard and low.

"Why are you so interested in my father?"

"What do you mean?"

"I'm just trying to understand—what is it about him that interests you so much? That all of a sudden you're so obsessed?"

"I don't understand what you're asking."

"Because this is not what he would have cared about."

I don't remember how I responded—I was upset but not confrontational—or how the argument ended; certainly we didn't reach a resolution. At some point we went quiet, went to sleep, and the matter did not come up the next day. But for a long time his comment ate at me. It was, I thought, unfair, ungenerous. What I was trying to do with this building seemed to me to be at worst innocuous. But why not righteous, why not good, why not meaningful, significant, sentimental?

A few months later, back in Poland, I interviewed a treasure hunter, Grzegorz, whose grandfather was Jewish and had been in the same concentration camps as Abraham. Grzegorz didn't see himself as Jewish, but was proud of his legacy, felt a responsibility toward his past. And he saw in me a kindred spirit. The first thing he said to me, as soon as I turned on my recorder, was "I am the same as you. Just like you follow your grandfather, I follow my grandfather." My instinct was to correct him, to tell him that Abraham wasn't actually my grandfather, he was my grandfather's cousin, but I held off, in the moment it didn't seem to matter. We were quiet for a long time; Grzegorz seemed to be contemplating what his grandfather had been through, and my thoughts turned to my grandfather, not Abraham, but my real grandfather, my father's father, who was also a survivor, who'd also been in the camps, but whose story has been lost, and I wondered what it would mean to "follow" my grandfather, I wondered if what I was doing with the reclamation constituted "following." And then I thought about what my father had said to me that night in the dining room, when he'd challenged me on my new-found family obsession, and I, sitting across from Grzegorz as he fought back tears, understood what my father had meant, what he'd tried to say.

It pained my father that I'd strayed from the path that'd been marked out for me when I was born, which was the path marked out for him, by his father, when he was born; he saw in my life decisions a rejection of the patrimony. And so this was what was behind his question about my newfound family obsession: All of a sudden out of nowhere I was re-claiming that patrimony? Had the chutzpah to *redefine* that patrimony? To insist I represented my grandfather and his wishes? That I was now so dedicated to his legacy? It was inconsistent, even hypocritical, in my father's eyes, to slice my grandfather's character like that, to pick and choose, to find meaning only where I wanted to find meaning, to uphold one kind of inheritance at the expense of another, more important kind. The reclamation was an assertion of a relationship with my grandfather, and of a relationship of a particular sort, and the fact of the matter is — so my father was saying — that this was not the sort of relationship my grandfather would have cared about, or at least not the kind he would have prioritized. I was saying to my grandfather, The building! You and I share this! And my grandfather was — via my father, the rightful or at least most qualified spokesman — responding, The building? Who cares about the building? That's not what I want us to share, that's not what I wanted you to inherit.

The most familiar form of non-material inheritance is sentimentalism. Wherein the object itself is less relevant than its spiritual load. We use the term "priceless" because we're talking an entirely different currency. It's a memory-value, which is a spiritual value. Or, if you will, a personal holiness. And that holiness can be passed down, can be cherished and re-cherished, even if along the way the holiness gets torqued a little: your grandfather cherished this watch and now you too cherish this watch but really you cherish your grandfather's cherishing. I think about sentimental objects not as a way to connect with those who are gone, but as a way to *describe* them. To ascribe verbs to them. Characterization. To bring them out of the universal and into the specific.

And though my family is astonishingly unsentimental—objects are objects are objects: never mementoes, keepsakes, or heirlooms—we are in fact exceedingly well practiced in let's call it the imposition of spiritual significance. Our ritual objects are sacred objects. Tefillin, shofar, esrog, kipah, Torah. These items are *kadosh*, are holy. But if the sentimental is a personal, or interpersonal, holiness, the *kadosh* is God-driven holiness. Tefillin are holy are holy are holy. They are no holier to me than to anyone else; the holiness exists independently of any individual.

Only when it comes to ritual does the holiness get particular: for all the thousands of rules in this religion, there are a million ways of performing them. It's *halacha*, the laws, versus *minhag*, the accretion of a family's quirks in how they fulfill those laws. After eating meat my family, as is tradition, waits before eating dairy. But we wait not six hours, as is standard, but into the sixth: five hours and one minute. There is no reason for this; it's simply our *minhag*. It's what we do. Or how we don't wear the little plastic cover on the *tefillin shel yad*, the box you wrap around your arm. This practice makes no sense. The cover has no religious function, it's just there to protect the tefillin's fragile corners from being blunted. But it's what we do. *Minhag* pushes beyond the irrational —which is a crucial ingredient for holiness—and into the anti-rational, which is a crucial ingredient for art, for love, and for tradition.

Minhag is spiritual lineage: families passing on, holding onto, protecting their particular religious identity, their spiritual personalities. And the war was a massive rupture of this lineage, and it's a rupture that rarely gets discussed, because you don't notice when it's gone, because the practice just reverts to the mean, you don't know what your grand-father did so you just do what everyone else does. It's a rupture that's neither institutional, historical, religious, nor communal in nature, but familial. These rules aren't written down anywhere; they're passed down via a kind of osmosis; it's a family's personal Torah. And all these Torahs were lost. No one had parents, and then no one had grandparents.

For forty years my father ended havdalah in the standard way: he put out the candle, drank the wine, got on with his week. But then he watched the video and saw his father do something different: he saw his father dab three drops of wine on his eyelids, put three drops of wine in his pockets. My father said, That's right, my father used to do that, I remember now.

10

Long ago, in the Owl Mountains, lived a man who possessed vast treasures, which he secured in his underground lair. Every New Year's, when the clock struck twelve, he opened the door to the lair and allowed anyone to enter and take as much treasure as they could carry. But the door remained open only as long as the twelve chimes of the clock — then the door shut, and the greedy ones were locked inside the mountain.

It is believed that in the early 1990s a great treasure was discovered in the Jeleniogórska Crevice, between Lubomierz and Radomice. The treasure included silver dishes, antique jugs, Turkish sabers, gold, and precious stones.

A year later, the voivode of Jelenia Góra received an anonymous letter offering information about the treasure in exchange for half its value and a guarantee of amnesty regarding the objects already sold. The voivode did not respond.

In 1993, the Wrocław-based Polish Exploration Society claimed they had discovered a large tunnel in the crevice, and that it contained gold, jewelry, amber, and the corpses of murdered German military officers, including a general in whose uniform were three Fabergé eggs. One of those eggs was reportedly later found in the home of Waldemar Huczka, a Romanian mayor from Nowa Sól who had been murdered. This discovery came to be known as "Hitler's Sesame."

Many explorers believe there is still a great deal of undiscovered treasure in the crevice. Others claim that Hitler's Sesame was a hoax, fabricated in order to camouflage illegal treasure trade by former Communist officers.

In the fifteenth century, a group of robber knights terrorized the Przygórze region, attacking merchants and travelers and plundering with impunity. No one knew where the robber knights' hideout was; no one even knew what they looked like. Occasionally, however, a group of well-dressed young men would come to the tavern, order an extravagant amount of food and drink, and dance with the girls.

Kinga was the most beautiful of the girls, as well as the best dancer. The mysterious young men would court her, prevail on her to come with them to their castle, but Kinga would always refuse. Kinga and a group of peasants, suspecting that these young men were in fact the robber knights, concocted a scheme to track down and raid their hideout.

The next time the young men showed up in the tavern and asked Kinga to come back with them to their castle, Kinga agreed.

They climbed the mountain, walking carefully between the rocks, and soon reached a small castle. One of the men whistled a melody, and the door opened. It was an old castle, but cozy and well appointed, and full of swords, shields, and loot.

Unbeknownst to the robber knights, a large group of armed peasants had followed them — Kinga had worn sharp heels that left marks
in the wet ground. When the peasants came upon the castle they waited
for Kinga's sign. Finally, when it was nearly dawn, Kinga appeared
in one of the windows. She stretched her arms and said, "Oh, everything is so far away from here!" This was a sign that the robbers were
tired.

The peasants stormed the gates. A fierce battle ensued, but the robber
knights were tired and drunk, and soon all were killed or wounded.

All of the robber knights' treasure was seized by the peasants, except
for two golden boxes, which could not be found, even after the castle
was demolished.

Two hundred years later, an old sorceress claimed the golden boxes
could be found in the following manner: on Christmas night, a virgin
bearing a torch can go to the castle ruins, alone, and at the spot where
the treasure lies, the flame will point downward.

None of the local girls was willing to attempt this.

In 1948 Russian engineers traveled throughout Silesia in order to mea-
sure uranium levels inside abandoned German mine shafts. The results
were very promising, and new shafts were quickly opened in Kowary,
Kletno, and Miedzianka; within a few years, more than a hundred miles
of mining drifts were being exploited for the metal.

The miners were paid extremely well, but worked under severe conditions, and under strict secrecy and security; some of the mines were
officially listed as "paper factory." Thirty minutes before the end of their
shift, the miners would carefully dust off, unroll their cuffs, turn out
their pockets; at the gate they would each be checked by a soldier with a
Geiger counter. If a speck of spoil was found anywhere on his body, the
miner would be taken away, and would not return.

Great wealth came to the mining towns. There were new movie

houses, community centers, homes, and motorcycles. But the miners suffered from black lung and cellular degeneration: the rock dust they breathed in contained radon, a product of decayed radium. Many children were born with tumors and disfigurements.

Cistercian Anselm recorded the following in a tavern in Reichenbach (Dzierżoniów) in 1524:

> One morning in 1483, a Corwin named Georg von Stein, known as the Prague Cleaner, arrived in Rogowiec. The robber knights Niclas and Hanz Schellendorf and their band of hard men, upon hearing of von Stein's arrival, shuddered in fear—von Stein and his army had a reputation of great strength and mercilessness.
>
> Soon von Stein's messengers delivered the conditions of our surrender. We were to abandon the castle and leave the area until the following evening.
>
> This caused a great uproar, as there were many precious treasures in the cellar. The robber knights did not want to abandon their loot.
>
> In the end, they decided to save their own lives, but hid the treasure well. Von Stein and his army searched for the gold and silver without success. Enraged, von Stein demolished the castle.
>
> The robber knights' treasure remains buried beneath the ruins of the castle until today.

In the last months of the Second World War, residents of the villages surrounding Owl Mountain heard frequent detonations, and witnessed the daily comings and goings of trucks, heavy machinery, and rows of slave laborers. Concentric rings of German soldiers kept the sites secure.

Residents were warned that anyone who approached the sites would be shot.

The Germans were constructing tunnels, the locals knew. But it was a subdued, fearful knowledge. Even after the war, most of them kept their distance.

In June 1985 in Środa Śląska, an excavator operator named Widurski uncovered a clay pitcher containing nearly four thousand coins and fragments of coins, mostly copper pieces from the fourteenth century.

Three years later, in the same spot, another clay pitcher full of coins was found during a demolition. Workers and onlookers fought over the treasure, and the police had to be called to quell the fighting and secure the coins. It is widely believed that a number of gold coins were smuggled from the site, and later sold or traded. There are many stories of children in Środa Śląska selling ancient coins in shops and bars.

Some of the treasure ended up at the local landfill—the police searched, but turned up very little. Local "pickers," however, were more successful, finding chains, golden eagles, knives, fruit bowls, and other valuables. Many who attempted to sell these objects were apprehended, but the problem was so widespread that the municipality declared an amnesty for those who voluntarily returned treasure.

Eventually much of the treasure, including the Golden Crown of the Czech queen, was recovered, albeit often in fragments or otherwise damaged. Some can now be seen in the museum in Środa Śląska.

Historians believe that the treasure had belonged to a Jewish banker, who had received it, perhaps as a loan repayment, from Charles IV of Luxembourg, the Czech king. It is speculated that the banker fled the city in the fourteenth century during the plague epidemic.

• • •

In the eighteenth century a man named Herzer, hoping to persuade Frederick the Great of the viability of Silesian minerals, secretly shipped cobalt from Saxony and "mined" it. Frederick paid for a large-scale survey, but soon discovered the hoax. Herzer attempted to flee but was apprehended and put to death.

In December 1972, in Komorowice, workers building a sheepfold found in the sand—which had been brought from the gravel pit in Kotowice—a pot containing silver coins and ornaments. The Kotowice treasure, as it came to be known, contained approximately 3,500 items, including Arab, Byzantine, German, and Czech coins from the end of the tenth century.

Much of the treasure was snatched by the workers. Some was sold to onlookers in exchange for beer. Some, however, was accidentally mixed in with the mortar and ended up in the wall of the sheepfold. Under police supervision, workers dismantled the wall and liberated the treasure. Many items were damaged in the process.

During the Thirty Years' War, in one of the many battles between the Swedish army and the German kingdom, a Swedish general was mortally wounded, and his body was buried at the top of Owl Mountain. But he had been a cruel and sadistic man, and his soul could not find peace; his ghost haunted the mountain.

Locals believed that great treasures were hidden inside the general's tomb, and many attempts were made to plunder it, but all ended in disaster. Once, a group of miners from Nowa Ruda reached the tomb, but the moment their tools touched the stone, the sky filled with terrible thunder, the heavy lid slid off of its own accord, and the ghost of the general appeared, wearing his uniform and boots and raising his saber. The miners fled.

Two hundred years after his death, the general finally found peace, and his ghost departed. The treasure is still in the tomb, but its location is no longer known.

In 1198, in Janowice Wielkie, Duke Bolesław Wysoki built a castle on the site of an ancient Slavic temple. Legend has it that in the castle's dungeon there is a treasure guarded by an enormous knight. For centuries, local villagers have avoided the castle, fearful of the knight.

For many years, villagers scoured the cavities in Owl Mountain for traces of gold. One day an old woman hid grains of millet inside one of the cavities. Since then—as if a curse had been placed—no one has found a single speck of gold.

Locals believe that the mountain will once again yield gold, but many years will have to pass—as many years as grains of millet the old woman hid in the cavity.

In the 1980s in Maślice a local named Wojtek Stojak discovered a massive cache of weapons—mostly of German origin, but also American, English, French, Canadian, Italian, and Belgian. According to Stojak: "We pulled out machine guns, both heavy and light; many old revolvers; some bayonets; and even one very rusty saber. We excavated a lot of weapons. Many MG-42 and Stg, a few Schmeissers and Mausers. I removed the cache with my excavator and took it home in my car trailer."

My father tells me that after the war my grandfather returned to Sosnowiec, to the apartment he'd grown up in, because his father had told him that he had hidden cash and jewelry inside the walls.

My grandfather searched, but did not find anything.

In the Middle Ages, the discovery of traces of gold in the sands of the Oder River set off a gold rush. The Piast princes, who owned the land

and everything it contained, speculated, excavated, brought in specialists from the west. Soon the mines were famous all over Europe, and the woods were full of gold-seekers.

From a March 12, 2014, article in *naTemat:*

> The American-based firm Amarante Investments is seeking seven exploration licenses, one of which concerns the area of Lwówek Śląski in Lower Silesia. For hundreds of years, gold was extracted from the sands and gravels of the surrounding streams. According to the data of the Polish Geological Institute (2010), gold resources in the Bóbr River sediments are estimated at 2.5 tons. "The entire area of the Kaczawskie Mountains is a prospective area in terms of gold and should be the subject of modern exploration work," says Professor Stanisław Mikulski of the Polish Geological Institute. Mikulski and other geologists estimate that nearby prospective areas contain about about 350 tons of gold.
>
> The enthusiasm of local gold-seekers has been whetted by the historical reports of extraction of large quantities of gold; the abandonment of unprofitable mines; and notable amateur discoveries. In 2008, gold-seekers were shocked to hear of the discovery of gold fragments weighing 57, 11.5, and 4 grams. Supposedly they were discovered in the gravel pits in the Kaczawa Valley.
>
> According to PGI experts, extending existing veins by several hundred meters and finding five new ones would make accessible 100 tons of gold. Significant treasures can be hiding under rocks —but to reach them, it would require drilling 100–300 meters.

In 1512 a robber knight named Christoph von Zedlitz, known as "Black Christopher," and his gang were caught and hanged. Their treasure, however, has never been found, despite being sought for more than five centuries. There are those who believe that the treasure was in fact discovered in the 1970s by a group of Germans, known in the region for their off-road vehicles and advanced exploration equipment.

The researcher Włodzimierz Antkowiak recorded the following from a man who worked for AEG during World War II:

> There is indisputable evidence that in the Kłodzko Fortress the Germans secured at least two large caches of valuable items, including antiques. One of them was discovered by employees of the AEG armaments factory during an underground expedition —what we saw was breathtaking! Real treasures! Under the walls were old shelves filled with various objects: porcelain tableware next to beautifully engraved silver cups. Old leather books and manuscripts on the floor. Dozens of oil paintings by the old masters. Satin dresses with gold and silver thread. A stack of pistols in the middle of the room. We figured out later that we had discovered the spot where the Nazis had hidden artifacts stolen from the Kłodzko Museum and the Wrocław Museum. Many AEG employees stole items and sent them to their families. Eventually the Germans realized that the hiding place had been discovered, and moved the stash somewhere else. Shortly after the Red Army occupied Kłodzko, they tried to find this new hiding place, but failed.

In the basement of the courthouse in Sosnowiec are rows upon rows of Forever Books, the historical ledgers in which sales of land were recorded.

In the Forever Book of plot number 1304 it is written:

In 1904, Joseph and Judessa Mangel purchased the property for 22,000 rubles. After their death, the property was divided up among their ten children.

In 1936 the Kajzer brothers, Moshe and Shia, bought the property from the Mangel children for 42,734 złoty.

No subsequent sales are recorded.

There is a legend, very popular among treasure hunters in Lower Silesia (particularly those from Jelenia Góra), that somewhere between Pilchowice and the quarry in Radomice there is an entrance to a mine blocked by an enormous iron gate with no visible lock and no hinges.

A local gold-digger reportedly knew the location of the gate, and for many years he struggled to figure out how to open it. He revealed the existence, but not the location, of the gate to four explorers, who spread the word. This gold-digger died under very mysterious circumstances.

In the early 1980s, the newspaper *Kurier Polski* invited readers to share any information they had concerning valuables hidden by Germans at the end of World War II. The series was titled "Where the Gold of Wrocław Was Hidden." The following note was published in the paper on July 5, 1983:

> Władysław T. worked in Miłków, where, toward the end of April 1945, eleven trucks escorted by a team of SS men arrived at the estate of Count Matuschka. On the trucks were metal crates. The next day, the crates were reloaded onto horse-drawn carts. The horses, SS men, and a group of French prisoners left the village, toward Bierutowice. In the evening SS troops returned to Miłków, but without boxes or prisoners. Supposedly, the French prisoners buried the chests and then were killed.

. . .

In August 2015, it was reported in the Polish media that two unnamed explorers had recently notified Wałbrzych city officials that they had discovered a buried World War II–era train; everyone immediately understood this to be the legendary Golden Train.

A few days later, at a press conference at City Hall, officials confirmed the reports, and also formally notified the Ministry of Treasury, Ministry of National Defense, and Ministry of Culture and National Heritage of the discovery. The explorers who had purportedly found the train were not present, but their lawyer, former senator Jarosław Chmielewski, was, and he vouched for their credibility and experience as treasure hunters, citing their thorough knowledge of World War II history and their many years of responsible exploration. Chmielewski said his clients would divulge the precise location of the train only if the government guaranteed them 10 percent of the value of whatever was eventually found.

Major international news outlets, including Reuters, BBC, Fox News, CNN, and Sky News, breathlessly reported the discovery of the Golden Train (or rather the as yet unsubstantiated *claim* of the discovery of the Golden Train—many publications hardly bothered with the distinction). Speculation ran rampant as to what was on the train. Gold bullion? Long-lost artwork? The tsarist amber chamber?

The media worked themselves into a frenzy; there was an avalanche of sensationalist reporting, particularly from abroad. A headline in Britain's *Daily Mail* read, "Poland Confirms Existence of Underground Nazi Gold Train."

The press's lack of skepticism was reflected and galvanized by the lack of skepticism among Polish officials. The deputy culture minister of Poland, Piotr Zuchowski, said that the images definitively showed a train. Zuchowski also offered a (unsubstantiated) backstory: these two explorers had learned the train's location from the deathbed confession of a man who'd helped hide the train seventy years ago. The general conservator of historical monuments—appointed by the prime minister to oversee the preservation and integrity of Poland's historical sites—said that, having seen the georadar images, he was 99 percent sure the discovery was legitimate.

Historians and explorers who urged caution, who noted that the discovery was still unconfirmed, were largely ignored; Golden Train fever had set in.

The precise location of the train remained a secret; most reports placed it somewhere along a four-kilometer stretch, between the sixty-first and sixty-fifth kilometers of the Wrocław–Wałbrzych rail line. Explorers from Poland and beyond flooded into Wałbrzych in order to search for the train; local and international media quickly followed. The attention and activity were unprecedented for Wałbrzych, a small, economically depressed town.

The general conservator soon issued an appeal to explorers to cease their searching, warning that the train might be booby-trapped, protected by mines, or full of dangerous gases. His appeal had little effect. The governor ordered police to block entry points along the four-kilometer stretch; some of the rail lines were still active, he said, and explorers could get hurt. A few days later, an explorer died after falling several meters into a mausoleum.

Golden Train fever continued apace. The train seemingly became less abstract by the day, and the legal and logistical implications of a Nazi train full of Jewish gold buried in the Polish countryside were setting in. Most pressingly: Who would get the gold? The CEO of the World Jewish Congress, Robert Singer, said in a statement that any valuables taken from Jews must be returned to their rightful owners or their heirs. A lawyer named Mikhail Joffe said in an interview that the train's contents belonged to Russia. "If the property was taken from territory of the USSR," he said, "then the cargo, in accordance with international law, must be passed to the Russian side." This claim was promptly rejected by Polish authorities, who said that all efforts would be made to return the property to its original owners; however, as numerous organizations pointed out, such a restitution would be tremendously complicated and contentious, and Poland has shown itself somewhat less than capable in this department. The Americans and Israelis took a quiet but active interest as well.

A few weeks later, the minister of defense ordered Polish military forces to clear and secure the site, check for unexploded mines and buried chemical weapons, and remove trees and shrubs to prepare for an underground survey.

In the meantime, the explorers—since identified by the media as Piotr Koper and Andreas Richter—had at last released their evidence. There were two key documents. The first was a readout, supposedly from a KS-Analysis GPR KS700, a high-end ground-penetrating radar device. The second was an image of a shaft. The train, Koper and Richter said, was at the end of this shaft. Whether or not these documents constituted proof of the Golden Train was ferociously debated.

On September 4, Koper and Richter—who had thus far kept a relatively low profile—went on television and, reading from a prepared statement, claimed to have conclusive evidence of the train's existence. They also claimed to have secured the funds for an excavation, and divulged—possibly unintentionally—that the train was located at the sixty-fifth kilometer. The explorers—and, in turn, the journalists and spectators—promptly moved their operations, concentrating and exacerbating the chaos.

The next day, Koper and Richter were expelled from the Lower Silesian Research Association, the exploration group of which they had been long-standing members. Koper and Richter had betrayed the association, the head of the group said, and, further, had not given due credit to Tadeusz Slowikowski, a retired miner who had been researching and tracking the Golden Train for decades. Slowikowski's family then accused Koper and Richter of stealing documents from Slowikowski.

Soon thereafter, a regional official pointed out that Koper and Richter had not secured a permit for their initial exploration, when they had first discovered the Golden Train; not only did they do not deserve any reward, the official said, but also they could face fines and/or prison.

More and more people flooded into Wałbrzych—more explorers, more journalists, more tourists, more government officials. A mishmash of agencies, including city police, state police, forest guard, military, and railway security, patrolled the area. On the one hand, the city was reaching a breaking point. On the other hand, this was also an unprecedented economic windfall. Hotels and restaurants were booked solid. There was Golden Train beer, "gold" bars of chocolate, all varieties of Golden Train tchotchkes. A Golden Train tourist package was slapped together to promote local sites of mystery. One official estimated that Golden Train fever had brought $200 million worth of free publicity to Wałbrzych.

There were attempts to dial it back. Various officials pointed out that Koper and Richter's evidence was far from conclusive. The minister of culture and national heritage said that the train was still nothing more than a legend. Complaints were filed against the general conservator: his premature confirmation of the train's existence, the complaints said, constituted a major breach of his official responsibilities.

But for the most part these words of caution fell on deaf ears. If anything they made it worse, served only to heighten the pitch, fuel the speculation. Someone must play the role of the skeptic—otherwise it isn't a real mystery, and the conviction of the believer is only hardened.

One of the few voices of reason, of moral clarity, was Deputy Prime Minister of Poland and Minister of National Defense Tomasz Siemoniak. Siemoniak did not opine as to whether the Golden Train was real or not. Instead he sought to remind everyone what this site actually was:

the train, the gold, whether or not it existed, was incidental; much more important was the fact that thousands of slave laborers had died here. This was a site of death, not treasure, and we should act accordingly. But his exhortation had little effect.

Finally, on November 10 — nearly three months after the first reports of Koper and Richter's discovery — a large team of researchers and explorers, including scientists from AGH University of Science and Technology in Kraków, as well as Koper and Richter, analyzed the site with ground-penetrating radar systems and magnetometers. The operation was partly funded by the Discovery Channel.

A month later AGH University researchers issued their report. No train, they concluded. It was possible that there was a tunnel down there, they said, but definitely no train.

The report was rejected by Koper and Richter, as well as a core of their supporters. According to one conspiracy theory, the train *was* there, and the researchers were well aware that it was there, but the university had covered it up; they were in cahoots with the government, which had an obvious interest in having everyone believe there was no train.

The report helped break the Golden Train fever; the world lost interest.

Undeterred, Koper and Richter announced they would excavate the site, and after a series of delays, they began digging on August 15, 2016. At a reported cost of $130,000, a team of sixty-four people, mostly volunteers, dug for a week, and found nothing.

It seems that the irregularities on Koper and Richter's initial readouts were due to an underground dome of loam, formed eons ago by an iceberg.

11

The Killer said a decision from the court was imminent but by this point I'd known The Killer for long enough, and was familiar enough with the Polish judiciary, to know that a decision could be "imminent" for months. The treasure hunters, particularly Andrzej, were constantly inviting me to come explore with them, see their new discoveries, but I begged off; I had had, for the time being, my fill of mystery.

I got it in my head to go to Sosnowiec, and not just for an afternoon, but for a few days, a week, maybe even a couple of weeks. There'd be some research to do but for the most part it would be open, aimless, missionless; I thought I should try to get in touch with the place. My grandfather was born here, had grown up here, he'd walked these streets: I was hungry for meaning, for some sense of my grandfather, and maybe, I thought, I could find it here.

I booked a hotel in the center of town, only a couple of blocks away from Małachowskiego 12. I probably could have stayed in the building.

Hanna had, more than once, offered to host me. And the year before —when this building was still the correct building, when it was still my grandfather's childhood home—I had nearly taken her up on her offer, but I'd gotten sick. Too bad, that would have been something. To stay in the building my grandfather had grown up in, had owned, but as a guest, but also as an heir? What a wonderfully fraught situation. But now it didn't make much sense, the meaning had drained: this was almost certainly the wrong building, and even if it was the correct building or if I could somehow trick myself into believing it was, it was still the case that it hadn't been my grandfather's childhood home, my grandfather had never slept here. But also I didn't want to interact with the residents, I didn't want to have a confrontation—even though it was almost certainly the wrong building, I remained a threat until I was definitely not.

I arrived in Sosnowiec, checked into the hotel, and hurried to meet Małgorzata, the translator from court, whom I'd hired for the day. By 5 p.m. I'd crossed off every research-related task I had on my list. We'd gone to the basement of the courthouse and flipped through the Forever Book of plot number 1304; we'd visited the museum, which was a fine municipal museum; we'd gone to Teatr Zagłębia, only to learn it was closed for the next two weeks.

Małgorzata went home and I went back to the hotel. I took some notes, uploaded photographs, took a nap. Then I took a short walk, came back to the hotel, had a light dinner. Then what? I didn't know what to do. I watched television, took some more notes, took another walk, which turned into a very long walk, but it did little to alleviate my restlessness. Nothing I saw felt particularly interesting or meaningful. Perhaps it was a failure of observation or of imagination on my part, but the city felt so sterile and cold. It got dark. The shops closed, people packed onto streetcars to go home. I found myself scanning faces. Who did I think I might see? Bartek, Hanna, one of the other residents, maybe the judge? I was lonely. I was in an increasingly ugly mood, full of spite (toward whom? I don't know) and self-pity and a sense of futility, a feeling I was wasting my time here. All I could see were ugly streets and ugly buildings; if there was in fact something here I didn't know what it was. Sometimes you can feel the absence, can sense what's gone, or at least can sense that something's gone, but here I just felt like a lonely cranky foreign pedestrian. I couldn't even get lost, though I tried. I kept walking past Małachowskiego 12, at first I thought accidentally but then I wasn't so sure. As I passed by I'd acknowledge the building with a nod, like it was an acquaintance whose presence would be impolite to ignore. I felt a strange antipathy toward it. Not to the people who lived there but to the building itself. Like it had lied to me, misled me, led me on. Soon the streets were nearly empty, and the only places open were a handful of unremarkable bars. I stopped at a few of the bars and had a few drinks. Nothing remarkable happened in these unremarkable bars. I didn't talk to anyone, no one talked to me, though heads turned when I ordered in English, people noticed. I drank alone and in silence. I was miserable and bored, and I couldn't even decide if my misery and boredom were useful or interesting, or if I was simply bored and miserable on the first night of what I'd planned as a five-day stay in a city where I didn't know anyone and to which I was no longer sure why I'd come at all.

It got truly late and still I walked the streets. Now I was miserable and drunk. No one else was out. I walked past Małachowskiego 12 and ignored it, didn't even turn my head. How naïve to think I'd encounter my grandfather here. Could I have forced it? I suppose I could have, I could have forced myself to imagine my grandfather as a child walking these streets, going to school, playing, I don't know, but what would that be worth? Then there was a man walking behind me. Where had he come from? Was he following me? It seemed he was. He kept a steady pace forty feet behind me. I sped up and it seemed he did too. I tried to get a good look at him—I didn't want to do anything too overt—but could only make out that he was slight and bald. I turned the corner and he turned the corner. I considered breaking into a run, screaming for help, charging him, taking him by surprise. I was afraid, but also, I admit, excited: getting attacked in Sosnowiec, now that'd be something. Then I turned a corner and entered the hotel and watched through the glass as he walked past. I had a very particular dream that night. It's so on the nose I'm reluctant to tell you but obviously I have to tell you: I am walking the streets of Sosnowiec, for hours, exactly as I'd done in real life. I have the distinct sensation of trying to avoid someone. I don't know who they are or why they are trying to find me or why I'm hoping they don't. But then all of a sudden someone is behind me, following me. I peek over my shoulder, but their face is shrouded. And yet I know with certainty who it is: it's Bartek, it's Hanna, it's any or maybe all the residents of Małachowskiego 12. I stop walking. I decide I won't be chased, and turn around, but as soon as I pivot, so does my pursuer, and flees from me. And as I give chase, I realize it's my grandfather, and I am filled with this terrible knowledge I'll never catch him.

When I woke up I had a bunch of messages from Joanna, inviting me to what she called a major exploration on top of Osówka. Many treasure hunters will be there, she'd written, and Andrzej asked me to make sure you come. He says you must do it for your grandfather. Not my grandfather, I thought, but at this point what difference does it make? When? I wrote back. She wrote back a few seconds later: Tonight! Immediately I packed up and checked out and headed to the train station.

It was an impressive, well-equipped campsite. A large tarp sunblocked a folding table laden with food and drink. There was an electric generator, water cooler, floodlights. An enormous cast iron pot dangled from a fancy special-purpose tripod over a low steady fire. Off to the side were a couple of oversized hammocks. Pots, pans, mugs, sausages, vegetables hung from strung-up wires. A dozen or so explorers lazed around on collapsible chairs, sipping beer and snacking on pickles and salami.

It was a lovely spot; from most angles you could not see any mysterious cement structures, it was calm cool Nazi-less forest all around. "The view from this place is beautiful," Abraham Kajzer wrote about one of the Riese worksites. "We are surrounded by forests and mountains. There is no trace of any buildings and the impression is that we are in the uninhabited wilderness."

Andrzej, his usual alpha self, greeted me as if we were long-lost fraternity brothers, big hugs, big yelps. He handed me a bottle of beer but then took it back in order to open it, which he did with a rusty machete, a hundred-year-old relic he'd found on a battlefield and which he apparently brought with him to the forest for the express purpose of opening bottles of beer.

Andrzej looked me up and down and grimaced. "Co to jest?!" *What is this?!* He was referring to my clothes—I was wearing jeans and a hoodie. He shook his head like my mother used to shake her head when she didn't approve of what I was planning to wear to shul. From the trunk of his Land Rover he grabbed a t-shirt and tossed it at me. Not unlike how a maître d' might lend a no-goodnik the house blazer. The shirt was army green and had on it the emblem of Andrzej's exploration group—a snarling wolf wearing an army helmet marked HUNTER above an intersecting coat-of-arms-style metal detector and shovel. In a triangle at the bottom was the motto, in English, STRONG TEAM. Everyone else was in fatigues, even the toddler (there was a toddler), and many of them head-to-toe, cap, shirt, jacket, pants. No one matched, each wore different combinations, different styles; but still it was, clearly, a uniform of sorts.

I took off my hoodie and put on the HUNTER shirt and Andrzej hollered his approval.

By dark there were twenty or so explorers, mostly middle-aged men, a few wives and girlfriends. I counted among them a retired army lieutenant, two retired miners, two electricians, a software engineer. Everyone settled in for a night of drinking around the fire. They teased and toasted one another, ate, drank, reminisced, drank, roughhoused; they laughed so hard so frequently it was difficult to carry on a conversation.

This was new, I hadn't yet seen this side of the explorers, I hadn't really understood how much *fun* the explorers had exploring. I'd imagined what you've probably been imagining: super-serious men with their impenetrable theories and secret documents and petty jealousies and fancy digging toys, hunting for treasure, plumbing mystery, unraveling conspiracies, and doing so with great gravity and solemnity. I'd had this image because this was the image that, when I'd met them one-on-one or in small groups, they'd done their best to project. But there in the forest I could see how it was softer, more social, more fun. I wondered if maybe on some level treasure hunting can be understood as an extremely elaborate excuse to hang out and get smashed with your friends in the forest.

The beer you were allowed to drink casually but the vodka had an enforced etiquette. It was called *nominatzia* and it was very simple and —insofar as it made the activity of getting shitfaced a more social activity—very effective. Whoever is nominated downs (along with everyone else) a shot, then nominates the next person, who downs (along with everyone else) a shot, then nominates the next person, and so on. So if you're nominated you can't say no, it messes everything up, everyone's drinking stalls.

I was nominated with alarming frequency. The explorers were giddy that I was there. Abraham Kajzer's grandson! "Manhattan, *nominatzia!*" (They called me "Manhattan.") I'd down my shot, nominate someone else, he'd nominate someone else, and then that someone else would nominate me. Sometimes the person I nominated nominated me right back. Manhattan, *nominatzia!* The metal cup I'd been given—Manhattan's designated cup for the night—kept getting refilled, I kept getting nominated, my half-polite, half-dire demurrals were laughed off, I kept drinking, it was not a sustainable situation. It was only a couple of hours in and already I was trouble having words. Manhattan, *nominatzia!* I developed a strategy. Once nominated, as I waited for the explorers to fill their cups, I'd sit and let my arm dangle nearly to the ground and surreptitiously pour out the vodka. Then I'd raise the metal cup and make the appropriate cheer and throw back the few drops that remained and mime the burn in my throat and the rush to my head. This strategy was at least partially effective, as I did not die that night, but still . . .

I vaguely remember at one point warning them that if they kept nominating me I'd forget to tell them about Abraham Kajzer's unpublished diaries. Ha ha ha! went the treasure hunters. Manhattan, *nominatzia!*

I vaguely remember offering my own theories about *Die Glocke*. I've seen it. I said. It's in Cleveland. Ha ha ha! went the treasure hunters. Manhattan, *nominatzia!*

I noticed something exceedingly interesting: a statistically significant number of these men were missing an incisor. What's that about, I asked. Ha ha ha! went the treasure hunters. Manhattan, *nominatzia!*

They were generous hosts. (Getting me drunk was absolutely a form of generosity.) They worried I was too cold, offered me sweatshirts and a better spot near the fire, made sure I had a comfortable chair, worried about the smoke, worried about the bugs; Andrzej insisted on opening my bottles of beer with his rusty machete. Whenever one of them addressed the group, telling a story or joke or whatever, he'd slow down and pause frequently so that the monologue could be translated, for me, the only one there who didn't speak Polish.

There was a little bit of serious treasure-hunting talk—sites, documents, strategies—but not much, as if that was work and right now they were off the clock. It was very chummy, the conversation of men who know one another very well getting very drunk together. They gossiped: which treasure hunter was up to what, what zany scheme this explorer had cooked up now, who was screwing whom over. One of the younger explorers, a fresh-faced shiny-haired twenty-something they called Kebab, told off-color jokes, which I see no need to repeat or comment on except to say that, at the titillating bits, like mentions of large penises or Vaseline (used for guess what activity), the explorers laughed so hard that I, as I waited blankly for the translation, kept wrongly assuming that the punch line had been reached.

They spoke of explorers' exploits, or, really, misadventures—somewhat loving, somewhat mocking, these stories were about other explorers, not present, whom this group considered more hapless, more amateur, more *nebach*. A number of the stories featured an explorer named Karol, apparently somewhat infamous for his ineptness and bad luck. Once, Karol broke into a strange, mysterious, seemingly abandoned house. (Why? I asked. To explore, obviously, someone said. But isn't that breaking and entering? I asked. No, came the reply, he was exploring.) In the closet in the master bedroom, Karol found a well-preserved Prussian officer uniform. Naturally he put it on, and continued his exploring thus. He turned a corner and came face-to-face with an old woman sitting silently in a wheelchair; behind her was a large portrait of a man in the uniform Karol was now wearing. They stared at each other for a few moments and then she asked him, quite sensibly I think, if he was a ghost. Karol, quick thinker, said yes, he was a ghost. The woman, unconcerned, perhaps accustomed to ghosts or ghosts wearing this Prussian military uniform, told him that she was very sad and very lonely, that she was a prisoner in her own home—her grandson, she said, had locked her in there, was giving her only the bare minimum needed to survive, while he, the grandson, cashed her social security checks. Karol said he would save her and, once he left the house, presumably still wearing the Prussian officer uniform, notified the authorities—though no details were offered on what Karol said to explain how he'd obtained the information—and was hailed as a hero.

The night went on, we drank, talked, laughed, it was a party in the forest, it was a party in the forest at the site of a Nazi underground structure where thousands of slave laborers had been worked to death, but that didn't seem to be on anyone's mind. I talked with this explorer and then that explorer and then I brooded alone—islanded, not unpleasantly, by the chaos and my lack of Polish—and then I found myself in conversation with Marcin, a software engineer from Łódź in his late twenties who was not a member of HUNTER and who didn't really know anyone, and Sławek, a middle-aged construction worker with a big hard belly and a kind gaptooth smile who knew everyone and was, he said, a founder of HUNTER.

I was feeling confounded. I wanted some insight. I was drunk and thus more susceptible than usual to meaning-cravings. Who were these guys and what were they doing? What was I doing? What makes you tick and what does this mean? It's a far drive from Łódź, I said to Marcin, why'd you come all the way here? It is my hobby, Marcin said. That explains everything, I said, but on the other hand it explains nothing. Sławek, who spoke no English, impatiently tapped Marcin's knee; he was eager to be included in the conversation. Marcin translated what I'd asked and what he'd answered and Sławek gave us a disapproving look. Someone said, Manhattan, *nominatzia!* Someone else fell out of a hammock. I poured out my vodka and then pretended to drink it. Do you want a potato? someone said. Fresh from the fire. Sławek touched his camouflage pants, camouflage jacket, camouflage cap. He said to me, via Marcin: Do these clothes look like the clothes of someone doing a hobby? But as Marcin was translating he did something—I don't remember exactly what, a gesture, an eye-roll, something like that—to show me that he, Marcin, thought it was all a little ridiculous. You're wearing camouflage pants, I said to Marcin. What are you really after, I thought but did not say aloud. This camouflage thing seemed in the moment to be the key to understanding everything. Marcin smiled and shrugged and said, These are the pants you are supposed to wear. It is annoying. They're expensive and they get very dirty, it doesn't make sense, but these are the pants you are supposed to wear. Sławek tapped Marcin's knee. Marcin translated our exchange or some version of our exchange. Sławek beamed. French, he said, referring to his outfit. I asked why French. Sławek shrugged; apparently he just liked the design. An explorer whose name I didn't know sidled up to show me a bottle of whiskey and a picture on his phone of what at first glance looked like a gold nugget, but I couldn't get a second glance because Sławek wanted my attention. French, he said, again, and then, perhaps to show me how idiosyncratic camouflage preferences can run, he had each of the explorers around the fire announce the nationality of their outfit. NATO, Polish, French, US Marines first Iraq war, US Marines second Iraq war. The differences were lost on me. I mean, I could discern the visual differences — colors, patterns, etc. — but the implications of the differences were lost on me. Only Marcin didn't know which country's camouflage he was wearing; someone else identified it for him: British special forces.

I still don't understand, I said to Marcin. You could go camping closer to home.

Yes but there is something special about Silesia, he said. There is a lot of mystery here.

I've been hearing that word for a long time now, I said, and I still don't know what it means.

No one knows what it means! he said, laughing. Sławek tapped Marcin on the knee; Marcin caught Sławek up and Sławek laughed.

I don't understand anything, I said.

Why are *you* here? Marcin asked.

Why am I here? Because you are here. Because of Abraham Kajzer.

You don't have family that's closer?

Manhattan, *nominatzia!*

I spent a year in Israel, said a pudgy explorer named Daniel who'd come out of nowhere. I was in the Polish army and we were sent over during the Lebanon war. In one day I went swimming in three seas: Dead Sea, Red Sea, Mediterranean Sea.

I poured out my vodka and pretended to drink it. I'm not Israeli, I said to Daniel.

When Marcin said "closer" I knew he meant closer physically, as in geographically, but the other meaning—viz. in terms of kinship—landed harder. I was having confused feelings regarding legacy. I felt weirdly disloyal. It had to do with Abraham Kajzer and/versus my grandfather. *If only the treasure hunters cared about my real grandfather!* I'd think, and then feel guilty about thinking. Someone poured vodka into my metal cup. Someone else showed me his bowie knife. But three seas, I said to Daniel, that's cool. Daniel said, It is an honor to meet the grandson of Abraham Kajzer. He's not my grandfather, I said. I don't understand, Daniel said. He's my grandfather's cousin, I said. He is the father of your father, Daniel said, or he is the father of your father's father? Yes, I said, fine, I concede, he is my grandfather. Myth is more persuasive, more seductive, than truth. From here on in I'll just go with the better story. I am Abraham's grandson. Do you think, I wondered aloud to Marcin, that there is an inherent tension between "adventure" and "memory"?

I am sorry, Marcin said, I do not understand your question. Manhattan, *nominatzia!* Someone poured vodka into my metal cup. I poured it out but unsurreptitiously, just dumped it on the ground, right in front of everyone, though no one seemed to notice. Sorry, I said, I'll ask my question again. I turned to Marcin and said, But don't translate this to Sławek, at least not yet? Marcin said okay. All these guys, I said, gesturing at the gathering of camo-clad men sitting in the forest nominating one another into oblivion, they come here to explore, to drink, have fun, whatever?

Something like this, yes.

So my question is, what about all the people who died here?

Yes, Marcin said. What is your question?

I don't know, I said. I mean, what do they think of that? Do they *know?*

Yes they know, of course they know, Marcin said. It is impossible not to know. Sławek tapped Marcin's knee; Marcin asked me if it was okay to translate. I nodded. As Sławek listened he put on his most serious face. Then he said: The dead are the most important.

Well, I said.

I said, Of course the dead are important. I know that, I know that you think the dead are very important. So maybe my question is something like: Which comes first? This place where we are right now, Osówka—is it a site of death or is it a site of mystery?

I had meant this question for Sławek but I had to ask through Marcin and so in effect I was also asking Marcin, who answered me on his own account: Why not this one and also this one? Why not both?

Desecraters! I thought. You are desecraters! But it turned out I did not think this to myself but in fact said it aloud. What, I am sorry, I do not understand, Marcin said. Are you talking about ghosts? Many explorers are big believers in ghosts. I was not talking about ghosts but maybe I *was* talking about ghosts, I said. Then I epiphanized: The ghosts are dead Jews are the UFOs. They appeal to a similar spirit of exploration, hold a similar grip on the imagination. Gold, rifles, *Die Glocke,* golden teeth, treasure, skeletons. Mass graves and underground tunnels. It all adds up to: *mystery.* I understand now, I said, the Jews are your ghosts! What, Marcin said. Nothing, I said, what did you ask me before?

Marcin said, It can be a site of death and also be a site of mystery. It can be both! Marcin was drunk, too, I realized. Somehow this hadn't registered before.

It can be both, it *is* both, I said, I know. But on the other hand, no one would show up to a place of death in an army costume.

Marcin: For me it is both.

A treasure hunter whose name I did not know sidled up and complained to me about the Polish law which mandates that anything found in the ground belongs to the government. That sucks, I said. Is it like that in America? he asked. I don't think so, I said. That's good, he said, then he told me that he once followed my grandfather's journey. He'd read his book many times, he said, and had done a pilgrimage of sorts, had followed his route exactly, had walked to each of the camps and worksites listed in the book. And what did you learn, I said. I don't remember, he said. I only remember that it rained and I was very angry at the rain. But you should do it too, he said. It is important. I said I would.

How many times have you been here? I asked Marcin. Not so many, Marcin said. How many times have you been here? I asked Sławek. Many many times, he said. How many times have you been here? Marcin asked me. Three, I said, and this struck me as an astonishingly high number. From the other side of the fire: Manhattan, *nominatzia!* I did not pour out this shot; I drank it. It hit hard and from this point onward I cannot vouch for what was said and who it was said by: I was taking notes but not responsibly, I wrote down the conversations I was having and I wrote down the thoughts I was thinking but I wasn't making distinctions between the conversation and the thoughts because in the moment everything made super-perfect sense but in the morning it was a jumbled heap of text. Marcin caught Sławek up. I nominated someone and then listened/reflected as Marcin channeled Sławek and here is what happened in my notebook:

> How confront/receive history? With intention; listen, receive. Explore = allow history to ask its questions. There is the dead / they are inside the questions // you think about the dead all the time? // that would be impossible / rather we listen. Sławek says I am distant from my own history and I agree // sure you're Abraham Kajzer's grandson (sic!!!) but what does that really mean (and also you're not even his grandson). You don't live it. We live it. Look around,

whose forest is this / the Jews'? the ghosts'? the treasure hunters'?
You are searching but we are <u>literally searching</u>. Your metaphors are
so weak.

Andrzej got up to reposition the floodlight but he stumbled and fell
and hit his arm on a rock; when he got to his feet and stood beneath the
floodlight—which spotlit him dramatically, as if he were starring in a
play in the forest—there was a thick streak of blood running from elbow
to wrist. *Kurwa*, he said; the other explorers, though not unconcerned,
laughed; Andrzej cursed again, then joined in the laughter. He wiped the
blood off with a paper towel, disinfected the wound with vodka, and,
from the same bottle, poured a shot and nominated himself.

12

It was, in fact, the wrong building. Hanna was right; of course she was right — it was her personal history against my secondhand Scotch-taped myth. This building, her building, was wholly unconnected to, had never been owned by, my family. Our stories did not intersect. Małachowskiego 12 — that is, the building that is today number 12, the building I'd visited, the building I'd persuaded myself I had an obligation to visit, whose inhabitants I'd persuaded myself I had an obligation to get to know, the building where Hanna and Bartek had lived their entire lives, the building with the Teatr Zagłębia backstory — was, just as Hanna had said, built in 1955, more than a decade after the history of my family in Sosnowiec had closed. I had no business here, I had no business being here.

Whence the confusion? The addresses had shifted. When this block of apartment buildings, Małachowskiego 10–18, was constructed, the numbers on the buildings farther down the street were bumped up in order to make room. Małachowskiego 12 became Małachowskiego 34. Such a straightforward explanation; yes, in retrospect it always seems straightforward. The reason it had taken me so long to figure out was that in his 1967 letter to my grandfather the trusty building manager Konrad Moszczeński had put down the old, incorrect address, number 12, and not the new, correct address, number 34. An oversight. He'd made a mistake. (What if it was *not* a mistake? What if Moszczeński had for some reason deliberately misled my grandfather? It's unlikely but not impossible but I refuse even to consider it: this is too deep a hole to jump into.) On the one hand I suppose it was an understandable error—his entire life it had been number 12 and now suddenly it was number 34—though on the other hand it had been twelve years already; but in any case this two-digit typo sent me down the wrong path, had me knocking on the wrong doors, for two years.

Eventually the address change was confirmed, first over email and then in person, by Sosnowiec's director of maps, something like the city's official surveyor. I sat in his office and—in a manner so straightforward it made me realize all over again how needlessly difficult and wearying these bureaucratic missions usually were—I gave him the info, he entered it into the computer, got the results, then fetched a large yellowed book and turned to the page and there it was, in exquisitely neat penciled script: plot number 1304, on Małachowskiego Street, with "12" crossed out and "34" penciled in, owned by Kaiser, Moshe and Sura-Hena, and Kaiser, Shia and Gitla.

It had an effect, seeing up close this official inscription. 34 12. A half-centimeter-long pencil mark. All that confusion rendered moot by this tiny stroke. A literal sliver of clarity and simplicity within an otherwise increasingly exasperating and confounding undertaking. More than that — this entry in the yellowed book was the first corroboration that the building was in fact owned by my family. Not that I had ever really doubted, but still — I was working within an opaque past, with no one alive to back me up or contradict or correct me; working against a foreign bureaucracy, in foreign languages, under seemingly increasingly antagonistic laws. Knowledge can start to feel slippery. My truth can be true and at the same time go unrecognized. I say: My great-grandparents are dead; the state says: Not so fast. Again and again you learn that you do not understand what you thought you understood, that you had it incomplete, or skewed, or that it's all irrelevant anyway. So it was affirming to see these names and numbers written in the ledger in the office of the director of maps. As if the city were saying to me: Okay, everything checks out, that's what we've got here too. It's our story too.

From a legal point of view the 12 34 revelation didn't actually matter all that much. This was a bureaucratic, paper-based reality; the reclamation would proceed (or wouldn't) within courthouses and archives, would happen (or not) via documents, records, petitions, judgments; no one cared which building I *thought* it was. This knot would have gotten disentangled eventually.

But beyond the legal implications — ? Did it matter? That I'd made such a fuss over the wrong building? Sunk all that time and energy? Barged into the wrong building and knocked on the wrong doors and harassed the wrong people? Yes and no. No, because this is part of it, this is how it goes, these stories will always have interesting and meaningful detours. Look what had turned up, look who I got to meet. If the treasure hunters had taught me anything it was that who knows what you'll find but it will be something. It's about the searching and not about, etc.

And a wrong address makes for great slapstick, sure. In a way it was perfect. Of course I was going to get the building wrong, of course all my ponderous moralizing was going to misfire and splatter.

But also yes, it did matter, of course it did. I felt terrible. I'd caused, I assumed, no small amount of distress among the residents, and for what? I'd done all these mental gymnastics in order to qualify and justify what I was doing, to make my intrusion less of an intrusion, turn it into something a little noble, even. But it was, it turned out, just an intrusion.

Remember Bartek? Bartek who lived on the second floor, who'd been so gracious, who'd so readily opened up, who'd told me about meeting his mother for the first time in thirty-five years, who'd introduced me to Hanna? A few weeks after we first met — by which point the inhabitants of Małachowskiego 12 understood what I was up to, what I was after, recognized the threat I represented, but before they or I knew that I had my addresses wrong — Bartek sent me an email:

> Regardless of how this turns out, keep in mind that for many of us, this building is our whole life (for me it is my family home, which I never really had). Teresa has been living here since 1957, Pani Hanna since I can remember. Some of the neighbors have already died (I do not remember some of them), some have moved out. Forty-two years in one place is a long time. I would say this is a kind of status quo — one cannot replant old trees.

Unfailingly generous, even as he was appealing to me to not upend his life and the lives of his neighbors, Bartek went on to write that he believed that it was fate that we had met, and wished me good luck on my journey into my family history. It was something, he wrote, he could relate to. I am sorry everything is so hard, he wrote.

Bartek, Hanna, Teresa, the other residents of Małachowskiego 12 — I'm sorry. I'm sorry for disturbing your lives, for the fear and anxiety I caused.

It is remarkable how long an act of violence can echo.

Our origin stories, our stories of where we come from, of where our parents and their parents and their parents come from, are riddled with errors. My grandmother's tombstone, to give a particularly blatant example — it's literally set in stone — says she was born in Oświęcim, but that's wrong, she grew up there but was born in Rzeszów. And I can't tell you how many times I've heard about someone schlepping to eastern Europe in order to trace their family story, to follow their memory-map, only to discover that they'd had their entire lives a major or minor detail incorrect — the dates don't add up, the train routes are impossible, this address never existed, the ghetto had already been liquidated by then.

It always *feels* surprising, bumping up against an error like this, but it shouldn't be. Family stories are poor preservers of history: they're fragmented, badly documented, warped by hearsay, conjecture, legend — of course errors are going to creep in. This seems somehow wrong, even blasphemous, at odds with the private sacredness we impute to our origin stories. But most stories in most families aren't meant or relied on as preservation of hard information, they're meant and relied on as preservation of soft information, of sentiment, narrative, identity, of who someone was and, subsequently, who you are. It tells not a historical truth but an emotional truth. I'd even argue that the built-in uncertainty — often unknowability — of details large and small is essential to the family mythos: we not only receive but also participate in the story; on some level we choose to believe. We ascribe.

And the truth is that the details most easily corrupted are not details most people care all that much about anyway. What's the difference between number 12 and number 34 when either building is on a funny-named street in a city you think about only in terms of dead Jews in a country your family fled from? The mistake on my grandmother's tombstone—I've been bringing it up for years but no one really cares, we're never going to change it, because the difference between Bubby having been born in Rzeszów and Bubby having been born in Oświęcim is, to us, her children and grandchildren who cannot properly pronounce or find on a map either city, negligible. And anyway the errors are almost never discovered. The stories sit undisturbed and unprovoked, congeal into lore, no one is any the wiser.

But what happens when the story *is* disturbed and provoked? When you seek to inspect or inhabit or engage with or build out parts of the story? Then the details do matter, especially the details you can touch and see and get up close to. Oświęcim and Rzeszów are more than two hundred kilometers apart. The difference between Małachowskiego 12 and Małachowskiego 34 is, when you're asserting your rights as an heir, immense. Once you enter the story, the where and the what matter, because those are your access points; those are the story's anchors, the myth-containers, and to get that wrong, to chase down the wrong building or go to the wrong city, is to get your story wrong, to misfire, to suffer that private but sharp humiliation of having cared in the wrong direction.

Or maybe even then it doesn't matter, maybe the relationship between our stories and the places they describe is more tenuous? Maybe it's just a phantom force, just us insisting there's something, pretending there's something, tricking ourselves into believing there's something? Earlier I wrote how these sorts of stories can flex, can absorb, that they'll always have interesting and meaningful detours, but maybe that's not true, maybe the detours in fact break the story a little, put into relief and reinforce the distance between you and whatever or whoever it is you think you're connecting with. Expose the fiction of sentimentalism, in other words. You thought this thing, this object, this building was meaningful, was special, but it turns out no, it's just an object, just another building, it means nothing to you, you were creating all that in your head. And if that feeling of meaningfulness could be so wrong and misplaced, then what is that feeling worth? What is that feeling at all?

Or maybe the sentimental history isn't erased but overwritten, maybe it retains the narrative of *having been* meaningful. In Jewish law, when an object that is *kadosh,* holy, loses its holiness—like a Torah scroll that loses a couple of letters and thus becomes unusable—it does not then become spiritually meaningless, does not revert to a mundane object; rather it becomes an object that once was holy, and must be treated accordingly: you cannot put it in the trash, you have to give it a proper burial.

An ignoble restart. Jason, Larysa, and I returned to Sosnowiec to see the new, by which I mean the correct, building.

Małachowskiego 34 was a three-story building on the corner. The exterior of the top two floors—the residences—was run-down, unlooked-after, a splotchy gray on grayer gray in the pattern of a skin disease. The ground floor, occupied by a pharmacy, had a fresh coat of beige paint and bright red awnings and signage. Later I would reread my grandfather's application to the Foreign Claims Settlement Commission and see (not for the first time but only now was I paying attention) that he'd cited the loss of a "Corner house / Apothecary on the ground floor."

Relative to number 12—a meaningless but unavoidable comparison—number 34 was a little smaller (so less valuable?) but on the corner of a busy intersection (so more valuable?); it was a little stranger, a little more baroque, much less Communist. Jason asked me what I thought about the new building, if I liked it or if I was excited or something like that. I shrugged. I wasn't feeling much at all toward number 34; it was a dry unsentimental encounter.

We got inside without a problem. The stairs were wide and wooden and run-down. It was shabbier than number 12, it was more despondent, it seemed poorer, but that might just have been the stairwell, for all I knew the apartments were newly renovated and expensively furnished. We walked to the top floor. A woman hurried past us and into her apartment, shutting and locking the door behind her. I stared at the closed door. An antagonism was creeping in. It felt different than it had in number 12, or rather I felt different—I felt hardened, ground down, ungenerous. Who were these people and what were they doing here and did they even know and how dare they? They didn't own their apartments; my family did; they were squatters or if they weren't squatters then they certainly weren't here with permission. The people who lived here had, even if indirectly and unwittingly, benefited from the wholesale murder of my family, were continuing to benefit from the wholesale murder of my family. I had never really faced that fact before; I'm not saying it's not more complicated; but it is the truth, or part of the truth, or one of the truths.

Larysa asked if I wanted to knock on any of the doors and I said, No, not today, I'm not feeling up to it right now.

We visited the pharmacy, which, to put together what Hanna had told us and what my grandfather had written on his Foreign Claims Settlement Commission application, apparently has been operating continuously since at least the 1930s. Inside it was, like many Polish pharmacies, quaint, fusty, inefficiently designed, with a tiny waiting area for customers and an expansive but barely used space behind the counter, where most of the items for sale were out of reach and out of sight. The walls had wooden paneling and I could see, in the back room, mortars and scales. I imagine it looked much the same in the 1930s, when my great-grandfather came to collect the rent. This was probably the most open portal to my grandfather, the best opportunity for my imagination and sentimentalism to worm their way in, but it felt only like a pharmacy, hardly more than that, something to which I had a personal connection but not that personal. We asked the woman behind the counter if we could speak with the owner. The woman said the owner wasn't in, but was happy to pass on her contact info; later I wrote to the owner to ask if I might interview her about the history of the pharmacy. She was open and forthcoming until she learned that my family had owned the building before the war, and promptly shut down the conversation. "I don't know what you want from me," she wrote. "There is nothing to discuss." I felt strangely satisfied. Let everyone be intransigent and suspicious; good, let everyone play their roles, let's embrace the stereotypes, I'll be the Jew coming back for his property and you be the fearful Pole.

You have every right to expect that I attempted to seek out the residents of Małachowskiego 34 the same way I'd sought out the residents of Małachowskiego 12. That I sought out their stories, that I tried to make this reclamation more human, less distant, less abstract. All of those arguments regarding empathy and responsibility still applied, right? At the end of the day *this* was the building whose inhabitants would be affected; this had always been the building.

I did nothing. I didn't knock, I didn't interview, I didn't engage, I didn't meet anyone, I didn't get rebuffed by anyone, I heard no one's stories, I heard none of the building's history. I left it abstract, unintruded-upon. I clung to, insisted on, number 34's real estate-ness.

I don't have an excuse. I was exhausted, which isn't an excuse. I didn't have it in me. The thought of knocking on more doors; of having to once again contort the truth of who I was and why I was there or risk being seen as a threat; of being seen as a threat in the long run no matter what I did—I just didn't have it in me.

I think in these stories of return and reclamation, of zany eastern European adventures, of trekking back to the *alte heim* and stacking myths and confronting ghosts, the emotional strain is too often tamped down, smoothed out. I don't mean the trauma, the psychical cost of delving into exceedingly dark family histories—that is often very movingly explored. I mean the much more banal truth of how *tiring* it is. How draining it is to keep pushing into spaces that really push back. The lies add up. The errors, oversights, unknowns. The posturing. The absorption of stories. The communicating via a translator. The dead ends. The traveling, the intrusions, the retreats, the deceptions. Stories like this are often presented and received as missions, and the protagonists, consciously or otherwise, as heroes. We like our heroes to be indefatigable. The unromantic truth is that it is very, very taxing.

A few days later The Killer sent me a message that the Sosnowiec District Court had come to a decision. It had not gone our way. Judge Wioleta Grabowska had ruled that my dead relatives could not be declared dead.

To understand why the judge had ruled the way she had we'd have to wait for the written decision, but at that point I wasn't even all that curious, I was resigned, I'd surrendered to the absurdity. The Killer told me the news and I blinked, sighed, said yes, of course, why should anything be rational or simple. Of course the court would refuse to acknowledge the deaths of my dead relatives.

That night I listened to the recording I'd secretly made of my court testimony. I listened to the judge's absurd questions, her demands, her brusqueness, her references to the building, and I began to suspect—I had a hard time not suspecting, I hated that I was thinking like this but I could not help it—that this wasn't about the deaths at all, this was about the reclamation, this was about property, this was about Jewish property: the deaths were a technicality, an excuse, a fig leaf, something the judge had seized upon in order to justify torpedoing the reclamation. Judge Grabowska could have affirmed the deaths—the judge in Będzin, presented with the same (lack of) documentation, had affirmed the deaths of Shia and Gitla Kajzer. But Grabowska had chosen not to. What could it be but sabotage? Did it go deeper? Did the judge's agenda in fact reflect the government's agenda? Was Judge Grabowska torpedoing my reclamation because the new nationalist, revisionist, judiciary-undermining government wanted her to, had directed or compelled her to? Or even if no one had said anything aloud she understood which decision her higher-ups would be happy with, she didn't want to step on any toes, hundreds of judges across the country had just been fired, better play it safe . . . ? I was paranoid. I had had the goodwill knocked out of me and now I was paranoid, I was being yanked back to my family's default attitude toward Poles—suspicion, mistrust, resentment. My father wasn't the least bit surprised at the ruling; disgusted, but not surprised. *Antisemitn,* he said. What did you expect.

A few weeks later we got the decision in writing and my suspicions weren't allayed in the slightest. As best I could tell—this was a translation, of uncertain quality, of a legal document—Judge Grabowska's reasoning seemed to be that since there were other Jews who'd been in similar circumstances who *had* survived (including, I suppose, my grandfather), it therefore could not be conclusively determined that my relatives had *not* survived. The judge was not saying, to be clear, that my relatives could not be declared dead because they might be alive—the judge did not believe that my relatives might be alive, because the judge was not an idiot. Her reasoning was more procedural: these deaths did not qualify, did not meet the state's standard of "death." The judge even went so far as to offer counterexamples, circumstances where death *could* be declared—such as a natural disaster—but not here, not in this instance, because, apparently, the Holocaust wasn't deadly enough . . . ?

If only there'd been a flood, I said to my father. Then they'd be dead.

In her decision Judge Grabowska cited a law, the Act of 23 April 1964, that seemed intended for *exactly* this kind of situation—i.e., those who went missing during a time of war can be declared dead one year after the war ends. But according to Judge Grabowska the act did not apply in our case because there were *some* Jewish survivors. It was an infuriating argument. If the existence of *any* survivors means the law does not apply, then it's a hollow and meaningless piece of legislation. A 99 percent mortality rate was, apparently, insufficiently deadly.

The arbitrariness was further underscored by the fact that the act of April 23, 1964, had been invoked by the Będzin judge: Shia and Gitla Kajzer's deaths were dated May 9, 1946, one year after World War II ended. Indeed, the final paragraph of the decision of the Będzin judge reads like a direct rebuke to Judge Grabowska, outlining why the lack of hard evidence of deaths isn't, in this instance, meaningful: *Undoubtedly . . . the legislators had also, or even mainly, in mind the many legions of people who died in labor camps and Jewish ghettos. With very few exceptions there are no eyewitnesses, because these eyewitnesses themselves were victims and died together with those for whom recognition of death is being sought. In this respect, the applicants' claims, given the historical circumstances, constitute sufficient substantiation.*

The generosity I'd come to the process with, that spirit of *what can you do, bureaucracies will be bureaucratic,* now seemed so misplaced, so naïve. Because all I was asking for here, really, was an acknowledgment of a supremely banal fact, that they're dead, that my relatives who died in the Holocaust are dead. What could be an easier-to-acknowledge truth? That the dead are dead? That those who died in the Holocaust died in the Holocaust? Yet the powers that be were saying: No. It was risible, it was outrageous. I had thought my story did not have an antagonist, but I was wrong, it does, I found my antagonist. Here it was. It didn't have a name, it was amorphous, it went beyond one judge in Sosnowiec—it was the system, the bureaucracy, the courts. Maybe it was even "Poland." The country, the history, the idea, I don't know.

What did this mean for the case? It was of course an annoying and dispiriting setback, now we'd have to appeal, and who knew how long that might take. But so what, who cared about the added cost and time? There were more disturbing implications—namely, the ugly abstraction of something so manifestly true, a truth that should be considered sacred: the deaths of Shoah victims! They were denying the deaths of Shoah victims! Even if "denying" is not the most precise verb here that's what I'll use, because that's what it felt like and, really, amounted to. For a minute I thought—kind of grandiloquently—that my frustration had something to do with closure, that the court's refusal to recognize these deaths was keeping something in limbo or whatever, but then I realized no, of course not, it had nothing to do with closure, I never knew these people, I wasn't in mourning or in any kind of psychic pain. Rather it was like I was being told that the truth doesn't matter. Yes they're dead but unfortunately that doesn't mean they're dead. Like I was being told: You have your story, we have ours. Your story isn't more true than ours. Your knowledge isn't actually the right kind of knowledge. People aren't dead just because you believe they are dead, just because you know they are dead, just because they are in fact dead.

13

A few days after I received the decision, Joanna called and said she had a surprise for me. She'd posted on Facebook, asking if anyone had any interesting Kajzer-related information. Most of the responses were from explorers who did not have any information for me but, being explorers, wanted to know if maybe *I* had information for *them*. But there was one interesting response, from an explorer who claimed to know the house Abraham Kajzer had hidden in during the waning weeks of the war, and said he was friends with the house's owner, a man named Jacek. Joanna had reached out to Jacek to arrange a visit. This was the surprise.

Jacek had stressed to Joanna that he himself was not a treasure hunter; he was, he said, extremely wary of treasure hunters. He was extremely wary of me. At first he said I could not visit; then backtracked and said okay; then backtracked and said no; then said I could come for one hour; then said I could not come at all; then asked Joanna for proof that I was related to Abraham Kajzer; then said I could visit but only for twenty minutes; then texted to say it wasn't a good day, let's try and reschedule, but by then we were already in the Land Rover on our way over so we just ignored the text.

Jacek lived on a narrow unpaved street on the outskirts of Głuszyca. His house was very big, and a peculiar combination of old and new—it had been expanded, renovated, altered countless times over the decades, and the scars showed.

Jacek met us at the gate and soothed the dog that was losing its mind. He was in his late thirties, which surprised me—I'd assumed he was older, mostly because he'd been so suspicious. He was blond, chubby, baby-faced, and wore a blue polo shirt, gray sweatpants, and Crocs, an extremely un–treasure hunterish outfit. For whatever reason (my Americanness; Joanna's celebrity), Jacek's suspicions of who I was and what I wanted evaporated instantly upon meeting us, as did any pretense that this was going to be a quick visit. We stood in front of the house as he spoke at length and with obvious pride about its history.

Jacek said that when he and his family moved in ten years ago, they didn't know anything about the house, were unaware of anything strange or noteworthy. But many things happened, he said, that made him understand that this was no regular house. (Ah, I said to myself, here we go; I'd spent enough time with treasure hunters to recognize their vocabulary; Jacek may not identify as a treasure hunter, I thought, but neither was he immune to the siren.)

One day, Jacek said, two Germans, an elderly man and his middle-aged son, showed up and began photographing the exterior of the house; when Jacek asked who they were, why they were interested in his house, the old man said that he had grown up here, had lived here until he and his family had been forced out in 1946. They assured Jacek that they had come strictly for sentimental reasons, just wanted to see the place, nothing nefarious, were uninterested in reclaiming the property or ripping out floorboards. A gracious and curious Jacek let them in, and they went through the house, room by room, as the old man reminisced, described what the place used to look like. And at some point during the visit, Jacek said, the old man mentioned that fifteen Jews had hidden here during the war.

Suddenly Jacek restarted the narrative; there was another house-related mystery that had to be told first. The previous owner of the house, he said, was murdered. Shot in the head six times. I don't believe in the supernatural but we definitely have a ghost, he said, then burst out laughing. The murdered owner had been an officer in the Communist secret police. (Ah, I said to myself; secret police are a staple of Silesian mystery, they are everywhere, in all varieties: KGB, CIA, Stasi, Mossad.) Six bullets in the head, Jacek emphasized. His body was found in the kitchen by his wife and daughter, I'll show you the spot when we're inside. Jacek paused; he was waiting for me to ask why the former owner had been murdered, so I asked why the former owner had been murdered.

There are three theories, he said.

One, it was a robbery gone wrong. An unfortunate and random act of violence. Nothing to do with the man's former career as a Communist secret police officer. This is a possible theory, Jacek said, but it was clear he considered this to be a preposterous theory.

Two, the murder was an act of revenge. An officer in the Communist secret police?—there are many people who would have wanted him dead. Joanna and Jacek nodded knowingly; I also nodded knowingly.

Three—something extremely secret. Like what? I asked. Jacek shrugged. I don't know, he said, and I also can't tell you everything I know. (Ah, I said to myself; these men, their exhausting insistence on the unutterable.) I found two hiding spots in the house that had been cleared out, he said. Who knows what was in there?

Anyway: the family of the murdered former officer of the Communist secret police didn't want to stay in the house, for understandable reasons, and sold it to Jacek. Though when they sold it they failed to mention the murder, I suppose also for understandable reasons; Jacek found out only after he'd moved in. I asked if it bothered him. Not really, he said. It makes it interesting. I told you—we have a ghost, and he burst out laughing.

Not long after he moved in, Jacek said, someone knocked on the door and handed him a book—*Za Drutami Śmierci*, by Abraham Kajzer. And when I read the book I understood that the house he describes is my house. What? I said. Who? Who was this someone? And why did they give you a book? And why that book? Jacek shrugged. I have no idea, he said. But that's very strange, I said. Jacek shrugged. It is strange but not so strange, he said. This is Silesia.

An hour after we'd arrived we went inside the house. It was refreshingly domestic—no exploring equipment, no Nazi memorabilia, no pseudo-military interior design. Jacek asked that we take off our shoes. The kitchen was a very nice kitchen and also a makeshift film studio, with fancy lighting equipment, softboxes, microphone, a high-end video camera on a tripod. Jacek explained that his wife, Dorota, produced and starred in a popular cooking show on YouTube, *Menu Dorotki*.

The house was enormous. You can't tell how big it is from the outside, Jacek said—thirty-seven rooms, 850 square meters (about nine thousand square feet). Jacek showed us what he called the least renovated room in the house; it looked like and was the size of the inside of a barn: 220 square meters, thirty-foot-high ceilings. It was cavernous, and, aside from some scattered junk—an orange plastic chair, an inflatable pool still in the package—entirely empty. Joanna and I gaped—to see a room this size inside a house felt surreal, like a violation of physics—and Jacek grinned.

We went across the hall and into the master bedroom. It was nice, modern, understated. Jacek stood against the wall. "Right here there was an enormous wooden cabinet," he said, "that had come with the house. My wife hated it so we decided to get rid of it. It took six men to move. And behind it, right here"—Jacek gestured toward the middle of the blank wall—"there was a small door."

Jacek said he opened this small secret door he'd just discovered in his bedroom and took a step inside—and fell or almost fell (I had some trouble understanding) a full story down. There was a gap between the walls; it was a false wall. Jacek, uninjured (so I guess he only almost fell, or was very lucky), examined the gap. There was a ladder. The ladder led down to the secret room, which we would go to now.

We exited the bedroom and went down a short flight of stairs and entered the room that had been the secret room and which was now a laundry room. Washer, dryer, hamper, cleaning supplies, everywhere piles of clothes. There were no windows, only the one (recently installed) door. The ceiling sloped so that I could stand upright only along one edge of the room; it was maybe twenty feet by ten feet, which made for a very nice-sized laundry room but impossibly tight living quarters for fifteen people. Jacek pushed aside laundry and toys and household detritus as he gave us a tour, told us what it'd looked like when he'd stumbled down here for the first time—he'd found some shoes, some pages from a book. I admit I had some trouble holding onto the significance of the site. It felt to me like a laundry room with interesting trivia. There is a site and there is its memory and these two things often don't align. It'd be, I bet, very illuminating to study Polish history through the lens of home renovation.

I had some questions for Jacek regarding the chronology of these discoveries: "So you found this room right after you moved in?"

"*Tak.*"

"So before the German father and son had shown up?"

"*Tak.*"

"So before you'd read Kajzer's book?"

"*Tak.*"

"So when you first discovered this room you didn't know anything about Jews hiding here during the war?"

"That is correct."

"So what did you think this room was?"

Jacek shrugged, rolled his eyes. A secret room, not such a big deal, not exactly major news. "This is Silesia," Joanna said, also shrugging. "*Tak,*" Jacek said. "This is Silesia, there are secrets everywhere."

Indeed there were: Jacek's tour was far from over. We went downstairs, put our shoes back on, followed Jacek outside. The property was a couple of acres in size, and unfenced, so it bled right into the surroundings —overgrown grass and rolling fields stretching to the mountains. We came to a small lake. This lake, Jacek proclaimed, makes no sense. For a long time we could not figure out the source of the lake, he said, the water seemed to come from nowhere. And then—Jacek had a huge grin on his face—we found a pipe, and below the pipe—at this point Jacek was basically cackling from excitement—there were underground railroad tracks.

Jacek lifted a makeshift wooden grating and illuminated the hole with the light on his cell phone. Below, five or six feet deep, there were, unmistakably, rail tracks. You can scoff all you want at these treasure hunters but occasionally they show you something really amazing. Who knows if they had anything to do with Nazis but still—there were underground railroad tracks on this man's property.

What was Jacek's theory? Jacek's theory had everything to do with Nazis. He said that he and Jerzy Cera, something of an elder statesman among the treasure hunters, believe that the lake hides a secret entrance to Sobon complex. They had also found a valve, which they believe controls the lake's water level. "Cera is very suspicious, so don't tell anyone about this," said Jacek, who, for all his talk of not being a treasure hunter, was clearly very much in cahoots with some of them; he then told us that Cera and other explorers stayed here, in fact, in rooms he rented out as a side business. This struck me as an astonishing coincidence—the house Abraham Kajzer had hidden in also happened to be the treasure hunters' lodging of choice?—though Joanna was unfazed. This is Silesia, she said.

Jacek brought us around the back of the house to a small staircase that led to the cellar. He turned to us, solemn. A speech before we descended. When we moved in, he said, this room was full of coal. We didn't think anything of it, we thought it was just storage, junk, whatever. But when the old German man entered the cellar he burst into tears and ran out. When we asked him why he was crying, what he remembered, he refused to talk about it. He would only say, It's too painful, I don't want to talk about it. Jacek shrugged his big innocent shrug. So I don't know.

Jacek warned us to watch our heads and led us down the stairs and through a narrow sooted corridor to a section of gray stone wall maybe three feet across and five feet high. "There is something behind this wall," he said. "We know absolutely there is something behind this wall. The layout of the house strongly suggests there's a room there." He pointed out a rusty remnant of what might once have been a door hinge.

Joanna got very excited—which I hadn't really seen before: this was *new* mystery—and she and Jacek began speaking excitedly in Polish. I couldn't follow, but after a minute I butted in and asked Jacek, "Have you considered taking the wall down?" I was so tired of all this inaccessible invisible mystery.

"That's what we are talking about," Joanna said.

"He doesn't want to do it?"

"I will do it," Joanna said. "He wants me to do it."

"We're going to do it now?"

"No, we don't have the equipment," Joanna said. "We'll come back and do it."

Afterwards we sat in the kitchen—where the previous owner's lifeless body had been found by his wife and daughter—with Dorota, Jacek's wife, who had taken notes when the Germans had visited.

The Germans' name was Kammler and the story was, naturally, a little thicker, a little more complicated, a little more heartbreaking than what Jacek had sketched.

The Kammlers were not in fact the original owners of the house. The original owners were the Kreins, who employed Mr. and Mrs. Kammler—the parents of the old man who'd shown up one day—as groundskeeper and maidservant. The Kammler family, mother, father, child, lived in a single room upstairs. When the Kreins' son, their only child, died in combat in World War I, they bequeathed the estate to Mr. and Mrs. Kammler.

In Dorota's notes there was a heading marked JEWS: *200–300 people walked by every day, on their way to work at Sobon; 15 people hid here during the war.*

Under the heading 1.05.1946: 3 a.m.: *The Poles came suddenly and told [the Kammlers] to pack their things. They planted a grenade in the house, accused them of being terrorists, and said they had to leave immediately. They were put into Polish trains and deported—the entire street of residents was deported . . . The Poles treated them very badly after the war. Russians were much better.*

We stayed and talked a while; the conversation turned to lighter subjects. Dorota told us about her cooking show, invited me to appear as a special guest. Jacek showed us UFO/Riese videos he'd posted to You-Tube, and brought out his copy of Kajzer's book for me to autograph. At some point Jacek and Dorota's twelve-year-old daughter joined us.

Her attitude to all this mystery was refreshingly teenage. Like her dad, she believed the house was haunted by a murdered former Communist secret police officer. But she was wonderfully blasé about it. Whatever, the house is haunted, who cares, what's the big deal, nothing to freak out over. I pushed: But what is that like, living in a house that's haunted? You must have some feelings about it. Whatever, she said. You get used to it. Okay but what about your friends, I asked, what do they think about the ghost? She shrugged and rolled her eyes, as if I'd asked her to describe what toast tasted like. I asked: What do you think about this mystery in your cellar? She said she found it interesting, but by "interesting" she clearly meant "the most boring thing in the universe," and the only reason she'd said "interesting" was that she felt she had to be polite in front of her dad and his ridiculous guests with their ridiculous obsessions.

It was the wrong house. A few months later I finally received the translation of Abraham's diary and it was immediately clear that the house Abraham Kajzer hid in had not been this house, was not Jacek's mysterious house. It is plain to see in the text. Abraham hid not in a secret room with fourteen other Jews but in a potato box, in the cellar, by himself. The German woman who hides him is unnamed but there are enough identifiers — she tells Abraham this is her father's house, and that she is there with her children — to rule out Kammler or Krein.

So the house wasn't the house, and the building wasn't the building, and Abraham wasn't my grandfather, and my dead relatives aren't dead, and myths are stubborn, and truths unravel, and fictions fit snugly.

Part IV

—

FOREVER BOOK

14

1. Kaltwasser: I drove toward Kaltwasser, a subcamp of Gross-Rosen, the first of eight Abraham Kajzer was interned in. Or, rather, I drove to where Kaltwasser used to be, because the camp itself—the buildings, the barracks, the fences, etc.—has been completely effaced; actually, "where the camp used to be" isn't accurate either, because no one knows with certainty where the camp used to be. Rather my destination was the long-lat coordinates for Kaltwasser as per en.wikipedia.org/wiki/Project_Riese, coordinates I later learned had, unsurprisingly, been worked out and uploaded by treasure hunters. There were coordinates for each subcamp and they were very precise, extending to the fourth decimal place, accurate to within eleven meters. I'd uploaded the eight sets of coordinates, virtually staked eight blue digital pins, created my own private Google map of Abraham's suffering. The fact that the map was accessible only to me was I'll admit a little bit thrilling; it was a thrill that was somewhere between the thrill of the explorer and the thrill of the pilgrim. Kaltwasser was my first stop because Kaltwasser was Abraham's first camp. I was tracing his journey: I felt I should go in order. My phone directed me through the village of Głuszyca to Gdanska Street, a street I was familiar with—this was the street Jacek and Dorota lived on, in a house that, despite the stubborn myth, Abraham did not hide in, although, that said, somewhere right around here was the house Abraham *did* hide in. The blue pin representing Kaltwasser was located (virtually, physically, historically, spiritually?) behind a new house that looked as if it was still under construction and not yet inhabited, so I parked on the unpaved driveway. As soon as I opened the car door, though, a dog from inside the house began barking. Still I was pretty sure that no one was home but even so I skirted the property, I was nervous about trespassing. Behind the house was an empty expansive field. How big had Kaltwasser been? I don't know. No one knows. "Several numbered barracks," Abraham wrote, "located fifty meters apart." So quite big. The scanty sources we do have suggest up to two thousand prisoners were housed here, somewhere around here, and now it's just field, uncut, growing wild, belonging to the owner of this just-built house, if not legally then de facto. The blue digital pin is deceptive. I labeled it "Kaltwasser" but Kaltwasser had dimensions, boundaries, measurements; the pin has none of that. The pin is a unitless point on a map: the most precise we can get is *around here somewhere*. What was this place? It was a field where once had been a concentration camp where once had been a field. I didn't expend any imaginative energy trying to see—feel?—sense?—understand?—the camp through—behind?—beneath?—via?—the field. Maybe this was because there was no physical remnant of the camp, no visual anchor. I walked to the edge of the field and discovered I was wrong, there was in fact a remnant: an old stone dugout that was part of Kaltwasser, and even if it wasn't part of Kaltwasser it was still part of Kaltwasser because here was the site of a concentration camp called Kaltwasser and here was an old stone structure; the association is so blatant there is no need for it to be factual in order for it to be true. The people who are living here in this new house, in whose backyard this stone structure is half-buried but hardly hidden—what do they make of it? I imagine, I like to imagine, that they have thought deeply about this strange stone ruin in their backyard. Have thought about the notion of *historical residue.* Have considered whether a place can become historically stained. But what if they don't even know about the concentration camp in their backyard? Then I think it's fair to say that they don't know about concentration camps, full stop, and ignorance like that is a kind of choice, if not a personal choice then a collective one. We choose to forget. We choose to allow this place to forget its history. Abraham was in Kaltwasser considerably longer than he was in the other camps, from August until December 1944. I walked a big circle in the field then returned to the car. I backed out of the driveway—relieved to no longer be trespassing—and drove back to the main road.

2. *Tannhausen:* I parked and crossed a deserted playground and then hiked though thick growth, there was no path, I had to push through painfully sharp and thick bramble to reach the back of a low ugly building that housed a company that made drive belts: here were the coordinates for Tannhausen, where Abraham stayed two weeks, in the camp hospital. He didn't do labor here, he wasn't beaten here, he recuperated here, he was relatively grateful for his time here—should I relate differently to this camp? Or is that too granular an approach? My wrists and my forearms began pulsing strangely; it was more worrying than it was painful; but then it was painful. Dozens of small red marks, insect bites, emerged up and down my arms. A deer rocketed past me, startling me so badly I nearly fell over. This back lot was a very ugly industrial mess. It felt more transformed, and transformed more irrevocably, than had the open field at Kaltwasser. Residential, commercial, farm—most any other sort of space seems to me to better allow history's whispers to be heard than an industrial space; this place had terrible historical

acoustics. Why had I come out here? What was the point of driving out to these blue pins? I think I wanted a better sense of the geography, wanted to earn a familiarity with this land so pockmarked by Abraham's history. I'd read Abraham's book but not through the lens of where this happened and where that happened. In general that's not the way you read these books: it rarely seems important to differentiate location, it's an uninterrupted undemarcated expanse of trauma. Yet Abraham's book has persisted and is celebrated *because* of its attention to place; and Abraham himself was meticulous about location, heading each entry with the camp he was in at the time. So there's that. And: if I believe that *place* has intrinsic meaning, i.e., if I believe that memory and history are somehow imprinted into, onto, place—and I don't know if I do believe that; this is the question that seems to me to be at the heart of everything I'm doing in Poland, from the building in Sosnowiec to the mishegas with the treasure hunters—but if it's something I'm even considering, wrestling with, then: then you go, you go to the place, you accede to the pilgrimage, you say yes to the obligation and you go. That's not true. It's something I might tell people and might tell myself, but the truth is I don't feel obligated. A more honest answer would be that I made this trip because I thought it would be useful: showing up in person can help force the insight to the surface. Put another way, there was nothing else for me to see: you do all this memory-work and you hunger for the unabstract, for place person object noun. The irony is that it doesn't really get more abstract than these eight blue digital pins; or maybe it'd be more accurate to say that the pins represent the *process of abstraction:* the concentration camp, its buildings and markers and fences, is seventy years later *not there,* is now a little blue digital pin on my Google map, which represents something like "place" but isn't exactly "place," it's rather an idea of place, something like the spiritual counterpart to the original place. The concentration camp has been reduced, abstracted, into a single unitless point, which cannot be seen, only visited — it has presence but not dimension — and, maybe, depending on your spiritual sensibilities, intuited and felt. I think if you take the concept of place seriously enough you will end up having to work within the spiritual, or at least work with a spiritual vocabulary, because an ether is required — how else can place and history touch?

3. *Wüstegiersdorf:* I returned to the car and doubled back toward the next pin, about half a kilometer away, and I could feel the area shrinking, which is what happens when a place becomes familiar, not unlike how a text you reread seems to condense. I think of this as a sort of submission, a surrender, of the space, of the text. Familiarity gives license to the imagination. After the war Abraham rode a bicycle from camp to camp, fetching the notes he'd buried beneath the latrines. Not the latrines but where the latrines used to be, because just a few months after the war some of these camps already didn't exist, had gone abstract, although the treasure Abraham was after was hardly abstract — the scraps of cement packaging he'd scribbled on and buried. He was on a holy errand. I wonder what he thought about the camps slipping into nonexistence. Did he prefer them effaced, destroyed, gone, or did he want them preserved and memorialized? Wüstegiersdorf had been inside a textile mill in the center of Głuszyca. Abraham stayed here one week, one of between seven hundred and a thousand prisoners. Now it's a supermarket parking lot. Which really took me aback — not because it's a parking lot (in certain ways a supermarket parking lot feels like the most natural endpoint for the site of a concentration camp) but because I'd been here, on the drive in I had stopped at the supermarket to buy a bottle of water. I thought what a coincidence and then I thought maybe not such a coincidence, maybe this region is so saturated with sites of concentration camps that it wasn't in fact so improbable that I'd unknowingly stopped at one. A

city needs its supermarkets and you have to put a supermarket some-where. It was a very hot day and I went inside the supermarket to buy more water and as I stood in line I realized that now I'd visited the camps out of order, I hadn't followed Abraham's route; though, of course, I hadn't known, my stop at the supermarket was a stop at the supermar-ket, it didn't mean anything, though then I had to ask myself what was the point of following the route in the first place. I had thought some meaning would emerge, but none had, and it would add at least an hour of driving to what was shaping up to be a very long day. So I decided to abandon that route and plot a new route, the one that was shortest. This had the icky effect of making the stops feel a little like errands, though if I'm being honest that had already been the case.

6. Schotterwerk: I turned onto an unmarked road and then onto an-other unmarked road and parked and walked to an open field. It was a stunning vista, gorgeous nearly to the point of cliché: rolling hills, fat brooding bales of hay, mountains in the distance. A handful of large modern homes spaced far enough apart that you read them as part of the scenery. It felt familiar or maybe I don't mean familiar I mean *expected:* here is how a place with the awfullest history looks, this is what happens when time has a go at it. The more sinister the history the more lush the landscape? Schotterwerk had at least eleven barracks and housed at least 1,250 prisoners. I didn't linger here; the picturesqueness annoyed me.

Detour: I drove toward Osówka, the Riese complex, because some-one had asked me to pick up a couple of copies of *Za Drutami Śmierci* and they were available at the gift shop. About halfway up the winding mountain road I had to pull over to make room for two vintage Amer-ican military jeeps coming from the opposite direction. Inside the au-thentic-seeming jeeps were men in authentic-seeming American military uniforms who were definitely not actual American military; I did not know who they were or what they were doing but I assumed they were, if not explorers (it was too neat, too organized, too matchy-matchy), then something explorer-adjacent, maybe reenactors, something like that. I resisted an impulse to chase them down. At the gift shop, as I was paying for my copies of *Za Drutami Śmierci*, I asked the man behind the counter if he'd read the book. He was young, early twenties, pimply, smiled easily. Of course, he said. What'd you think? I asked. He made a sound of exclamation and said he thought it was an incredible book, there was so much detail in it, everything felt so real, so true, except for maybe all the beatings, maybe that was too much. What do you mean, I asked, too much? He said, I don't know how he could survive, I don't know how it would be possible for someone who had so little food, who was worked so hard, to survive beatings like that. I asked—genuinely, not confrontationally—You think he made it up? I don't know if he made it up, he said, but maybe also it is not exactly historical. He wrote a book and this is his story. Ah, I see, I said. Thank you! I did not tell the man behind the counter that I was related to the author, or that I was spending the day visiting the camps in which he may or may not have been beaten as badly or as often as he claimed to have been, or that I was writing a book about him. I didn't see the need to embarrass the man behind the counter and I didn't feel all that compelled to defend the memory of Abraham and/or the accuracy of Abraham's book. The skepticism of the man behind the counter was a strangely sympathetic sort of skepticism. Back home, skepticism toward a Holocaust narrative is beyond the pale: you must not challenge in any way the veracity of the account, *especially* as it relates to details of suffering. We guard vigilantly against myth (though of course it's there, it's everywhere) because we worry "myth" is not sufficiently historical and we worry that what is not historical is antagonistic to history and thus too close to *false,* and we feel duty-bound to enshrine *truth* and to stamp out the merest hint of *false*. So it's all true, it must be true, every word is true.

7. *Dörnhau:* The location of Dörnhau, unlike the location of the other camps, is known with precision; there is an extant map, drawn by a prisoner named Henryk Sussmanek. The camp was inside a carpet factory, and the building still stands, occupied by a company called John Cotton, which, according to its website, produces high-quality pillows and quilts. I parked in the large empty lot and walked past an unmanned guardhouse into the inner yard. There was a truck, empty, open, waiting. A forklift backed out of the bay. I took a photograph and walked back to the car. The camps, my experience of these camps, were starting to bleed together. I'm guessing something similar is happening on your end. I flattened my notebook against the roof of the rental car and made notes, mostly in order to be able to tell the camps apart later. It was important for me to be able to do this but I don't think it's important for you. Dörnhau was the seventh camp Abraham was in, and then after a transfer out and then another transfer back, was also the last camp he was in, was the camp he escaped from. I wanted to try to trace his escape route; I wanted to see if I could figure out or at least make an educated guess which house he'd hidden in. But regarding his escape Abraham doesn't get very specific: the only clues offered are the direction — northwest, in the direction of Kaltwasser, where he knew there were some houses — and that he followed a country road. I drove around the corner and down an unpaved road into the open field separating Dörnhau and Kaltwasser. I passed a fence, in relatively good condition, whose posts were cement and had that familiar menacing curl toward the top. The camps were not far apart, less than a mile. What country road? On my map there was no road. I toggled the view from "Map" to "Satellite" and now there was a road, or a path, or something. It was just a little farther ahead but from where I stood it could not be seen, owing to the height of

the grass. It was more or less where you'd expect it to be, a road between the camps that an escapee might have followed, it certainly could have been this road, this was the best tense I could hope for: *could have been.* I drove toward it and a man on a tractor thirty meters away stared at me for a very long time—we were both driving very slowly—and I turned onto the maybe-escape road, which I wasn't sure would be wide enough for the car—if it wasn't I would have walked, part of me wanted to or maybe even felt like I was supposed to walk—but it was fine, it was wide enough. I followed the road toward Kaltwasser. It continued beneath the forest canopy and terminated at a lot behind Gdanska 4. This could be the house Abraham hid in. But no, Abraham makes note of passing houses, so it couldn't be the first house. But of course maybe this wasn't even the right country road in the first place, maybe he went the long way, skirting the forest and emerging on the other side of Gdanska. It would be helpful to know whether he crossed the street. It's true that the text does not say "I crossed the street," and, under the circumstances, crossing the street would have been a dangerous and memorable act. But, of course, the omission of "I crossed the street" does not mean he did not cross the street; you can't close-read the text like that; Kajzer's book isn't meant to be geographically traced. It is a narrative, not a map. I'm doing it regardless. Throughout the day I wondered to what extent I was approaching the text like the treasure hunters do, them with the tunnels and me with the camps. Joanna was of the opinion that the house Abraham hid in—once it was determined it could not be Jacek's house—was an inn; and Joanna had sent me a prewar photograph of the inn she thought it was. I drove back down the maybe-escape road and circled back to Gdanska Street. Outside Jacek and Dorota's house I saw Dorota signing for a package, and I stopped and said hello, showed her the photograph of the inn, asked if she knew which building this was; she didn't, but called over Jacek, who pointed to a white roof peeking out from over the trees. I continued down the road. The inn, the former inn, was large and wooden and had once upon a time clearly been grand and stately; now it was abandoned and dilapidated. Now *this* could be the house Abraham hid in; in fact it *felt* like it was the house Abraham hid in, but I knew I was probably responding more to the fact that it was abandoned and run-down than anything else. Intuition should be celebrated, examined, investigated—but not relied on. I investigated, I did my due diligence, I compared the building with the building in Joanna's photograph, compared the angles, the driveway, the details of the roof. It was inconclusive. It was always going to be inconclusive. What do we do with the unknowable? What can we do but embrace it? Let us let our stories leak, become diffuse and imprecise. Maybe this was the house Abraham hid in and maybe it wasn't the house but it's now part of the story. Same as Jacek's house. Same as Małachowskiego 12. I've come to acknowledge a broader definition of "story," one that includes the misfires, that incorporates the misinterpretations and mistakes. The story anoints a place and when it's found to be the wrong place it does not revert to being meaningless.

4. Larche: I continued driving down Gdanska until the street went no farther. I parked and continued on foot into the forest. There was no path. I oriented myself toward the blue pin, like a digital North Star. My phone, more omniscient by the day, knew not only my location but also the direction I was facing. I walked uphill through a muddy ravine, attempting to stay on as straight a path as possible. The concentration camp is over here, my phone says, just this way. For ten then fifteen then forty minutes I walked farther into the forest. Had I been doing this via written-out directions, with an analog map, I would have abandoned the effort almost immediately. The digital map was reassuring, it knew where I was, it knew where the camp was, I felt accompanied. (Though if I lost service I'd be hopelessly lost, I hadn't been paying any attention to where I was going.) Then I was there. A brick wall, low, only two or three feet high, at least twenty feet long. The wall was half-consumed by the forest. A little bit farther uphill was a collapsed cement building, similarly ceding to its surroundings. Of all these camps Larche has the most extensive remains. The preservation is accidental, a function of its remoteness—the camp was built here so that the prisoners didn't have to travel too far to the worksite, which was not about mercy but efficiency. The conditions in Larche were particularly bad: the inmates lived in plywood barracks that offered no protection from the cold, and in the winter and spring, when the snow melted, water freely flowed inside. The pin was very precise, by the way, the camp was exactly where it was supposed to be, which made me feel more confident in the other coordinates, though I recognize the irrationality therein. Because of the hike, because of the nature of the ruins, Larche felt the most like a pilgrimage. I sat on the low brick wall for a while to cool down; I was sweating profusely.

8. Erlensbuch: I drove halfway around the mountain, parked, crossed a bridge to where the Erlensbuch camp was pinned: a clearing at the edge of the forest that contained a single man-made object, a utility tower. In the Museum of Gross-Rosen there was an undated photograph of this clearing, and it was from this vantage: the view is exactly the same, down to the utility tower. Not a photograph of the camp but a photograph of where the camp used to be. It is a photograph of the abstraction, an iteration of memory. I got back in the car and continued driving around the mountain when I came up behind the two vintage American military jeeps, and in the back of the leading jeep—I hadn't noticed this before —were two children and a dog. I followed them for a bit and when they pulled to the side of the road so did I. The men in American military outfits climbed out (the dog and kids stayed inside) and unstrapped large gas canisters from the side of the jeeps and began to fill up. I approached them and asked about the uniforms, about the jeeps. They were Czech, they said, and this was their hobby. They didn't seem sheepish but neither did they seem particularly proud; I would have expected one reaction or the other. The jeeps were in fact authentic, the men confirmed, had been used in the first Gulf War. The uniforms too, they said. One of them unfolded an enormous laminated map. (I didn't see any phones; I assumed this hobby had a rule against phones.) Do you know where is the rocket? they asked. I knew what they were referring to: right outside the Rzeczka complex there is, for no good reason, a full-scale model V-2 rocket. I showed them on the map. They thanked me and piled back into their jeeps and drove toward the rocket.

5. *Wolfsberg:* Wolfsberg was the largest Riese subcamp. It held at least 3,100 prisoners. The pin was easy to find. It was right there on the side of the road where a prominent stone memorial reads, in four languages: "IN MEMORY OF THE PRISONERS OF WAR, FORCED LABOURERS AND PRISONERS OF THE GROSS-ROSEN CONCENTRATION CAMP MURDERED IN THE OWL MOUNTAINS 1943–1945, PEOPLE OF THE WALIM COMMUNE IN THE YEAR 2010."

15

In the plainest sense *Za Drutami Śmierci* is a first-person chronicle of the eight brutal months, August 1944 to April 1945, of Abraham Kajzer's internment in concentration camps, first in Auschwitz and then in various Gross-Rosen subcamps in Lower Silesia. It is a blunt, sober, ungentle read; the material is not padded and is not introduced gradually. The first sentence is "We are on the train." Abraham and his wife and child have just been deported from the Łódź Ghetto and are being taken to Auschwitz (which even in August 1944 was something of an unknown: Abraham's wife asks, "What is Auschwitz?" "A town in Upper Silesia," Abraham responds). Immediately upon disembarking Abraham is separated from his wife ("Women to the right! Men to the left!") and then his son ("[The SS officer] takes my child and says: 'Children with the women.'"). The scene is told quickly and with blank resignation.

Abraham does not tell us the name of his wife. He does not tell us the name of his child. What that means I can't really say, other than it is clear that this is how Abraham prefers to present his ghosts.

The disembarkation and separation occurs on page two. Every subsequent page is marked by pain, privation, suffering, decay. I don't know how to summarize a book like this. It is a litany of inhumanity. An endless series of beatings at the hands of Germans, Ukrainians, and kapos; laments of hunger; obsessive descriptions of pathetically meager rations; machinations of survival; ravages of lice, frostbite, infections; the body falling apart; the mind falling apart.

It is an astonishingly unsentimental book, hauntingly (and, in a literary sense, admirably) unadorned and straightforward. The bleakness is unmodulated and unadulterated. This is not a story of hope or faith or even of perseverance—that Abraham happens to survive is a meaningless accident, not fate but chance. God or any parallel power is absent. The universe is cold and dead. But you can't even contemplate that, because you're too hungry. If occasionally Abraham does ask grander questions, one gets the sense that it's only when he cannot help himself, that he is of the belief that even to wonder is a kind of capitulation. What is there to say? Life has been reduced to a black narrow corridor. Wake up, work, absorb the kapos' sticks, eat your soup, try and stay warm, try not to die (or when the time comes try and figure out how to most effectively kill yourself), try to stay sane.

The question at the book's core is not whether Abraham will survive —a foregone conclusion—and not even really how he survives—scavenge, steal, and luck, like everyone else—but why: Why hold on? Why not just let go?

> They only want to murder us with this work anyway. Is my work not a curse? Am I not prolonging my suffering in vain? Oh, how good it would be if I died! How blissful! How quiet! I would not feel anything anymore! I would not think anything! I would be

liberated! No, I can't think about it! I have to live! Maybe my child is alive? Maybe he is living in better conditions than me? And what will he do without his father when the war is over? I must live and endure everything. I cannot orphan my son, and leave him in neglect. And maybe my wife will survive? I have already failed enough, giving up my child without a word of protest. Why did I do this? Why? When the SS man told me to leave them, I didn't say anything and left my child at the mercy of fate. No! Not in the hands of fate — in their claws, in the claws of those tormentors and predators! No! Worse even: not predators — German SS men. Why didn't I immediately realize the horror of my act? Oh, if I were with my child! I would live only for him! I would know at least who I am suffering for, and that it is worth suffering! No, I have to live ruthlessly!

Now I decide. I have to live like an automaton, without thoughts, without feeling. I have to persevere to the end for my child, whom I hurt so much, giving him to the SS man without a word.

In his child Abraham has found a will to live, but it is precarious, built from the flimsy stuff of ghosts and hopes. A few months later Abraham encounters a friend from Łódź who had been a *Sonderkommando* in Auschwitz. Abraham asks if he had seen his wife and child. The friend from Łódź replies that not only did he see them but in fact he took them to the ovens himself. Fighting to remain calm — he wants the truth, not sympathy — Abraham asks the friend from Łódź whether he's sure. The friend confirms: "What, you think I didn't know your wife and child? I will tell you how they were dressed. Your wife was wearing a bright English coat, and your son was wearing brown knickers and a turtleneck."

His reason to live is dead; Abraham decides to kill himself. "How should I do it? Hang myself? No! Too much pain. I'll throw myself in front of the train! It will kill me quickly! I will be rid of my thoughts, suffering, feelings, and trouble. Only one moment—and then a great eternal rest!" The next day Abraham, feeling content, fulfilled, determined, even happy, lies down in front a moving train. But he is thwarted, even here, his body on top the vibrating tracks awaiting release. The train does not crush Abraham, only slides him harmlessly forward. He grabs at the ground to increase his resistance, but to no effect. The train stops and he's still alive. There is no out; the suffering is bottomless.

In April 1945 Abraham makes a relatively undramatic escape to a nearby village and persuades an unnamed German woman to hide him in her cellar. He stays there for a month, living in a box meant for storing potatoes, until a Soviet soldier opens the lid and shines a light in his face and tells him he's free. Reluctantly he leaves his hiding spot, wanders about. He finds peas on the ground and begins to collect them. A Soviet soldier stops him and brings him to a ransacked shop and tells him he can take any foodstuffs he wants. Abraham pretends to choose something as he waits for the soldier to leave, then returns to collect the peas and put them in his pocket, "as if they were an incredible treasure." No happy ending, no redemption, no moral, no hope. Just brokenness. Collect the peas scattered on the street. "Where will I go," Abraham writes, "to where will I return? Who is waiting for me? Who do I need? Who else remains in this world?"

Za Drutami Śmierci is a stark and powerful book, if in most respects a fairly standard Holocaust memoir. (Anyone who spends time with the genre will quickly apprehend the ancillary tragedy that it's a *genre:* these mind-shatteringly horrific stories are common enough and familiar enough that they can feel ordinary, even banal, sometimes even clichéd.) Yet—treasure hunters aside—it is unknown and unread, one of thousands of similar books, a tiny unit of a very large body of work that is critical but in a collective, superliterary sense. Even if there are too many

Holocaust memoirs to be read in one lifetime there is nonetheless great moral significance in that fact.

That said, in certain ways this is a very notable, strange book, and that's even before we get to the treasure hunters and the esteem in which they hold it.

First, this is a *very* early Holocaust memoir — the Hebrew version was published (if totally ignored) in Israel in 1952, the Polish in 1962 — and is one the few accounts we have of the Gross-Rosen/Riese subcamps; much of what we know about these camps comes from this book. The Museum of Gross-Rosen's main exhibition — a small maze in the gate-house of the Gross-Rosen concentration camp — is more or less built around excerpts from it.

Second, the story behind the book — how it was written, how it was assembled, literally and editorially, how it was published — is a doozy. Here we must introduce Adam Ostoja, secretary of the Łódź Association of Polish Writers, and editor of *Za Drutami Śmierci*. His short preface begins: "In 1947, Abraham Kajzer came to me with a rather unusual proposal. He wrote, or sketched, rather, a camp diary and wanted me to develop it into a literary work." Ostoja continues:

> Abraham Kajzer was a simple man, a Łódź worker, a weaver by trade. He brought with him a large manuscript and a pile of gray, thick paper torn from the packaging of cement bags. These scraps were covered on both sides with lopsided and crudely written letters in the Jewish language [i.e., Yiddish].
>
> "You see, sir," he said. "This is my 'diary.' Every day, I hid in the latrine of the camp and feverishly recorded my experiences. I kept these notes in various places until I was notified that I would be transferred to another camp, when I gathered them together and nailed them to the bottom of a latrine board."

"No one noticed?" I asked.

"No. I wouldn't be alive."

"How did you get them back?"

"After the war, I borrowed a bicycle from the woman who saved my life. I traveled to most of the camps where I'd stayed, and I retrieved these pages."

It was amazing. I had before me a man who passed through several extermination camps, referred to by the Germans as "labor camps." He was possibly the only survivor of a transport of eighteen thousand men and, still, he managed to keep a "diary."

In the camps, he had no more than a striped uniform, a thread from which he tied a small mechanical pencil, with which he scribbled his notes. This was his greatest treasure.

Even within a genre whose origin stories are astonishing nearly by definition, this is an astonishing origin story. Abraham risks his life by jotting journal entries on stolen scraps of cement packaging. Whenever he's set to be transferred to another camp, he hides his "diary" beneath the latrine. Against all odds he survives, and in the weeks after liberation, he borrows a bicycle from the woman who'd hidden him and rides from camp to camp, collecting his notes. (What an extraordinary image: Abraham riding a borrowed bicycle into the concentration camp, riding right up to the latrine, or the spot where the latrine used to be, dismounting, digging out his notes, getting back on the bicycle, riding to the next camp.) A couple of years later he schleps the thick gray proto-manuscript to Ostoja the editor, and together they labor to turn it into a "literary work."

"It contains nothing but the truth," Ostoja writes. "I kept everything, without revision, that Kajzer wrote, said, and what could be read of his remarkable 'diary.' These are his authentic words and thoughts, his views and feelings, and, in many cases, even his style. This book was written by Kajzer. I just organized it and, as far as I could, 'polished' it."

The result is not quite a diary and not quite a memoir but something like a diary wrapped inside a memoir. The first half or so of the book, written in the years after the war from Abraham's (excellent) memory, consists of long undated chapters. Then there is this passage—

> For several days now, I've had a pencil I found in the *Baustelle* [worksite]. I would very much like to keep a diary, but there is nothing to write on and nowhere to write. If I was noticed in the block, everyone would think I was a madman, but I feel an unspoken need just to take notes. Perhaps the paper from which the cement bags are made would work for this purpose? I could hide the notes in the latrine. But where to write? Maybe also the latrine? I feel the need to share, even if it's just for myself, my own thoughts and insights, so that, when I am a free man, I can re-create it all again, and, if I die, I might leave this faint mark behind.

—and immediately, in a kind of Nabokovian realization of a described text, we are presented with the entries that Abraham has just been contemplating writing; we are reading those scraps of cement packaging. The entries are relatively short and headed by the location—that is, the concentration camp Abraham is in—and day of the week. Though I think it's safe to assume that at least some of what's being presented as diaristic is artifice—I can't imagine that recovered scraps, hidden for months underneath a latrine, would be perfectly legible (and Ostoja himself seems to admit as much)—I don't believe that this detracts at all from the effect.

The book thus shifts from memoir to diary, from postwar recollection to intrawar experience, even on some level from book to artifact, and I wonder: Does, or should, this shift impact how we read, how we receive? Do we "trust" the diary more? Is this mode more authentic because less time has passed between occurrence and recording? Is it more raw, more real, less edited, less mediated? Or does it just appear that way? In a manner that I don't think is accidental — or even if it is accidental I don't think it's any less pressing — Abraham's book, a book explicitly concerned about the writing of itself, raises sticky questions about memory, narrative, mediation, and myth.

Once Abraham escapes — without his pencil, without his scraps of cement packaging — the headings are dropped, the mode reverts to memoir, it's once again recollection.

Ostoja and Abraham worked on the book for a year, until 1948. But for maddeningly vague reasons ("The circumstances were such . . .") the book was not published in Poland until 1962, fifteen years after Abraham first showed up at Ostoja's office. It's possible the delay had something to do with Soviet censorship. But who knows.

By this point, Ostoja tells us, Abraham is long gone. He moved to Israel years ago. Ostoja claims that he and Abraham corresponded for a while but then Abraham stopped responding, and left no forwarding address. Ostoja does not know where Abraham is, does not know how to reach him, does not even know whether he is alive. "Maybe I can find him and then he will know that this, what he wrote — as though in his own blood, daily enduring death, agony, and torture beyond human comprehension — has seen the light of day."

In 1962 Abraham was alive and well and living in a suburb of Tel Aviv.

Ostoja makes it sound as if he and Abraham had simply, innocently fallen out of touch, that their relationship had faded blamelessly, as relationships do. I am skeptical. Abraham goes AWOL and in effect severs himself from a book he risked his life to write . . . ? It is hard not to see Abraham's decision to disappear (from Ostoja, that is) as somewhat deliberate. At the very least, clearly there is a lot more to this story than

what Ostoja is telling us: the nature of their relationship, in both a professional and personal sense, is elusive. Throughout the preface Ostoja
repeatedly gets details about Abraham wrong. For example, he writes
that Abraham's "whole family—wife, child, brother—all died" in the
war and that Abraham moved to Israel, where his distant relatives lived.
But Abraham's entire family didn't die—two siblings survived—and
it wasn't a distant relative who was living in Israel but his sister. Maybe
Ostoja forgot or maybe for some reason Abraham lied to him, but the
impression one is left with is that of two men, author and editor, way
out of sync, more than a decade out of touch, their only link a long-dor-
mant book project that belongs to both and to neither. Indeed, at times
Ostoja's preface feels like it's being written about an entirely made-up
version of Abraham:

> "How did you know that you wouldn't die?" I asked, moved. He
> smiled gently and wagged the stumps of his fingers, lost in the
> camps.
>
> "I didn't stand a chance," he replied. "But I had faith. I was
> deeply convinced that I would survive."
>
> He owed his salvation not only to his faith, but also to a whole
> set of extremely fortunate circumstances, and, above all, to his
> amazingly resilient character, the strength of his nerves, and his
> indomitable physical health.

Maybe this conversation or a conversation resembling this conversation did in fact happen. (Though unless Ostoja kept detailed notes, I'm
not sure why we should be expected to trust his recollection: it had been
fifteen years since Ostoja met this "simple man," whom Ostoja admits
he was skeptical of and initially uninterested in publishing.) But even
so, this is a reading that surrenders to or at least overindulges mythos
and sentiment in a work that allows for neither. Abraham was deeply

convinced that he would survive? He owed his salvation to his amazingly resilient character? Abraham frequently prays that he will die. He lies down in front of a moving train.

There is a disconnect, clearly. I'll take it further—not only did a schism open up between these two men, but also the book itself split into two. Ostoja had his version, and Abraham had his. I mean this in a more literal sense than you think I do.

When Abraham immigrated to Israel he brought with him a copy of the Polish manuscript and had it translated into Hebrew. *Bein Hamitzarim,* or *Dire Straits,* was published in Israel in 1952, a full decade before the Polish. Ostoja, clearly, was unaware. *Bein Hamitzarim* is presented as a standalone work: Abraham excised the backstory—no preface, no acknowledgments, no Ostoja. The translator is given a byline but there's no mention of what the original language was.

A cursory examination reveals *Bein Hamitzarim* as a relatively faithful translation of *Za Drutami Śmierci,* or, more specifically, of the manuscript that would eventually become *Za Drutami Śmierci. Za Drutami Śmierci* and *Bein Hamitzarim* tell the same story, in more or less the same style, using more or less the same language.

Yet they are different books: they exist on different planes. They entered distinct worlds with no tether between them: *Za Drutami Śmierci* was published without Abraham's knowledge, *Bein Hamitzarim* without Ostoja's (and I am almost certainly the first person since *Bein Hamitzarim*'s translator to have compared the two)—and with different intentions, receptions, legacies. So much more than language separates these books that the descriptor "translation" obscures more than it clarifies. *Za Drutami Śmierci* and *Bein Hamitzarim* are read differently, valued differently, understood differently.

To wit: *Bein Hamitzarim* is a noble but insignificant book; *Za Drutami Śmierci* is a significant but ignoble book.

Bein Hamitzarim was ignored and forgotten. Not many in Israel in the early 1950s wanted to hear *Bein Hamitzarim*'s hard bleak truths; in that time and in that place the Jewish historical narrative was being forcefully bent toward heroism, bravery, resilience; what had happened in Europe was tragic, shameful, and best left unspoken. Later, after the Eichmann trial, after a sea change in public consciousness, after the deluge of books and films, *Bein Hamitzarim* was already long out of print. *Bein Hamitzarim* is probably best described as a carrier for Abraham Kajzer's memory. Its protagonist isn't a hero but a witness: "I feel the need to share, even if it's just for myself, my own thoughts and insights, so that, when I am a free man, I can re-create it all again. But if I die, this poor diary will be my hand and memory." *Bein Hamitzarim* is testimony, even if no one is listening.

Za Drutami Śmierci is very much alive, very much in print: the Museum of Gross-Rosen puts out an updated edition every year. The book is sold in the Riese gift shops, at Książ Castle, at other tourist sites across Silesia and beyond. *Za Drutami Śmierci* is valued, studied, dissected, and it is valued, studied, dissected for reasons that are if not contrary then certainly alien to Abraham's authorial intentions—not for the hard bleak truths, its depictions of cruelty and suffering, but for its most incidental details. For the stuff in the far, far background, for what the average non-treasure-hunting reader would regard as crumbs of information —which worksites, which tunnel, what construction material. For the treasure hunters it's an extractive read. Everything else can be skimmed and discarded. A passage wherein Abraham describes forced labor is important not for its depiction of brutality or subjugation but for the particulars of the labor. *Za Drutami Śmierci* is the textual equivalent of a treasure map. And in *Za Drutami Śmierci* Abraham *is* a hero, because he, regardless of what he thought he was doing when he jotted those notes on scraps of cement packaging, successfully preserved those crumbs of information. "I am amazed by my own stubbornness," Abraham writes. "Who am I writing these notes in my diary for?"

. . .

Here is a passage the treasure hunters highlight:

> In the face of our apathy, dejection, and determination, one needs
> to have a lot of cunning in order to identify and employ the right
> tactics. In any case, it will always be the tactics of a fly against a
> spider. You can try to explain yourself or take your punches silently,
> waiting for your assailant to tire. You can try to shout or, despite the
> repeated blows, grab a pickaxe and blindly chip away at the stones
> or the earth in front of you. In this situation, only the sharpness of
> the mind will save you from the massacre and so, to avoid it, every-
> one tries to keep their place. It's not easy, since the companies con-
> stantly report different needs and each day the camp kapo forms
> the "kommandos" differently. There are a few companies that use
> our slave labor, namely: Sago and Werner, Seiden, Spinner, Lentz,
> the Bahnhof Kommando, and others.
>
> The work is also incredibly diverse. Beyond the forest, in the
> mountains, is a huge *Baustelle*.
>
> There are diggers, drilling machines, and borers here. All day
> long narrow-gauge trains run, carrying sand, gravel, crushed stone
> from the quarry, bricks, cement, and pipes. Lines run between
> construction sites, which are scattered in various places among the
> mountains.
>
> Some groups work on putting in a sewage system. Standing an-
> kle deep in water, at a distance of five meters from one another,
> the prisoners beat at the hard ground with pickaxes. Where the
> rock is exceptionally hard, a machine drills holes that are then filled
> with dynamite. After the rock is broken up, the group collects the
> stones by hand. Others are busy clearing the forest and removing
> tree trunks. The next group unloads wagons of cement. The same
> group works offloading stones from freight cars. The car is pushed

to the edge of the mountain, where part of the group holds it steady so that it doesn't fall into the ravine during unloading. After the stones are unloaded, they are pushed into the gorge with shovels. As it's filled in, the track is laid along the newly formed edge using special mallets. Still another group unloads sand, which is offloaded here day and night for unknown purposes. Other teams are involved in the construction of new tracks—they lay rails and the foundation, prepare the ground, and drive piles. Others deal with unloading and laying brick or laying pipes. A group from Elektrica digs holes for electric wire. A dozen or so prisoners carry dirt from the freight car to fill the ravine. After being reloaded, one of the *Häftlings* [prisoners] is assigned to direct the car's axle, pressing on it with a rod, after which the car, with its own weight, begins to roll down the slope in the direction of the ravine. Just before the ravine, the prisoner then applies force with the rod to stop the car's momentum, calculating the exact distance by which the car travels right along the ravine's edge. This work requires skill and a sharp mind. The smallest mistake can cause the car to fall, along with the man, into the ravine.

Here is another:

Today I worked in another group—with the Magyar [Hungarian], in the tunnels, in tunnel number 4. We are dismantling the tunnel equipment—we remove huge, long, heavy pipes. We bring them out and stack them in front of the tunnel. Every hour a car arrives and we load it with iron. The tunnel is big, humid, and cold. The foreman and the guards watch over us. We have one hour of rest during twelve hours of work. Many of us are subjected to various accidents every day. People are knocked down by iron beams, pipes fall on their feet, they faint under their weight, but still, they bustle

about quickly, in fear that they might be roused with a rifle butt
or a rod.

Not wanting to feel their weight, I force myself to think about
something completely different. Mostly I think about what the
world and life will be like after the war.

There isn't actually all that much Riese-relevant info in *Za Drutami
Śmierci*. A few robust passages like these, some other details scattered
about, but really not much, and little that struck me as revelatory or crucial. On the one hand, it shouldn't have been so surprising, this scarcity
—it isn't what the book is about: Abraham had not set out to solve the
mystery of the Nazi project he was being forced to work on—but on
the other hand, given *Za Drutami Śmierci*'s outsized importance to the
treasure hunters, I was expecting a lot more about Riese.

To some extent this is a function of how little material there is anywhere else: this is comparatively a gold mine of intel. It's more than that,
though. *Za Drutami Śmierci* is held in esteem by the treasure hunters
for reasons that go beyond the scraps of information that can be gleaned
from it. The book, and subsequently the author, have entered the realm
of myth. Abraham's book is totemic; it's almost like a religious text. It
transcends mere research material. Jerzy Cera, the renowned treasure
hunter, told me he's read *Za Drutami Śmierci* more than forty times.
Many explorers told me about making a pilgrimage, tracing Abraham's
journey camp to camp, worksite to worksite. They weren't doing it to
learn or uncover anything, it wasn't an exploration; they were doing it to
experience something, something I'd have trouble relating to or articu-
lating but that they, clearly, found meaningful. Many explorers asked me
to sign their copy of *Za Drutami Śmierci*. Every time I was weirded out
—this book is a Holocaust memoir, and also I am not the author. But
they didn't think it strange at all.

· · ·

Even after reading *Za Drutami Śmierci* many times I had little idea who Abraham Kajzer was, really; I knew him only through the prism of myth. In his book there are no details from his prewar life, no reflections from his postwar life. The more time I spent with Abraham-as-myth the more acutely I felt my ignorance of Abraham-as-person.

I sought out his family. Abraham's only child had died in Auschwitz. But his sister Necha had two daughters, one of whom was still alive, and seven grandchildren — this had been Abraham's family in Israel. And Abraham's brother Chaskiel, who had escaped to Argentina before the war, had four children, three of whom were still alive, and though they hadn't known Abraham well, they had met him a few times.

I tracked down my new relatives, spoke to them about their uncle Abraham. These meetings were strange and poignant, sometimes stilted and awkward, sometimes affecting, always interesting. Ultimately, though, I didn't learn much about Abraham, certainly little that carried insight into who he was. It is difficult to get to know a man refractively. By the time I showed up Abraham had been dead for almost forty years. After that amount of time I suppose what sticks are untextured impressions and quirks. He was kind, he was gentle, he was stuck in a severely dysfunctional marriage, he was desperately addicted to cigarettes, he trained pigeons, he grew strawberries in a barrel in his backyard, he rode a motorcycle. To them he was Uncle Abraham, lovable, scarred, low-key, eccentric, aloof. No one I spoke to seemed to have known Abraham intimately; I got the impression that no one, save for his late sister Necha, had *ever* known Abraham intimately.

Nonetheless, these visits provided a meaningful corrective: here was the anti-myth; here was Abraham-as-person. I couldn't gain access, I could only orbit, but I could see that it was there. None of his relatives knew, or really cared, about the tunnels, about Abraham's Riese legacy; his wartime experience was, to them, tragic but remote. None of them had read his book; most of them had never known about it, or had forgotten that it existed.

Speaking of myth: there is some confusion as to how many fingers Abraham had—how many fingers he had when he was born; how many fingers he lost; and when and how he lost them. The myths, you might say, do not agree.

Abraham Kajzer had nine fingers. He was born with ten fingers, a full set, but in the early 1930s, in order to avoid being drafted into the Polish army, he cut one of them off. "He used a large tool," his niece told me, "a bolt cutter, or shears, in order to make it as quick as possible."

Or he lost the finger during the war. Maybe he lost more than one. Ostoja writes in the preface that "[Kajzer] smiled gently and wagged the stumps of his fingers, lost in the camps."

Although there is no account in Abraham's book of how he lost his finger(s), the missing finger(s) themselves do come up:

> I developed a way to ease the pain. I tell myself that what hurts me physically does not hurt me, only my body—I should not care. Me, this is me—the one who thinks, understands, and feels, while my body is just an object, an instrument. It's just like the piece of finger now missing from my hand. Maybe that piece of finger, rotting somewhere, can feel pain. Perhaps the muscles, bones, tendons, red and white blood cells ache, but I don't feel the pain anymore. Although it is a piece of my own body, at the moment, I'm estranged from it, I have nothing to do with it—just as I do not want to have, and often do not have, anything to do with the rest of my body. I try to turn off my body, separate it from the rest of me. In this way, it's easier for me and I don't feel pain, like before, when I'm beaten.

Curiously, if not necessarily meaningfully, this section is only in the Polish version, and not in the Hebrew. Perhaps Abraham deleted it, perhaps Ostoja inserted it.

Or Abraham had eleven fingers. Or at least was born with eleven fingers. The condition runs in the family. In the 1980s Abraham's grandniece Osnat gave birth to a baby with six perfectly formed fingers on one hand. This sort of polydactyly, the doctors said, is extremely rare, and is a genetic condition. Mira Meir, the baby's grandmother, said yes, that makes sense, her uncle Abraham was born with eleven fingers. Mira, an accomplished poet, and one of the most famous children's book writers in Israeli history, soon thereafter wrote a poem called "A Sixth Finger":

A Sixth Finger

A.

For five generations the sixth finger waited, dormant
latent in the DNA, passed down
in an invisible relay race. The superfluous sixth finger
is removed. Nobody need know that it once was.
A bond of silence. But it won't give up
as if to say the bond is like a pact
and continues to flow.

B.

The infant's sixth finger
something superfluous. A little terrifying, maybe.
Should we ask the doctors? Maybe
I'm mistaken and it's not so. Maybe it's just a dream —
it popped up suddenly, out of nowhere. Who knows
what was in the past

the generations dissolved in a fog
in the end, a small, superfluous finger
is removed in the cold, sterile operating room
anesthetized and sanitized as prescribed.
We begin, anew.

אצבע ששית

א

חמשה דורות חכתה האצבע הששית רדומה
ב .D.N.A זורמת בחשאי נמסרת
במרוץ שליחים סמוי. אצבע ששית מיתרת
מוסרת. איש אינו צריך לדעת שהיתה.
קשר של שתיקה. אך היא אינה מותרת
כאלו אומרת קשר כאלו חותם
וממשיכה לזרם.

ב

אצבע ששית של תינקת
דבר מיותר. אולי מעט בהלה.
לפנות לרופאים בשאלה? אולי
טעיתי וזה לא כך. אולי רק חלום-
מאין היא צצה פתאם. מי יודע
מה היה בעבר
כל דורות ההורים כלו בערפל
אצבע קטנה מיתרת בסופו של דבר
מוסרת בחדר נתוח סטרילי וקר
מאלחש ומעקר כנדרש.
מתחילים מחדש.

• • •

According to the Museum of Gross-Rosen, Abraham was buried in Holon, a suburb of Tel Aviv, along with his wife, Sophie. According to the Internet there was only one cemetery in Holon.

The cemetery was much larger than I'd expected, which was an unwarranted and dumb expectation, I admit. I suppose I'd become accustomed to tiny Jewish cemeteries in eastern Europe, less cemeteries than remnants of cemeteries, really, and which were usually small enough and run-down enough that if there's an intact, legible tombstone in there you can find it. But there were thousands of well-maintained graves here; I had no idea where Abraham's was; an undirected search would take hours.

I followed the "Cemetery Director" signs past a row of open-air eulogy rooms and a small prayer room and into a cluttered, musty office. An old man with a long white beard and a black kipah sat behind the desk, talking softly on the phone. Sitting beside him was a second old man also with a white beard and a black kipah, though much less kempt, and not doing anything, just sitting there, languidly watching the first old man talk on the phone. Cemetery intern, I said to myself. Neither the director nor the intern paid me any attention as I entered the office. I sat down on a bench against the wall to wait out the phone call, giving me time to formulate precisely my request; my Hebrew, limited to begin with, was rusty.

A few minutes later the director hung up the phone and I approached the desk and told him, in deceptively fluent Hebrew, that I was looking for the grave of Abraham Kajzer. He nodded, tapped on the keyboard, and asked, "His father was Fyvush?" I said yes, and when I said yes I felt a flush of pride — I may well have been be the only person in the world who could confidently answer that question. The director grabbed a photocopy of a map of the cemetery (there was a whole stack of them;

apparently requests like mine were common). He highlighted the relevant section, and, on the bottom of the page, wrote down the row and plot.

The section I found easily enough, but the rows weren't marked, and I wandered back and forth among the graves, searching: I'd stand in the middle of a row and scan the sea of tombstones in either direction for רזיק — the Hebrew spelling of Kaiser — or some variation thereof. But I couldn't find it. I had to get more methodical. I began walking down each row, checking each tombstone. It took a long time — the section must have contained four, five hundred graves — but at last I found Abraham's. Of course I'd missed it at first: the tombstone was only a few inches high, a low stone rectangle, with the inscription on top, facing the sky; in order to read it you'd have to be standing in front of it, looking down. Actually even then you wouldn't be able to read it, because a thick brambly bush had grown right over it, and it was covered in dirt and tree debris. Sophie's plot, similarly obscured, was nearby, but not adjacent — the couple were separated by a double plot containing Mr. and Mrs. Poterkovsky. This was either outrageously poor cemetery planning or an eternal testament to a very dysfunctional marriage.

I got on my knees and, wedging my body between the tombstone and the branches, cleared the dirt from Abraham's tombstone, and then cleared the dirt from Sophie's. The dirt was heavy and damp; it had been storming on and off all week.

There was no epitaph, just the name. I stood up and the branches overhead snapped back and reobscured the tombstone. I was filthy, my hands were caked with dirt, I had dirt on my face and in my hair. How forgotten these graves were. If Abraham had been buried in Silesia the site might very well have become a shrine. At the very least it would have been well maintained and -visited. But here in Israel he was just another survivor from Poland. Dead, childless, and remembered by a rapidly diminishing number of people. He was dead and his memory was dying. No special myth attached to him here. I have a question but I don't know if it's appropriate and I also don't quite know how to articulate it. I want to ask: Which is preferable? The celebrated myth, which is at least partly false? Or the uncelebrated person, the memory of whom so quickly disappears?

Before I left the cemetery I returned to the office, to the two bearded men behind the desk, the director and the intern, and told them there was a bush blocking Abraham's and Sophie's tombstones, that the tombstones were obscured and filthy, and that the cemetery was responsible for unobscuring and cleaning them. Or at least I tried to tell them this; I sputtered in my clunky Hebrew. I don't know what I succeeded in getting across. The director smiled and nodded and tapped at his keyboard, and the intern didn't do anything.

16

We appealed the ruling of Judge Wioleta Grabowska of the District Court in Sosnowiec. We believed we had a good case, that our arguments that my relatives who had died in the Holocaust were dead were strong; that a higher court would recognize the inconsistent rulings of the two lower courts; that a higher court would recognize and overturn the Sosnowiec court's arguably anti-Semitic casuistry.

The hearing was set for early September 2018 in the Regional Court in Katowice, and again I was called to testify as proxy for my father and my aunt. But I'd just moved to New York and couldn't justify the cost and inconvenience of flying to Poland for a day or two. And anyhow it wasn't obvious that this second trial would be all that different from the first trial: new judge but same procedure, same arguments, same documents, same testimony. The Killer represented me in my absence.

The morning after the trial I got on the phone with Grazyna and The Killer to hear how it had gone. It was a characteristically frustrating conversation; I wanted to hear everything, from the color of the walls to what was happening on the judge's face, but they didn't seem to think there was much to report, only that The Killer had argued the case and now we had to wait for the decision. Start from the beginning, I said. What was the courtroom like? Grazyna said that she didn't know, she hadn't gone inside—only her mother had been allowed in. I asked Grazyna to ask her mother what the courtroom was like. My mother says it was a courtroom, Grazyna said, in the Regional Court in Katowice. Does your mother think it went well? I asked. My mother submitted the documents and made the arguments and now we wait for the decision, Grazyna said. Did the judge say anything unexpected? I asked. My mother says there were three judges, Grazyna said. Three judges? I said. Is that normal? Grazyna said something about a rule change but I couldn't get straight what rule had been changed, whether it applied to all appeals cases or just inheritance claims or what.

Three judges! Had I known there'd be three judges I would've flown to Poland, expense be damned. That there were three judges—a goddamn tribunal, and three appellate judges, no less—tasked with deciding whether or not my dead relatives were dead pushed the absurdity past its breaking point; it was now state-sponsored farce. Can you imagine? Three judges, in their robes, on the bench, pursed lips, furrowed brows, listening to The Killer's arguments, evaluating the Sosnowiec judge's decision, gathering in closed chambers to debate whether or not these four dead Jews were dead. (To aid your imagination: all three judges were women in their late forties or early fifties, which I thought was a weird demographic coincidence, especially considering that the judge in Sosnowiec was also a woman in her late forties or early fifties; The Killer agreed it was strange but offered no further insight.) That the issue would be discussed out loud, not just privately mulled, that it would be debated, that a consensus would have to be reached—it supercharged the preposterousness. I imagine the discussion got pedantic, technical, even metaphysical. What does dead even mean? If a Jew dies in the forest and no one is there to record it . . . ? Can, for the sake of expediency, the Holocaust be considered a natural disaster? I imagine that at the outset the judges were split on the matter: one was of the opinion that these Jews should be declared dead; one was of the opinion that these Jews should not be declared dead; and one was undecided, could see both sides. I can see both sides, says the undecided judge, who is sitting in the middle. On the one hand they are dead, but on the other hand maybe they are not technically dead. I am having trouble deciding. Of course they are dead! says the judge on the right. We all know it. We know our history. All the Jews died! We also know math. If someone was born in 1888 how old would they be today? They are dead. What else is there to talk about? Interesting argument, says the judge in the middle. I can see your point of view. Idiots! thunders the judge on the left. You perverse commonsenseniks! Did you not swear to uphold Polish law, to the let-ter? Of course, says the judge in the middle. We did, says the judge on the right, though more begrudgingly. Then tell me, says the judge on the left, what does dead-ness have to do with anything? We are not here to decide whether these Jews are dead! We're not? says the judge in the middle. No! says the judge on the left. We're here to decide if they *qualify* as dead, regardless of whether they are literally dead. And on this point the law is clear: they do not qualify. Do we know the date? Do we know the cause? Yes, says the judge on the right, we do know the cause! The cause was the Holocaust! Not specific enough! says the judge on the left. Nowhere near specific enough! Hmm, says the judge in the middle. Also an interesting argument. I can see your point of view as well.

I badgered The Killer a while longer, did my best to get a sense of how the hearing had gone, but she was her usual terse cryptic self. What hap-pens if we lose? I asked. The question seemed almost to offend Grazyna and The Killer; they offered another bromide about waiting. Yes, I know, I said, but if we lose, we can appeal, right? Yes, Grazyna said, we may appeal, the next court would be the Supreme Court. I laughed. Partly in disbelief and partly from the shot of maniacal joy it gave me to imagine arguing this in front of the Supreme Court.

Frustrating legal implications aside, there is something profound in the distinction between "dead" and "gone" — it points to the obligation of the living to record death, that is, to remember. Death demands acknowledgment.

A few weeks later The Killer sent me a message that the Regional Court in Katowice had upheld the decision of the District Court in Sosnowiec; our appeal was denied, in other words; the three judges agreed that my dead relatives could not be declared dead.

Now it wasn't a fluke. Now it wasn't a funny story of one hyper-stringent local judge. Or even a (somewhat) less funny story of a local judge whose hyper-stringency was a semiconscious cover for what I was trying my darnedest not to see as anti-Semitism. Now it felt aggressive, like they ("Poland") were fucking with me. Now it was underlined and bolded, this exasperating pedantry, this radical abstraction of death, this gross insistence on denying the most banal fact, that these people were dead. Now the system was implicated. One judge comes up with some cockamamie reasoning as to why your dead relatives can't be declared dead and it's silly and annoying and you question that judge's impartiality; three appellate judges declare the cockamamie reasoning to be sound and you wonder what logic this universe is adhering to. The absurd ruling wasn't so absurd after all, just the first checkpoint of a surreal system.

The good faith with which I'd begun my Polish legal journey was shattered. I'd fortified myself from, even scoffed at, the prejudice against Poles that was, back home, a passed-down norm. But it was now even harder not to buy into that prejudice. I didn't want this to be the case —I wanted any difficulties I encountered to be purely bureaucratic; if

I were to be stymied by the Polish courts I wanted it to be on account of inefficiency or poor historical recordkeeping, not bias—but, yeah, it was, at this point, very hard not to buy in to. To the Supreme Court, I said to The Killer.

And then, as in so many other instances throughout this story, it turned out I had it wrong, it turned out I had no idea what was what, legally speaking. Like my grandfather more than fifty years ago, I had misunderstood the instructions.

There were, I learned, *two* processes, with different criteria and different implications, wherein the state ratifies death (three if you include the standard death certificate issuance): *declaration of death* (*stwierdzenie zgonu*) and *recognition as deceased* (*uznanie za zmarłego*). To have someone "declared dead" you need to be able to establish the specifics of said death, that is, the when and where and how; to have someone "recognized as deceased" only a certain amount of time has to have passed from when that someone went missing (how long depends on the circumstances; ten years is the maximum).

The two lower court judges, the one in Będzin and the one in Sosnowiec, had not in fact disagreed; they had, rather, ruled on separate procedures.

The judge in Sosnowiec, Judge Grabowska, had considered *only* whether or not my relatives could be "declared dead," and ruled they could not, because the conditions were not met. When did they die? Where did they die? How did they die? It was all blank. There were no eyewitnesses; they didn't show up on any concentration camp lists; their location during the war was unknown. Judge Grabowska had not malevolently twisted the law; she'd offered a technical argument regarding a technical requirement. (A perhaps troubling corollary is that Poland/1939–1945/Holocaust is too abstract/loose to qualify as place/time/ method of death, which on the one hand, sure, that *is* abstract and loose, but on the other hand, one might contend that the Holocaust should be considered at least as "deadly" and "specific" as a natural disaster.)

The judge in Będzin, however, had considered whether my relatives could be "declared dead" *or* whether they could be "recognized as deceased." And while she agreed with Grabowska that they did not qualify for the former, there was no question they qualified for the latter.

I tried asking The Killer about the discrepancy, tried to get her to explain to me why it had gone our way in Będzin but not in Sosnowiec, which procedure she had requested of the courts in the first place, but of course this went nowhere, I couldn't get straight answers, so I ended up hiring another lawyer, Szymon, to explain my lawyer to me. I sent Szymon the relevant documents and a week later he sent me a seven-page memo that explained, in marvelously clear English, what had happened.

The Killer had filed the wrong motion. She had asked for "declaration of death," which my relatives absolutely did not qualify for, and not "recognition as deceased," which my relatives absolutely did qualify for. The judge in Będzin had been gracious about it and granted "recognition as deceased" anyway; the judge in Sosnowiec had not been gracious about it, had played it by the book, and ruled against us.

So it had been my (really The Killer's) fault, not the judge's. My suspicions were unfounded, all my hollering was misguided. (True, Judge Grabowska *could* have been gracious about it—she understood what it was we were there to do, she understood The Killer had made a mistake, she could have allowed us to proceed anyway; one could, if so inclined, read into Grabowska's decision a certain degree of maliciousness. But at the end of the day being a stickler for the rules hardly amounts to sabotage.) This was good news, I suppose. We were still in the realm of exasperating bureaucracy, nothing uglier was afoot. But the fact that I had to start over—appealing to the Supreme Court was a nonstarter; there was in fact no basis to overturn the lower courts' decisions—was frustrating and dispiriting, not only because of how much longer this now might take, but also because it exposed, again, how little I understood, how unprepared I was, how interminable this process might be, how not in control I was. The antagonist was even more abstract than I'd thought: the antagonist was the process itself.

The Killer—whom I did not fire, because this blunder notwithstanding she seemed to be doing a good job, and because she was affordable —filed a new motion with the court in Sosnowiec, seeking to have my relatives "recognized as deceased." It was back to square one. We placed an ad in the newspaper, again, asking anyone with information on the whereabouts of Moshe, Sura-Hena, Michoel Aaron, and Tamara Kajzer to please come forward in the next sixty days.

17

From chapter XXVIII,
Za Drutami Śmierci by Abraham Kajzer,
ed. Adam Ostoja

I thoughtlessly directed my steps down the country road. I walked like a ghost, like a specter from another world. I was completely resigned. My chance of survival was zero. I watched the houses unthinkingly. I stopped and asked myself: Maybe here? It seemed to me that I had gone a long way, that I had gotten far away from the camp. I staggered. Unknowingly and completely by accident, I passed a detour and entered an alley.

I hid from the nagging wind behind a door and I stood there for a long time stupefied, indifferent, having no idea what to do next. I couldn't think straight, I couldn't even grasp the hopelessness of my situation. I stood calmly, leaning against the wall, glad that it was night and that everything around me was sleeping, that no one could see me.

It was barely dawn when I heard someone's footsteps. Instinctively, I straightened up, clinging to the wall, wanting to hide from the view of whoever approached. Small and noisy steps approached slowly. My heart beat harder, my breathing sped up. Thoughts flashed like lightning through my head and then disappeared. Only now I realized the horror of my position.

Then, somewhere nearby, the steps stopped. I peered out carefully to see whether the danger had passed, and I saw a woman in front of me with a jug in her hand. She stood about five paces away from me, waiting, uncertain.

When she saw me, she dropped the jug, and covered her face with her hands, as though she wanted to block out the image of something terrible and monstrous. Then the fingers of her hands turned into predatory claws, ready to fight this terrifying ghost who stared at her. Slowly, without a word, she began to back up. It looked like her eyes would fall from their sockets with fear. Her horror restored my sense of balance. I took a step forward, and she stopped on the spot, her mouth open, her eyes wide, staring, spellbound.

Quietly I said, in German:

"Frau, do not be afraid. I will not harm you."

"But you escaped from the camp . . . They will catch you and hang you!" she said in a horrified voice.

"There is no need for that," I replied.

"Get away from this house!"

"No, I will not leave. Don't you understand I have nowhere to go?"

I saw the hesitation in her eyes.

"Frau," I said, "the war is coming to a close, Americans, British, or Russians will be here soon, and then it may be very bad for the Germans. If you hide me, you will have an excuse—I will plead for you, I will defend you, then you will not be threatened."

I tried to make my words sound convincing, but, in fact, I didn't really believe these words, because I didn't know what the future would bring.

"When I don't even have my own flat," she replied in despair. "I am a refugee from Breslau. I found shelter here with my five children, at my father's."

"I do not want a flat . . . I can stay in the cellar or in the basement, or in the attic . . . anywhere."

"And when they find out? They'll hang me together with my children . . . Maybe somebody saw you?"

"Nobody has seen me. I have been in this passageway for several hours. Anyway, I will not give you up, even if they skin me alive. Quickly, quickly, because we will be seen!"

"And you're certain that no one saw you? You're sure of it?"

"Yes!"

She stepped away from the house and looked around. She looked on all sides, finally returned, and with a firm motion she took me by the arm and led me to the basement.

We stood facing each other—her, slender and pale, and me, wretched and unfortunate. She took my hand, and, to my great surprise, a warm tear fell. I stood motionless, silent, and full of some inner trembling.

After a long moment, she broke the silence.

"We are wasting time," she said. "It's already dawn. Soon some Polish women who work for us will arrive. Do not betray your presence to anyone. They come down here to get water. Remember, do not trust anyone! Don't show yourself!"

I noticed a few long chests standing against the wall. I went over and lifted the lid—and saw the potatoes. I greedily grabbed the potatoes and, ignoring the presence of my savior, began to eat them. Maintaining any restraint was beyond my control. I unconsciously chewed and swallowed the potatoes, and didn't even notice that the German woman had left the basement. I saw her again, after devouring several raw potatoes. She had returned with linens and food.

"Eat," she said. "And in the meantime, I will prepare a hiding spot in this box, since it's already dawn and soon they will come down here for water."

She set down the food and took care of transferring the potatoes from one chest to another. I started to swallow huge chunks of cake. I took no time to chew. After a few minutes, everything was eaten. I walked over to her and helped her move the rest of the potatoes.

When the chest was empty, she put down a feather bed and a small pillow and two blankets, then looked at me and asked if I wanted more to eat.

"Yes . . . but bring only bread."

I was sorry that I ate so much cake. After a while, she came back with four slices of bread and a liter pot of porridge with milk.

I ate that in no time as well. Then she helped me lie down in the chest, and closed it up—and I was alone.

I fell asleep. When I woke up, I saw her leaning over me. She watched me with concern and anxiety. Seeing me open my eyes, she breathed a sigh of relief.

"Thank God," I heard her words. "I thought you were dead. You slept twenty-four hours straight. Did anybody see you?"

"No," I replied.

"You have . . . to eat and drink. Tomorrow, I will come again, and now I must leave, because I am afraid that someone will see me."

I was alone again. I lay quietly and listened. I heard people entering the neighboring cellar room; how they rattled empty buckets; how they pumped the pump. There was the sound of a bucket filling with water, the sound of footsteps on the stairs. From time to time, someone sang a song. Through the cracks in the chest, I watched the dawn and the falling twilight. I was often worried that my savior would change her mind . . .

Every day, I waited twenty-four hours for her to come. I greeted her always with unrestrained joy and when she left my heart sank. A strange joy filled me when I heard her words, which she repeated almost every day:

"Did you sleep well? Good-bye. Until tomorrow."

Then she would close the lid and leave the basement. I was left alone again. I listened again — the steps, the clatter of buckets, the splash of water, the detached words, the steps again — and then twenty-four hours of surreal silence.

After a few days, I could no longer lie in the chest. At night, I woke up and walked very quietly around the basement. Freezing, I finally returned to the chest, wrapped myself in blankets, and dreamed of once again hearing the sonorous voice of the one who saved my life — I fell asleep.

One day, unexpectedly, she brought a chair with her to the basement. She put it in a corner and said:

"Come out and sit a little at night but be careful . . . quiet."

I didn't manage to thank her before she disappeared like a shadow.

In those days, my only joy was her visits. Her voice made my heart beat faster. There was so much, so much I wanted to say, tell,

ask—but I did none of that, because I had to constantly take care,
watch, listen. With an excess of questions crowding my lips, I often
couldn't utter a word. The words died on my lips, and I was afraid
of my own voice, that if someone heard it, they might grow suspicious and suspect something.

One day in 1998, Shimon and Rochel Plonsker, an elderly couple from
Ramat Gan, Israel, were in the Frankfurt airport, maybe they'd just arrived, maybe they were about to head home, but in any case something
had gone wrong, there was an issue with the airline, and they were getting into it with one of the employees; the argument got heated.

A man named Alexander Fruhlich happened to walk by, took notice
of the tumult. Fruhlich worked for the airline—though on that particular day he wasn't working, just passing through with his wife on their
way home to Berlin—and intervened, came to the Plonskers' rescue.

The Plonskers, grateful, invited the Fruhlichs to lunch.

At lunch, Alexander, upon learning that the Plonskers were from Israel, told them that he had a special connection to someone in Israel,
though he wasn't sure where in Israel this someone lived, or even if he
was still alive; it had been some time since they had been in contact. His
name was Abraham Kajzer. Did the Plonskers know him by any chance?
No, they said, they did not. But what was the story? What was this special connection? Alexander said that more than fifty years ago, in 1945,
in the last weeks of the war, his mother, Gertrud Fruhlich, had hidden
Kajzer in the cellar, inside a potato box, had saved his life. After the war
Gertrud and Abraham had stayed in touch, Alexander said—Abraham
even visited once, in 1965—but they later lost contact. Gertrud was still
alive, Alexander said. She was ninety years old, and had never forgotten
Abraham. She still had a photograph of him on her wall.

The Plonskers were very taken with this story, and over the following months they spearheaded an effort to have Gertrud recognized as a Righteous Among the Nations, accorded by Yad Vashem to non-Jews who, at great risk, had saved Jews during the war. They submitted as evidence the section just quoted from Abraham's memoir; a letter from Alexander corroborating the story; a 1965 German newspaper article about Gertrud's heroic act; a photocopy of a Christmas card that Abraham had sent Gertrud and her children; a photograph of Gertrud holding a photograph of Abraham; and a photograph of three Abraham-related objects in Gertrud's possession, laid out side by side: the aforementioned photograph of Abraham, a copy of *Za Drutami Śmierci* that Abraham had given her, and a plain metal fork, submitted without comment.

Their efforts were successful. On March 29, 2000, Gertrud Fruhlich was honored as a Righteous Among the Nations in a ceremony in her home, in Streganz, Germany (she was not well enough to travel to Israel). The Israeli ambassador presented Gertrud with a medal and certificate, and her name was added to the Wall of Honor in the Garden of the Righteous in Jerusalem. The event was widely covered in the German press. Gertrud, the articles said, did not know whether Abraham was still alive—it seemed no one had told her that he had died more than twenty years earlier.

Gertrud Fruhlich died less than six weeks later, on May 9, 2000.

Now the story turns, for a few pages anyway, from Abraham to the woman who saved Abraham, Gertrud Fruhlich, although Abraham never calls her anything more specific than "my savior." This is a shift of protagonists. It is also a loosening of the story, Abraham's salvation story, which up until now has been constrained to a few harrowing but undetailed paragraphs in his memoir, terse as a myth, perspective limited to the inside of a potato box; now we get to flip Abraham's story over, pry it open, glimpse the mass of understories thrumming inside.

I was able to contact Alexander Fruhlich easily enough—the phone number he'd listed on his letter to Yad Vashem twenty years earlier was still active. He said he would be very happy to speak with me. He also put me in touch with his two older sisters, Rita and Helga.

On New Year's Eve—exactly one year after I'd flown to Israel to speak with Abraham's family—I flew to Germany to speak with the family of the woman who'd saved him. Alexander, Rita, and Helga were each in their eighties, in good health, had outlived their respective spouses and now lived alone. Over the course of three days I traveled to each of their homes and asked about their mother, the war, and Abraham. Alexander was formal, proper, if very friendly and kind. Rita and Helga were loud, colorful, excitable, funny. They had each prepared cookies and cake and tea for my visit. They were all very proud of their mother, and excited to talk about Herr Kaiser.

What I learned cleared up some mysteries, and introduced new ones. The myth got tweaked, became altogether more tragic, but also more affecting. It became a love story of sorts. I am getting ahead of myself. Let us begin at the onset of World War II, in 1939.

Gertrud and her husband, also named Alexander, had five children: Dieter, Rita, Helga, Alexander, and Adolf. They lived in Breslau. They were not rich, Alexander told me, but they had what they needed. When the war broke out, Alexander Sr. was drafted into the Wehrmacht and sent to the front in Italy. He was killed in Padua on April 27, 1945, one day before British forces liberated the city. The family, however, was not informed that he had died: something had gone wrong with the death notice, it was sent but for some reason never arrived. For years they lived with the ever-dimming hope he might still be alive. Not until 1992 did they receive an official notification.

So when Alexander left his family in 1939, that was it, he never came back. Helga and Alexander Jr., who were five and four years old respectively in 1939, told me they had no memories of their father. Rita, seven at the time, did; she told me, repeatedly, even kind of insistently, that she was her father's favorite. She showed me a letter he had written her from the front. It is heartbreakingly ordinary, full of a father's soft questions and promises of gifts and references to minor family rituals. On some level, Rita told me, she understood or intuited even then that he wasn't coming back.

The war raged on; the situation in Breslau grew dire — there were severe shortages of food, medicine, supplies. At one point all five children came down with scarlet fever; all five had to be hospitalized. Adolf, the youngest, Gertrud's baby, died.

In January 1945, Gertrud and her children fled the city — part of or just prior to the civilian evacuation mandated in preparation for the Soviet siege (what would come to be known as the Battle of Breslau). The children remembered and described to me the steady stream of Breslavians, mostly on foot, in the freezing cold, their possessions strapped to their backs or stacked on wagons they pulled, soldiers everywhere.

The family went to the village of Dörnhau, to live with Gertrud's father in his apartment in a large guesthouse. Two other refugee families were also living in the guesthouse, and perhaps two dozen Polish women, forced laborers, were interned on the top floor.

Alexander, Rita, and Helga told me about their grandfather, their Opa. He was proud, they said. Fearless. He was a patriot, and had been a World War I hero — there was a medallion of some sort on the wall, celebrating his valor — but he was, they insisted, opposed to the Nazis.

They told me about their lives in wartime Dörnhau, how they lived in such close proximity to concentration camps — there was one just up the road, and at least two more within walking distance. This is a perspective you don't often hear, of German children living and playing near the camps, children who are not at all blind to what's going on but are living their lives regardless. They told me they saw Jewish prisoners all the time, marching to work, marching back to the camp. They saw, often, transports of corpses; all the kids in the village, they said, knew where the mass graves were. Rita said that Gertrud would cook extra food and have the children distribute it to the prisoners, but they were caught by German soldiers and warned not to do it anymore, and Opa said it was best to listen. Alexander told me a story about how, one day, he buckled under peer pressure and snuck into a concentration camp with some of his friends. He told his grandfather, who punished him for it, said he should never do it again, and he obeyed, he never did it again. Alexander wouldn't or couldn't describe to me what he saw inside the camp.

One early morning in April, Gertrud stepped outside and came face-to-face with a skeletal prisoner, an escapee from the concentration camp, a Jew, cowering in the alley. In his memoir Abraham recounts how he pleads with the terrified German woman to hide him, makes the case that it is in her best interest: the war is nearly over, he says, and then it will be bad for the Germans; I will defend you, he says. Initially she wavers, she's afraid, she's a refugee herself, but then relents. She takes him to the cellar, to the potato box. Abraham does not mention the grandfather, Gertrud's father, not then, not later. Gertrud's children said it happened a little differently: they said that Gertrud did not make the decision on her own, that their Opa knew about Abraham, had given his approval to hide the Jew. According to the children, which is to say according to Gertrud, it was even more dramatic than what Abraham had described: they said that German soldiers arrived soon after, searching for Abraham; Gertrud, her children said, had poured water on the steps in order to mask Abraham's scent from the dogs. Rita claimed that a soldier even opened the box Abraham was hidden in — but did not see him, as he was well concealed beneath the potatoes.

Abraham stayed in the cellar, in the box, for more than a month. Alexander and Helga said that they had no idea anything was amiss. Rita said that she did know, claimed her mother had confided in her and occasionally tasked her with bringing food down to Abraham. Alexander and Helga said they had noticed their mother making extra food and disappearing into the cellar, but had never suspected anything. Alexander said that, later, after the war, Gertrud had said to him that he had been the most difficult to deceive, because he, the youngest, was always following her.

Abraham writes that he spent the month in isolation, punctured only by his savior's nightly visits. The children told me that Opa would also go down and visit Abraham; Alexander said that Opa would bring Abraham clothes and liquor, and that sometimes at night he would bring Abraham out to the yard.

By all accounts, including Abraham's, including the children's, liberation happened very suddenly. Helga and Alexander told me that that morning they were in the attic, watching through the window as German soldiers retreated and Soviet soldiers emerged from the forest. (Rita was not home; she told me she was likely at the hospital, where she worked as a nurse.) At some point the children came downstairs or were beckoned downstairs and encountered in the kitchen the two adults they knew—their mother and their grandfather—and one they did not, a man wearing the striped uniform, an inmate of the concentration camp, a Jew. (Abraham had been given new clothes by Gertrud but had put on the concentration camp uniform in preparation for his liberation, probably in order to help explain to the Soviet soldiers who he was and that these Germans had saved him.) Abraham described the moment of his liberation differently. He wrote that he was inside the potato box when he heard frighteningly unfamiliar footsteps, and suddenly "someone opened the lid with a strong jerk, brutally threw back the blanket, grabbed my neck, and shined a flashlight in my eyes. I was terrified." It was a Soviet soldier. "You're free!" he said.

Abraham wrote that he walked outside, contemplated his freedom, and then his unnamed savior took him by the arm, led him back into the house so he could wash and shave, and then he left again, presumably for good. This is the end of the memoir. What he does the next day

—it does not say. The years Abraham spent in Poland after the war had always been opaque to me. All I knew was that at some point Abraham brought his manuscript to Ostoja, and in 1948 or 1949 immigrated to Israel.

From Gertrud's children I learned that Abraham did not in fact leave Gertrud. He stayed, for months, for a year, for perhaps as long as two years, stayed with Gertrud and her children and her father. Abraham and Gertrud had a relationship; they were lovers. The children adored him. They called him Poppa. Alexander told me stories of going fishing with Abraham, and how his mother and Abraham went for bicycle rides in the countryside, often sharing a single bike. Opa and Abraham would spend hours together, the children told me, drinking homemade liquor and chatting. Abraham took on the role of the breadwinner. There were severe shortages, the family didn't have enough to eat, so Abraham traveled to Łódź to dig up the valuables he had hidden before the war (of course this myth—whether it's true or somewhat true or not at all true —existed here too) and returned with suitcases of food. This was the story behind the photograph of the fork sent to Yad Vashem as evidence —Abraham had brought this fork back with him from Łódź, Alexander told me, and Gertrud held onto it for the rest of her life. Abraham often stepped in with local authorities, using his newfound influence to help Gertrud and her family. He vouched for them. When the Soviets were confused by Opa's World War I medallion on the wall and suspected he was he a Nazi sympathizer, Abraham intervened. When a local politician made advances on teenage Rita, Abraham intervened.

Gertrud and Abraham: Can we understand the relationship, given its origin? What did that sense of absolute dependency turn into once the danger had passed, was it something like love or beyond love or not at all like love? Or maybe I'm overthinking it, maybe it was exactly love?

Abraham wanted to marry Gertrud; Gertrud wanted to marry Abraham. Rita and Helga each said to me, many times, that they wished

Abraham had stayed with their mother; their lives would have been very different, they said. Alexander was more circumspect but seemed to believe this too. When I showed Helga a photograph of Abraham — the same photograph her mother had had in her house for forty years — she held it and addressed it directly, lovingly: Why didn't you stay with us?

The children told me that their mother, who never remarried, thought about Abraham for the rest of her life.

What cleaved them apart? History, you might say. The war ended, Silesia was given to Poland, Dörnhau became Głuszyca, the ethnic Germans were forcibly evacuated, the State of Israel was founded. Gertrud asked Abraham to come to Germany with them, but Abraham wouldn't go to Germany, that was apparently too much for him; he asked Gertrud to come with him to Israel, but she said no, not with her four children, that was apparently too much for her. And she was still technically married, though her husband was almost certainly dead maybe he wasn't . . . ?

Opa always said that if they ever forced him to leave his home he'd kill himself; the day before Polish officials were going to force him to leave his home he killed himself. He did it upstairs, he put his head through a noose tied to a rafter. Alexander and Helga said they remember seeing Opa's body swaying from the ceiling. (Rita said that Opa died from a bad heart, but I don't know if this is something she actually believes or if she said it for my sake.)

Abraham intervened one last time: he helped get the Fruhlichs' deportation delayed a week, so that arrangements could be made for Opa's burial. (This delay had lasting consequences, as decisions in times of chaos and upheaval so often do: the family had been set to be moved to West Germany, but they missed that transport, and were sent instead to East Germany, behind the Iron Curtain.)

And Abraham? My insight is limited; no one in his family, at least that I spoke to, knew about his relationship with Gertrud. Perhaps he would have gone to Israel even if Gertrud had stayed in Dörnhau. Perhaps Abraham's decision to stay in Poland as long as he did had nothing or at least not everything to do with Gertrud. Perhaps; but it's not the story I choose. I choose the story that Abraham stayed in Poland only because of Gertrud—why else would you stay in the country where your wife, son, parents, siblings, and most everyone you knew had been murdered? Once Gertrud was gone, Abraham stuck around only long enough to get his manuscript in order, then moved to Israel. He soon got remarried, to Sophie, also a survivor. Sophie suffered from paranoid schizophrenia, she used to rage at the radio and television, convinced she was being spied on. She and Abraham had no children. Rita and Helga told me their mother never knew that Abraham had gotten remarried. According to Alexander, she did know: the reason Abraham gave Gertrud as to why he could no longer be in touch was, Alexander said, that it bothered his wife.

And Gertrud? Her children told me that she considered the two men, Alexander and Abraham, to be the great loves of her life, and the great tragedies of her life. Her husband, whom the war swallowed up, who was gone but not entirely, who wouldn't fully release her for forty-seven years. And the prisoner she saved, and then loved, and then could not be with. I cannot help but note the irony—the sort that history can always be counted on to furnish—that the German soldier died while his wife was keeping alive the Jewish prisoner who would become her lover.

After meeting Gertrud's children, after learning the truer story of Abraham and Gertrud, I reread the passages in Abraham's book that mention Gertrud, or, rather, his unnamed savior; it now felt acutely poignant, even or especially the fact that he kept Gertrud anonymous. It now felt coded, all these buried truths and sentiments, as if Abraham had smuggled into his wartime account of survival his postwar feelings of affection. "I greeted her always with unrestrained joy and my heart sank when she left. A strange joy filled me when I heard her words." "In those days, my only joy was her visits. Her voice made my heart beat faster."

I probably should abstain from wondering into their heads and hearts. But how can I not? Their story demands it, you can't help but try and peer in, fill in the long blank epilogue. Whether what we imagine is historically accurate or not is not the point; stories like this, stories that go so suddenly dark, have momentum, they invite us in, invite us to imagine . . .

Gertrud, in East Berlin, later in Streganz, raising four children who soon enough were raised and gone, and then she was alone. She thinks daily about the war, about her dead child, her dead father, and her husband, maybe dead, probably dead, almost certainly dead. She thinks about Abraham. Does she pine? Yes, or maybe that's the wrong question, the wrong word: there is too much loss, too much suffering, too much tumult and mourning, and what Gertrud feels in those years and decades after the war toward Abraham cannot be disentangled from that. Yet what she feels toward Abraham is the tip of the spear, what she feels the sharpest, what keeps the wound open, because only regarding Abraham was there ever any choice—even if in fact there wasn't any choice, only the illusion of choice—and so it's where regret settles. So she aches. It isn't something as simple, as manageable, as forgettable as a past love, because what they had was anchored by her act of salvation, this singular act of courage, something she went nearly her entire life unrecognized for but that nonetheless defined her, and also that counter-defined her as a German citizen. She aches. The pain gnaws, Abraham is gone, but not dead, and this pain beckons and merges with the pain of the incremental loss of her husband; this pain beckons and exacerbates her guilt over her betrayal of her husband. Where is he, she thinks. Where are they? Where is Alexander, she feels she is still allowed to ask, though she knows she shouldn't. Where is Abraham? He used to write letters. He even visited once. But then the letters stopped, and she no longer knows whether he is alive.

And Abraham, in Holon, taking care of Sophie, trying to soothe her as she raged that they, whoever they were, were watching her through the television. Whenever he has the chance he jumps on his motorcycle and rides to his sister, Necha, to drink tea and reminisce and talk of their life before the war, about their home and parents and siblings and friends, now all gone; or perhaps they didn't, perhaps their mourning was diffused and spread out thinly over thousands of hours of untragic talk. Does he tell his sister about Gertrud? And if he does, does he tell her the whole story, or a bowdlerized version, a version more in line with prevailing postwar attitudes and sentiments regarding Germans, and Germans-and-Jews, attitudes and sentiments that can include acts of courage and selflessness but not love, nothing like love, because love between those who inflicted the suffering and those who suffered would be too scandalous, disgusting, treacherous? He thinks daily of Gertrud. He aches too. It isn't something as simple, as manageable, as forgettable as a past love, because what they had was anchored by her act of salvation, her grace and courage and his state of helplessness, his utter dependency. He'd lost everything, he'd lost everyone, but at the end it was love, why can't it be love, but here comes the pain of the loss of his wife and the pain of the loss of his son: the love of and for the woman who saved him is, always will be, attached to the pain of the loss of the wife he couldn't save, of the son he couldn't save, and now here comes the guilt, too, though he knows he should forgive himself, has every right to forgive himself, but how? They're dead, and he is not. What was this love of Gertrud? Was it a betrayal? And now he loves, or at least is dedicated to, Sophie — is this in turn a betrayal? Of Gertrud? Of his first wife, Chana? Where is Chana? She is dead. Where is Sophie? Physically, she is at home, but where is she? And where is Gertrud? He used to write letters, he even visited once, but he had to cut her off, for her sake, for Sophie's sake, for his sake, and now he no longer knows whether she is alive.

18

The Killer assured me a thousand times that once my relatives were officially dead the reclamation was as good as done, the last step was a formality, the judge would walk downstairs and open the Forever Book and confirm that the last listed owner was indeed my great-grandfather and that'd be that, the inheritance would kick in and the building would be ours. Early on there had been some indications that our case was being prioritized, or at least being attended to. A decision was imminent, The Killer said.

A month passed, then two, then three.

I bothered The Killer to bother the courts, find out what the holdup was, see if we couldn't get this expedited. The Killer did what she could. She sent registered letters to the court, made calls, tried pulling strings. Nothing came of it. We were screaming into a bureaucratic void. There was an enormous backlog, The Killer said, because of the judicial reforms; everything was in disarray. I couldn't decide if this was a reassuring explanation. Six months passed, a year. I stopped bothering The Killer. Another six months passed. My expectations withered. You get stuck for long enough in a process you don't understand and can't see the end of and eventually you just accept your stuckness as the default. The Killer told me not to lose hope, insisted we were inches from the finish line. But were we? The longer it dragged on the less I believed her. Even if and when I got my day in court, why assume it'd go according to plan? Nothing had gone according to plan. Something would go wrong—a clerical error, a typo, a law we'd misinterpreted, new judicial reforms, The Killer would mess up, we'd get sidelined by some villain or catastrophe we hadn't anticipated. This was going to go on forever.

I had hoped to conclude my story properly, satisfyingly. Fade out on a successful reclamation of my ancestral property, a triumphant finishing of my grandfather's unfinished business, hurrah, mission accomplished, how glorious, how touching, with so many beautiful important lessons learned along the way. Or, plan B, I'd fail, come up empty-handed, have my mission crushed (this would probably be a richer, more interesting, more poignant ending, truth be told; certainly there'd also be many beautiful and important lessons learned). But neither of these outcomes has come to pass. It's been nearly five years since I first sat down with The Killer, since I took those first steps toward reclamation, and I have neither succeeded nor failed; this is an open-ended ending. My lawyer (and the lawyer I've hired to explain my lawyer to me) and others who've been through this tell me that my case isn't unusual, this is how it goes, this is how long it takes, but five years is five years, and it's all so indefinite, I don't know how long it will be before the issue is resolved in either direction, until I reclaim the building or it's determined with finality that I cannot. It could be months, it could be years, it could very well be never.

It's not the ending I'd hoped for but maybe it's a truer, more appropriate ending. Because at heart this was never really about whether or not I was successful in reclaiming family property; those stakes are hollow.

Let's say I did in the end get it back. Then what? Would I have "won"? Completed my memory-quest? Beaten the final boss? What epiphanies would be suddenly realized, what sentimental circuit would be suddenly completed? I can't even say for sure that it would have been what my grandfather wanted. Maybe he would much have preferred that none of his descendants ever went back to Poland than that his father's investment property be reclaimed. Maybe he'd gladly have given up the building if it meant I wouldn't write about the dispute between his children. Maybe he'd have been outraged that I erased his eldest son from the Polish legal record. It's less about the building than what the building stands for, and in turn what the reclamation stands for; and these are open-ended questions. What matters here is less the name on a deed than trying and failing but trying still to understand what it means to have, to lose, to take, to take back, to intrude, to inherit, to define your legacy, to declare your legacy, to impose your legacy, to misread your legacy, to impute value—historical, material, sentimental—and then immediately doubt that value, to assume the role of the protagonist in a story that isn't yours and that you can never understand, to unpause someone else's moral journey, to trace the ouroboric spiral of questions of family, history, justice, money, religion, ego, object, memory, meaning. This isn't a mission, in other words, that can simply be completed. Yes: the more I think about it the more I think that in the most morally honest version of this story the reclamation would be perpetual, irresoluble, Sisyphean; my children and their children should inherit not the building but the struggle to reclaim it, the struggle to understand what it is they're trying to reclaim.

When I first told my father about Abraham, about how I'd discovered this new relative, he was incredulous, he was sure I was making a mistake. "It makes no sense," he said. "How could it be, he asked me, that my father had a first cousin who survived the war, who lived in Israel, who even published a book, and either my father didn't know—which is impossible—or never mentioned it, which is just as impossible?" It was a good question. For a while I wondered if maybe my father was right, if I was in fact making a mistake, if somehow I'd gotten confused. But then I learned that Abraham's brother, Chaskiel, the one who'd escaped to Argentina before the war, had had a crystal company, Kaiser Crystal, and this jogged my father's memory—he remembered that when he was a kid a relative had come to the house with his crystal wares, had offered my grandfather a job; and my father remembered that some of the crystal that he and my mother had inherited from his parents—a vase and a set of shot glasses, which I'd always loved—was in fact Kaiser Crystal, samples from Chaskiel. It was conclusive, but hardly comforting —because while it meant that Abraham was in fact who I thought he was it also meant that my father knew even less about his father than he'd realized. For months afterwards, every time my father and I talked, he'd come up with fanciful scenarios in which his father wouldn't have told him about Abraham, or, even more fanciful, wouldn't have known about Abraham. He was rattled, I could tell. And later, after all my missteps, my misconceptions, I could see how this was but the beginning of a pattern I'd never break: at every step my grandfather's legacy seemed to retreat. (Here is the building he grew up in but in fact he didn't grow up here and also this isn't the building.) I ended up finding, falling into, another legacy entirely: the ease with which I was able to enter Abraham's story put into relief just how inaccessible my grandfather's was.

I wish I knew my grandfather. I wish I knew his history. It's a kind of longing for longing: I want to be able to mourn.

I do not trust the genre I am writing in, that of the grandchild trekking back to the *alte heim* on his fraught memory-mission—it's too certain, too sure-footed, meaning is too quickly and too definitively established; there is no acknowledgment of the abyss, the void, the unknowable space between your story and your grandparents' story. (I admit I'm also jealous—all the other grandchild authors seem to be able to so easily access the memory and the meaning of the memory of their grandparents.) I get why we write these stories this way, why we frame our memory-descents as missions—it's what's expected, it's what works, it's what's most suspenseful and most accessible and most marketable, and also when you're in it it *does* feel like a mission; there are places to go, obstacles to surmount, clues to discover—but it's a lie, or at least not the truest truth, because "mission" suggests the possibility of completion, redemption, catharsis, but there can be no completion, redemption, catharsis, because our stories are not extensions of our grandparents' stories, are not sequels. We do not continue their stories; we act upon them. We consecrate, and we plunder.

For nearly as long as I've been writing this book I've been asking myself if I've been going about it wrong, if it had been a mistake to write it as a memoir, if I should have written it instead as a novel. That it's nonfiction made it easier to set the stakes, made it easier to get you to care, but the limitations have become clear: if this were a novel I could have dumped everything into a narrative that could roam, stretch, fabulate, that could assert meaning with impunity. Right now I'm confined to the truth and the truth is that I know very little about my grandfather. If this were a novel I could conjure him.

He would be the protagonist, not me. It'd be him trying to reclaim the building, not me, and it would be *his* building, or rather his murdered father's building, though that only makes it more charged. The legal issues and bureaucratic issues and the issues with the residents would be his to deal with, not mine. The stakes and conflict would be immediate and unmediated; the trauma of the war and the trauma of the loss of his family would be immediate and unmediated. His motivations needn't be qualified or explained, he has to get the building back because he has to, his sense of displacement and vindication is immediately understood and accepted, nothing need be speculated about or presumed. There'd be no need to exhaustingly delineate between what's known and what's unknown, to chew these questions of legitimacy until everything's mush; instead there'd be the expansive solidity of the imagined. I could swap out my real grandfather, whom I do not know at all, and insert my fictive grandfather, whom I know perfectly. And I'd have no need of this stand-in grandfather, the one so revered by treasure hunters (or, of course, I could simply incorporate him into my fictive grandfather).

In the novel that this could have been, I'd almost certainly have the protagonist get the building back, succeed in his mission, taste that victory; in the novel that this could have been, redemption makes sense. But it would be short-lived; before long there'd be intense emotional fallout. Because it's not in fact a story of reclamation, it's a story of loss —and not loss of real estate, not of anything recoverable. The reclamation was but a desperate response to the loss, and the building was but a symbol—which the protagonist had lost sight of: he'd gotten fixated on the mission itself, had bought into the fiction that if the mission could be accomplished then maybe the loss could be undone. But once he's successful, once the building has been reclaimed, the loss is re-exposed, and to a certain extent re-experienced. The building now stands for nothing and therefore is nothing, all there is is loss, there's nothing standing between him and the void. He tumbles in. He drowns in grief, for months, maybe years. And then I think I'd have him burn the building to the ground. Raze it, destroy it, erase it. Maybe you'd read it as an act of madness, maybe you'd read it as an act of perfect sanity; it doesn't matter, it isn't an important distinction. Among the ruins he'll install a memorial to his disappeared family. A tombstone, or four tombstones, in any case something simple, but permanent. And I think in the final scene—if I'm able to pull it off—my grandfather places a pebble on top the tombstone. Perhaps his son is with him.

EPILOGUE

The last time I was in Poland I met a man I'll call Steve. Lawyer from the Midwest, mid-sixties, gray goatee, baseball cap. Very affable, a touch cynical, though really only on a midwestern scale. Steve and I had met by chance, or what passes for chance in Kraków — Yechiel, the local macher who'd introduced me to The Killer, had met Steve at the kosher shop and invited him out for a beer and I happened to walk by.

It was the first day of Steve's first trip to Poland and he was astonished by all the things that Jews who are in Poland for the first time are astonished by. The architecture; the tourists; the weird Jewish energy. He told us he was here as part of a group of 250 people, all of whom had roots in Sosnowiec/Będzin. Oh! I said, and told Steve that I also had roots in Sosnowiec and Będzin. Well, the truth is, Steve said, it's not my roots but my wife's — her father, my father-in-law, was from Będzin. But he never talked about it with her, only with me, and so here I am. He asked me what I was doing in Poland and I offered the usual spiel—ancestral property, Abraham Kajzer, treasure hunters.

Hmm, Steve said. That is interesting. That's very interesting. I have a story for you. You're talking about buildings and treasures—I think you'll find this story very interesting. Steve pulled his chair closer to the table. There is actually another reason I came to Poland, he said.

In Będzin my father-in-law had a jewelry shop, Steve said, right below his apartment, and, long story short, before he was deported, he took all his gold, melted it down, molded it into ten eggs, which he hid in the attic. He never had the chance to retrieve them. He used to talk to me all the time about the eggs. He told me very precisely where they were: in the attic there are two windows facing west, about twenty feet apart, and the eggs are beneath the smaller window, right-hand side, two bricks up from the ground. He even drew me a map, Steve said. He showed me on his phone:

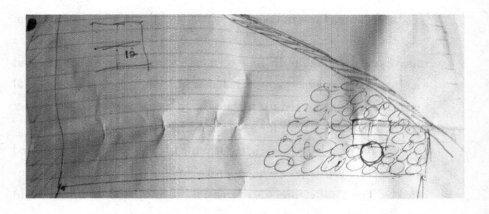

Yechiel asked how much the eggs were worth. Each egg is ten ounces, Steve said, so a hundred ounces in total. Yechiel looked up the price of gold—around $1,200 per ounce. Fuck! Yechiel said.

That's remarkable, I said. It was a remarkable story but also it was another remarkable story. This place is saturated with remarkable stories. I'd been hearing remarkable stories about Polish treasure for years. All my life I'd heard stories of Jews hiding treasure in walls—including one about my own great-grandfather, hiding treasure in walls. I have not heard many stories of people finding treasure in walls.

I know Będzin a little, I said—what's the address? Steve smiled and said, not unkindly, I can't tell you that. I was charmed that he wouldn't tell me, that he felt possessive of his myth.

Of course, I said, I understand. Are you planning to go to the house?

I don't know, he said. I'd like to. It would mean a lot to see the apartment. It would be really something to search for the eggs. I know exactly where they are. But we'll see. Steve was nervous about going in cold, just showing up and knocking on the door. He preferred something more official, more intermediate. He had contacted lawyers, tried to determine if he had any legal recourse. But his father-in-law, long since deceased, hadn't owned the house, so reclamation was out. (Consider yourself lucky, I said.) And it's not as if there's a law that permits you to enter a property that isn't yours in order to retrieve an item that belonged to your dead relative, especially an item whose provenance can't be verified and to which the current residents would almost certainly not readily relinquish their claim. Steve had even considered holding a press conference—rustle up some publicity, make it a cause, try and work out a deal with the authorities and the residents. But he didn't know anyone in Poland. He didn't know whom he could trust. And he was here for just five days. His only option was to knock on the door and see what happened. He wasn't bullish on his prospects. I doubt whoever lives there will talk to me, he said, let alone let me in, let alone let me search their attic. So we'll see. I recognized Steve's hesitancy. The sentimental obligation bumping up against decorum, this reluctance to trespass, this wish to not disturb others' lives, to avoid confrontation (and no matter how polite you are, it is a confrontation). You should do it, I said. I told Steve about my own experience knocking on unknown doors, how uncomfortable it had been initially. But I guarantee you'll have an experience.

Yeah, he said. He seemed to take this to heart. We'll see, he said.

The truth was that I was less interested in Steve's father-in-law's golden eggs than I was in these 250 people with roots in Sosnowiec and Będzin who'd come to Poland to do their memory-work. I wasn't sure what to make of it. It felt a little like they were crashing my party. Like 250 strangers had suddenly joined my solo hike. Steve invited me to the hotel for the kickoff dinner that night; I readily agreed.

The dining room was full of fressing Jews, plus a handful of fressing non-Jews. That nervous energy of individuals congealing into a group. Everyone had just arrived, everyone was just meeting everyone. It was a mostly middle-aged crowd, a few seniors, including at least two survivors. Everywhere family stories were being swapped. My father, my mother, my grandmother, from there, survived like this, moved here. People propped up little placards at their place at the table, listing not their name and hometown but the name and hometown of the family member they were there representing. Reunions were erupting all over the place. Siblings, cousins, relatives figuring out they were related. Most had never been to Poland, and would likely never come again; for them this was a pilgrimage. Poland was less a destination than something to be overcome, an obligation to be fulfilled.

The organizers gave me a schedule and invited me to tag along to anything I wanted.

A couple of days later I took a bus to Sosnowiec and easily found the group — 250 wandering tourists are not an everyday sight in Sosnowiec — and stood with them in front of the train station, in an awful heat, as the mayor unveiled a plaque commemorating the city's Holocaust victims. Memorials are good and important — it is good and important that memory be imprinted onto space; otherwise it's abstracted, memory seeps out, the space is allowed to forget. A plaque, though, is the least intrusive sort of memorial; it almost immediately becomes invisible. I don't know. It was fine. Certainly better than nothing. I should stop being cranky about stuff like this. I spent most of the ceremony chatting with Steve, for whom I'd become a sort of guide, a helpful insider.

In the afternoon there was a piano concert in a performance hall not far from the city center, featuring a renowned Polish pianist. The renowned pianist was very good but I left after twenty minutes. I had had my fill. Events like this feel like a charm offensive. Two hundred fifty relatively wealthy foreigners were visiting the city and it was pulling out all the stops, dedicating plaques and organizing concerts and crafting the message these foreigners want to hear, namely: We take your history seriously. But how seriously, really, did they take it? Look at all the trouble I had to go through for them to recognize the deaths of my dead relatives. I don't know. Maybe I should stop being cranky about stuff like this, too. Many in the audience seemed to be moved, or at least to be enjoying themselves.

In the evening there was a banquet. A few local politicians spoke, as did the head of the Warsaw Jewish community. The theme was unity.

The next morning there was a ceremony at the ghetto memorial in Będzin. It is an impressive memorial, very much not a plaque—a few meters of oversized train tracks that start abruptly and end abruptly in a square in the middle of what used to be the ghetto and is now a rundown section of the city. It's a poignancy coupled with irrelevancy. It disturbs the cityscape, sure, but the only people who ever see this memorial are the residents, and who knows how they see it, and the vanishingly small number of people who travel very far in order to pay their respects. Although on this particular morning there were 250 of those people here. There were speeches. Local television covered the event. I stood to the side, in the shade, schmoozing with Steve. Then Steve was called up to the makeshift stage and sang, in Yiddish, without accompaniment, reading transliterated lyrics off a sheet. He was very good.

When he was done he rejoined me in the shade. I complimented him, then started to say good-bye, that I'd see him when he got back to Kraków, but Steve said I should stick around—in the afternoon he'd be going to his father-in-law's apartment with Piotr, a local activist who had talked to the group earlier, and I should come with. We talked it out a bit. I asked if he was going to try to get to the attic. Steve shrugged. I don't know, he said. I'll have to play it by ear. But what'd you tell Piotr, I asked—did you say anything about the eggs? No, Steve said. I just told him that this was the apartment my father-in-law had lived in before the war, that I wanted to try and see it, that it would mean a lot to get inside, which is all true. You have to tell Piotr, I said, or at least you have to tell him something. It'd be a lot to spring on him in the middle of the visit. Like, Hey this is going well, can you ask her if we can go upstairs and poke around for ten golden eggs? Steve conceded the point. He said he'd tell Piotr—if not about the eggs outright, then at least a heads-up that there was something in the attic. Something sentimental, maybe, if not necessarily all that valuable. Maybe like a prayer book, I offered.

Steve was uncomfortable, I could tell. It wasn't about saying something to Piotr—who was an admirably dedicated protector of Jewish history in Będzin—it was more that, after he'd guarded this information for decades, the secret was starting to come undone.

A few hours later I had just put in an order for lunch when Steve and Piotr found me and told me it was time, we were going to the apartment now.

We walked up a hill and around the corner and found the address. It was a plain two-story building on a main street, a couple of hundred meters down from the Góra Zamkowa castle. (This is as specific as Steve is allowing me to get.) Steve recognized the building immediately from his father-in-law's description. We walked a little farther down the street in order to get a better view of the roof: there were the two attic windows, facing west. This is it, Steve said softly. Oh my god. Piotr and I stood by, respectfully. Piotr had done this before, had accompanied sentimental Americans to the homes their parents/grandparents had lived in before the war. It's profound and meaningful and at the same time very ordinary. Piotr knew, as I knew, that we probably wouldn't get in. It was lunchtime on a weekday; there was a good chance no one was home. And even if someone was home, there was a good chance they wouldn't let us in. Perhaps they'd say no politely, perhaps not so politely. Steve knew it, too, if a little more abstractly. But Steve was on his mission. Getting turned away is not at all the same as never visiting.

Before we went into the courtyard Steve turned to Piotr and said, nervously, I have to tell you something — it could be that there is something in the attic. Like an heirloom. It might come up, I might say something, depending how it's going I might ask if I can see the attic. (I remembered the soft lies Larysa, Jason, and I practiced before heading into Małachowskiego 12.) Piotr shrugged. Sure, he said, no problem.

The door to the courtyard was open, as was the door to the building, which meant we wouldn't have to buzz, which was good, usually you've got a very small window of opportunity to explain who you are and what you want — if it's too confusing they'll usually just withdraw — and it's easier to do this face-to-face, people are more sympathetic to a person than they are to a disembodied voice. (Also, for similar reasons, I think it's easier to lie, and also to get away with your lie.)

We walked up to the second floor; the stairs continued up to the attic. It was blocked by a padlocked wooden door, but it wasn't much of a deterrent, it wouldn't have been all that hard to climb over the banister.

There was only one apartment on the floor. Piotr knocked and a woman in her twenties opened right away, she must have been standing right there, with a three- or four-year-old boy pulling on her pants, trying to get her attention. The woman looked exhausted, impatient. Not unkind, she just had her hands full. Piotr began his spiel and the woman blankly stared at him, at us, and it was clear there was no way she was going to indulge us. We attach such high stakes to our memory-journeys, and apply such strict binaries to the people we encounter along the way—they either help or they frustrate, they either care and are open-hearted or they are fearful and closed-hearted. But often it's so much more banal. It was easy to see that this woman would beg off, politely or not so politely, because she couldn't deal with this right now, these three men, three strangers, including two from another country, who'd knocked on her door and were chattering on about World War II.

But in fact that's not what happened. Without saying anything, she turned inside and called for her mother, who came quickly. Piotr began his spiel again. The mother was confused, and in a very hoarse voice she talked quickly, excitedly. I stole glances with Steve. It's a strange moment, when the door is (literally, metaphorically) open but it's not yet clear if you're going to be allowed in. Often, even if they aren't initially suspicious they start realizing that they *should* be suspicious: any mention of "property" and "war" and "Jew" can set off alarms. It's (usually) unfounded, not based on anything they know—in my experience they don't usually know much about the provenance of their own home—but it can tap into a general, more diffused fear, an awareness that here lies trouble. Sometimes you can actually see the suspicion seep in: facial features harden, bodies stiffen with defensiveness.

But she was extremely unsuspicious—I don't think it even occurred to her that there was anything she should be suspicious about—and friendly. At Steve's request I won't use her real name; let's call her Justyna. Justyna was excited. She nodded along as Piotr explained who Steve was, that his father-in-law (it may have become "father") had lived in this apartment before the war. She nodded vigorously and said in her raspy Polish, Yes, I remember you. That's impossible, Steve said. I've never been to Poland before. The woman shrugged and said, You were here a long time ago, eighteen or nineteen years ago. Steve said again that it was impossible. Well someone was here, she said. She shrugged and laughed and beckoned us inside but then ushered us back out and made us wait while she brushed her hair; then beckoned us inside again. The living room was nice, modest, clean. An enormous television was playing an episode of something like *Cops,* not on mute. Steve said again and again how meaningful it was for him to be here, to see this apartment. Justyna had lived here only since the 1970s; she didn't know much about the history of the place.

We walked out to the small balcony, barely big enough for the four of us. There was a clear view of the Góra Zamkowa church, where a priest had granted refuge to Jews fleeing from the synagogue that the Nazis had locked and set on fire. I'm going to do it, Steve said to me.

My father-in-law, Steve said to Piotr, and Piotr said to Justyna, watched the synagogue burn from the attic. (Was this true? I don't know. I don't think so.) It would be very meaningful to me if I could go up and see the attic, he said.

The request didn't immediately register—Justyna was jumpy, things were getting lost in translation, she kept going back to the little bit she knew about the church. But once she understood what Steve was asking she said, Of course.

She fetched the key and opened the padlock and we walked up the wooden stairs into the attic. It was extremely attic-like—unfinished, creaky uneven wooden floors with raised beams, sloped roof. Some junk scattered about, but not much, it wasn't used as storage. It was clear that no one ever came up here.

This is it, Steve said. He walked to the window. This was the larger window. Maybe twenty feet away was the second, smaller window, beneath which should be the eggs, but the attic had been partitioned, there was a wall separating the windows. Steve and I walked to the partition, careful to keep our weight on the support beam. We looked through a hole in the dividing wall. There it was, we could see it, the second, smaller window. Steve asked Justyna if there was a way to access that part of the attic, where the smaller window was. That was the window my father-in-law watched from, was the excuse he gave, though by now it didn't matter, Justyna didn't care, she wasn't at all suspicious. She shrugged. She wasn't sure, she never came up here. She said it might be possible via the neighbor's apartment. So the four us went down into the yard and knocked on the neighbor's door, but there was no answer. Steve and I, giving whatever excuse, went back to the attic by ourselves. Maybe there was another way to get to the second window, maybe via the roof.

In the attic by ourselves, without Justyna, without Piotr, we could machinate freely, which was good, but was also on some level uncomfortable, because we were, it was getting harder and harder to deny, intruding: Justyna had given us permission to come up here but we were rapidly approaching the limits of what that permission had implicitly covered. We were stepping into deception territory.

Steve was excited, and nervous. I think this was the moment when it all became frighteningly unabstract. Are you going to write about this? Steve asked. He was protective of the story. I don't know, I said. Certainly not without your permission. Okay, he said, that's reassuring. It isn't my story, I said, it's yours, but yet it feels close to mine. Maybe as an epilogue. But nothing without my permission, right? he said. Right, I said. Whatever you want me to leave out I'll leave out. Okay, we'll see, he said, but maybe don't use my real name. Of course, I said.

Getting to the second window via the roof was dangerous. The only viable option was through the hole in the partition.

Steve had something the matter with his leg, and couldn't do it, but I could, and said I would. Are you sure? Steve said. I think he felt a little guilty. I assured him how much I wanted to. We are right there, I said, we are so close to being able to check those bricks. I got on my back and slid forward, wormed my way through, then walked to the outside wall and crouched in front of the second window. There was no pane, it was just a square hole in the wall, covered by a wooden board held in place by two metal wires strung across.

The window was four brick-levels up from the floor. According to Steve, according to his father-in-law, the eggs would be inside or behind the brick that was under the brick that was under the window on the right-hand side. Steve got on his stomach and poked his head through the hole in order to see. Wow, he said. That's it. You're there. You're actually right there. This is incredible, he said again and again.

Steve directed me from his perch; this was his show; I was his stand-in. Are the bricks loose? he said. Are you able to pry them off? They were not. Steve got up and rummaged around the attic to see what he could find to help me pry the bricks off. He came back with a nail, which he passed to me through the hole.

Using the nail as a chisel and a brick I'd found on the floor as a hammer, I chipped away at the mortar that secured the top brick. I did this for a while and made some progress but it was very incremental, and very painful. My fingers began to burn; my legs and my back, too, because I could get at these low bricks only from a crouching position. I was also increasingly uneasy. We'd galloped way past "deception." We were literally destroying someone's home, and someone who had been nothing but welcoming. False pretenses were one thing; unsanctioned brick removal felt like quite another.

So it didn't feel right and also we weren't really making progress; I put down the nail and brick and Steve and I discussed our next move. What if, I said, you offered her a cut of whatever you find? Like one of the eggs. Ten percent. Steve demurred. He wasn't greedy but he was nervous that if Justyna understood we were literally looking for treasure she'd get rid of us pronto. She'd been very gracious until now, it was true, but who knows what would happen if she understood that in her attic might be ten golden eggs worth $120,000. So we tweaked that plan: Steve would offer a bit of money, say we're searching for something, the implication being that it was something sentimental, but that we would have to remove bricks, and if we actually did find the eggs we'd nonetheless give her a cut.

Steve went downstairs to Piotr and Justyna.

I continued to chisel away, slowly and painfully. It was scorching in the attic. I was filthy, drenched in sweat, but focused and determined and feeling bizarrely content. I kept laughing to myself. Here I am in Będzin in a stranger's attic, chipping away at bricks, searching for ten golden eggs. Of course this is how my story has to end, I said aloud to myself.

Steve returned ten minutes later. Great news, he said. He'd offered Justyna $100 to search in the attic, to remove a few bricks, and she agreed, gave him carte blanche, didn't ask any questions, was incurious and gracious about it. She'd even given him a hatchet, which was the only tool she could find. Steve passed me the hatchet through the hole.

I chopped away at the mortar with the hatchet. It was easier than it had been with the nail, but it was still slow going. Steve had a better sense of brick-removal than I did, and directed me to use the hatchet as a wedge, to drive it between the bricks until they popped off. I used a brick to hammer the hatchet. It was very painful. My palms began to blister and my fingers were starting to give out; I was having trouble gripping the brick. But we were making progress. We were approaching the point where the eggs were either there or not-there, as opposed to maybe-there.

Steve and I talked throughout. Steve commented how wild this was, how he'd gotten so much further that he had ever expected. Then he said, Maybe don't write about this part, the searching. It's your call, I said, but that's the whole thing, that we're searching. I can't excise that part. If you don't want me to put that in then I would have to omit everything. Which again is your call. Steve thought about it for a moment. If we find anything, Steve said, don't put that in. He was nervous for two reasons. First, he was nervous that if we found something and I wrote about it he wouldn't be in control, and he saw this, had always seen it, as a very private story. This story belongs to me, is what I understood Steve as saying to me in that moment. And second, Steve, a practical guy, was already thinking about taxes, import duties, etc. Of course, I said. It's your treasure. It's your story. I'm just your accomplice.

I got the first brick out. I was exhausted, my hands were shaking, I could barely bend my fingers.

Piotr called to Steve and Steve went downstairs. I continued to work, making painful progress on the next brick. A few minutes later Steve returned and told me that Justyna had offered Steve the whole apartment for $10,000. Steve seemed actually to be considering it. Then he shook his head. I don't want the apartment, he said. I didn't come here for the apartment. I came for the eggs. Actually not even the eggs. I came here to search for the eggs. And if we find the eggs I'll give her $10,000, gladly.

It took me another twenty minutes, painful minutes, until the next brick was ready to come off. I looked at Steve, on his stomach, staring. Oh my god, he said.

ACKNOWLEDGMENTS

This book would not exist if not for the kindness and generosity extended to me by so many people.

It doesn't always come through on the page but virtually every person mentioned in the text—everyone I spoke to, interviewed, bothered—was exceptionally accommodating and patient, no matter how annoying or uninformed I was. Joanna Lamparska, especially, opened every door for me, and did so over the course of a very long time: the chronology in the book is a little fuzzy, I know, but my time with Joanna spanned *years*. Larysa Michalska, too, deserves special mention for helping me so many times with so many tasks. Thank you to the residents of Małachowskiego 12, particularly Bartek Piotrowski and Hanna Dobiecka. Hanna, an unparalleled chronicler of Sosnowiec real estate, and a loving mother and grandmother, passed away in 2018; she was immensely helpful and kind to me. Thank you to The Killer and Grazyna for their hard work;

one day we'll have that party. And, of course, thank you to the treasure hunters, particularly my fellow members of HUNTER. I hope you find what you're looking for.

My family grew. Shula, Rafi, Beni, Dorit, Sharon, Osnat, Oren; Albert and Maria; and Alexander, Helga, and Rita (who are family, even if not by blood)—they welcomed me into their homes, told me their stories, and allowed me to tell Abraham's. I am forever grateful.

Thank you to the staff of the Gross-Rosen Museum, particularly Dorota Sula, for their research help, and, more generally, for their work in preserving the memory of Abraham Kajzer and the other prisoners of Gross-Rosen.

Justyna Kramarczyk was the absolute best research assistant I could have hoped for.

Michael Bazyler, the preeminent authority on Holocaust restitution, guided me through the intricacies of Polish inheritance law; it was he who alerted me to the fact that there were two different types of death recognition. Thank you, too, to Szymon Gostyński for his exceptional legal advice and insight.

Malwina Tuchendler, Luba Shynder, and Gosia Wieruszewska were my interpreters for some of the longer, more intense interactions with the treasure hunters; these assignments, believe me, were no picnic, but they never faltered.

Lotte Thaa helped immeasurably with German documentation and my trip to Germany. That I had the opportunity to meet Gertrud's children was only because of her.

Thank you to Denise Grollmus, Dalia Wolfson, and Shoshana Olidort for their superb translation work.

I would need another book to properly thank everyone in Poland who has made my time there so special, but a particular thanks to Anna "Spinyawa" Rozalka and Patrycja Pikul for their long-standing friendship, support, housing, and occasional medical assistance; and to Maria Bilyk for, well, a lot. To Yak and Mechel, *yasher koach* and *jeszcze jeden*.

Thank you to those who've helped along the way: Elias Altman, Arielle Cohen, Daniel Cowen, Natalia Czarkowska, Maayan Dauber. Lidija Haas, Yonah Krakowsky, Josh Lambert, Agi Legutko, Anthea Malone, Sheila Miller, Ezra Seligsohn, and Rebecca Wolff. And to the Fulbright Fellowship and Wexner Fellowship for their support, and to my teachers and fellow students at the University of Michigan.

Dana Hammer offered invaluable feedback on the manuscript, and has loved and supported me in so many ways; my life is so much better with her in it. She is in a narrow but nonetheless profound sense my role model.

Jason Francisco is the kindest and most generous person I know, *and* an incomparable artist, scholar, and photographer; what a blessing to have him with me on those trips, what a blessing to be able to call him my friend. He has reminded me many times what it means to create. Jason, consider yourself shmucheled.

Maia Ipp has been there for me from the beginning, has supported, advised, encouraged, celebrated, edited, chastised me, and always with such love and patience and intelligence. At every point in this project, it's her I've turned to, relied upon, leaned on.

Thank you to Janet Silver, without whom I'd have gotten nowhere —her judgment and guidance have been everything.

Thank you, endlessly, to Deanne Urmy, for her stewardship, for her vision and enthusiasm, for making it all happen. Her support and belief in the project—and in me—were unwavering; in my darker moments, when I couldn't see the point or how it could be done or why it mattered, it was her confidence that gave me mine.

To those who feel that I had no right to broadcast or at least should have been more circumspect about family matters—I get it. The question weighs on me. There was no easy solution. It is the writer's curse, to try and tell your story as honestly and fully as possible while minimizing the details others might consider gratuitous or shameful. Perhaps in this regard I failed. I hope, then, that you can forgive me.

Reva, Tehila, Batsheva, Shalom, and Miri — I love you, and love that we're stuck with one another.

And finally, thank you to my parents, who give and give and give, and who taught me the value of tradition, what it means to care about and for your past, to celebrate your *yichus*, to honor those who came before you.

NOTES

This is a book of nonfiction, it's all true, it all happened, but certain caveats apply. The dialogue is not necessarily verbatim — I didn't always take notes or record conversations, especially early on — and my memory isn't perfect. Some names were changed in order to preserve anonymity, and "Yechiel" is a composite character.

Chapter 1

Polish names and Polish places have been spelled in Polish, except for the first names of my relatives, which have been transliterated into English. For example, instead of "Mosze" (or "Moszek") — which is how my great-grandfather's name was spelled on the Polish documents — I use "Moshe." I made this exception because these names are not in fact Polish, but Hebrew/Yiddish; they were already transliterated, in other words — the English spelling is just as true, so to speak, as the Polish.

Chapter 13

A few weeks later Joanna and I brought Andrzej to Jacek's house to try and figure out was what behind the mysterious wall in the cellar. We were unsuccessful. Andrzej, using a cartoonishly long drill bit—it was at least a meter long—drilled a hole through the wall, then attempted to coax through a plumbing camera, but he couldn't get it to go, there was too much debris.

Chapter 14

I did eventually figure out which house Abraham hid in, or, rather, where the house had been. When I visited Alexander Fruhlich, Gertrud's son, he showed me videos from his trip in the early 1990s to Głuszyca, and there was footage of the house—a pleasant-looking two-story cottage. But it had since been demolished, and Alexander did not remember the location of the lot.

Later I went over my footage of his footage (I had recorded it on my phone) and noticed that directly across the street from the house was a metal swing set, painted a distinctive red. The playground had also since been demolished, but Joanna found photographs of it in the archives, which let us pinpoint its location, and in turn the location of the house: it is now an open field on Kościuszki Street, on the west side, not too far from the cemetery.

Chapter 15

Bein Hamitzarim is, as I described, a relatively faithful translation of *Za Drutami Śmierci*, but it is far from a perfectly faithful translation, fascinatingly. There are dozens of divergences between the two texts. Most are minor, having to do with word choice or style—the natural by-product of a translation—or the peculiarities of the respective languages. *Bein Hamitzarim* employs more biblical and religious language/imagery, for instance, but that's a feature of vernacular Hebrew. And some of the changes can likely be attributed to the fact that *Za Drutami Śmierci* was published in Communist Poland in the early 1960s. In *Bein Hamitzarim*, for instance, there is an unflattering mention of a Communist block commander followed by further unflattering remarks about the political criminals in the camp. But in *Za Drutami Śmierci*, "Communist" becomes "bureaucrat," and the bit about political criminals is deleted.

Some of the formatting is different, too — chapters and sections break at different locations. I don't know what to make of that.

Somewhat stranger are the disparities of facts and figures — measurements, estimates, distances, number of prisoners, days of the week. I'm not sure what to make of these, either. Was Abraham, in *Bein Hamitzarim*, correcting *Za Drutami Śmierci*'s inaccuracies? I suppose it's possible, although given that many of these are in the section of the book that was ostensibly written as an as-it's-happening diary, that doesn't really make sense. Maybe Ostoja had misread or for some reason changed what was in the diary, and *Bein Hamitzarim* was, in fact, a corrective. Maybe it's the fault of the Hebrew translator.

There are also more drastic variations. Sentences and sometimes entire paragraphs have been omitted/added/moved. A few of these edits seem traceable. About halfway through *Za Drutami Śmierci* there is a heartrending passage wherein Abraham laments the loss of his son and wife; in the corresponding passage in *Bein Hamitzarim*, however, there is no mention of his wife — presumably Abraham decided to remove her from the text (because otherwise it would mean that Ostoja, of his own accord, wrote the wife into the passage, which seems improbable). Who knows what Abraham's motivations were, but I think it's pertinent that Abraham had since gotten remarried. But most of these more drastic variations are opaque, because we don't know the direction of adaptation. Presumably there was an original Polish manuscript agreed upon by both Ostoja and Abraham, which Abraham made changes to when publishing *Bein Hamitzarim*, and which Ostoja made his own changes to when publishing *Za Drutami Śmierci*—so with respect to any given variation we don't know what's original and what's tweaked.

I found Ostoja's role in this story so strange and so patchy that I actually began to doubt his existence, began to wonder if he hadn't been invented by the publisher in order to better present Abraham's book or something. But while I was never able to learn all that much about Ostoja, I did eventually at least confirm he was a real person. I'll tell you how it happened; it'll give you some sense of the weird charged serendipity that seems to so often propel these Polish memory-adventures.

I went with a friend to Łodź to visit the grave of Abraham's father and my great-uncle Fyvush—as far as I know the only extant Kaiser grave in Poland—and afterward we called a taxi and asked the driver if he could take us somewhere where we could warm up and have a cup of coffee, anywhere he recommended. He dropped us off in the city center, at Piotrkowska 86, a gorgeous restored building with a café on the ground floor. As we walked in I realized that, even though I'd never been to Łodź, I recognized the address: it was on the copyright page of the original Polish version of *Za Drutami Śmierci*—this had been the address of the long-defunct publisher, Wydawnictwo Łódzkie. For months I'd been trying to find someone who had worked there or knew the whereabouts of their files in order to learn more about *Za Drutami Śmierci* and Adam Ostoja, but had gotten nowhere.

We asked the waitress if she knew anything about Wydawnictwo Łódzkie or the history of the building. She did not, but said the owner might, and brought us over to meet him. The owner said he didn't know anything either, but perhaps his father would—after Wydawnictwo Łódzkie had moved out, the owner explained, his father's publishing company had taken over the space.

The owner of the café called his father, who didn't know anything but suggested we ask his good friend Ryszard Bonisławksi, a senator in the Polish parliament and an amateur historian whose office, as it happened, was across the street; the father of the owner of the café put us in touch with the senator, who was happy to meet with us.

Senator Bonisławksi—who turned out to be an amateur explorer—knew the Ostojas well: Adam Ostoja's son Andrzej had also been a senator, as well as a science-fiction writer of some note.

The next day, in Warsaw, we went to the Polish Writers' Union and looked up Andrzej Ostoja's books and discovered that he had co-written two books with his father, *Tirolinka* (1968) and *Waleczny Domek* (1969). From the flap copy we learned that Adam Ostoja had died in 1963, only a year after publishing *Za Drutami Śmierci*; he had almost certainly never again spoken to Abraham.

Chapter 17

Gertrud, in Abraham's account, says she has five children living with her. But in fact there were only four children: Gertrud's youngest, Adolf, had by then died of scarlet fever.

Chapter 18

The ownership of the building breaks down as follows.

The entirety of Moshe Kajzer's 68 percent stake was passed to his only surviving child, my grandfather.

Shia had no children—or at least none that survived—so his 32 percent stake went to his siblings, only two of whom, Moshe and Fyvush, had children who survived the war. So half of Shia's share passed to my grandfather and half to Necha, Chaskiel, and Abraham.

So my father, my uncle, and aunt own 84 percent of the building; Necha's and Chaskiel's children own the remaining 16 percent.